D0468168

SINK THE RAINBOW!

Rainbow Warrior

PHOTO: FERNANDO PEREIRA, GREENPEACE

SINK THE RAINBOW!

An enquiry into the 'Greenpeace Affair'

by

JOHN DYSON

(With Joseph Fitchett in Paris)

LONDON
VICTOR GOLLANCZ LTD
1986

Books by John Dyson

Novels

THE PRIME MINISTER'S BOAT IS MISSING
BLUE HURRICANE
CHINA RACE

General

YACHTING THE NEW ZEALAND WAY
BUSINESS IN GREAT WATERS
THE HOT ARCTIC
THE SOUTH SEAS DREAM

*With my warmest appreciation to
David, angler for books and trout, and
Paul, surfcaster for books and snapper*

First published in Great Britain 1986
by Victor Gollancz Ltd,
14 Henrietta Street, London WC2E 8QJ

Copyright © John Dyson 1986

British Library Cataloguing in Publication Data
Dyson, John
    Sink the Rainbow!: An enquiry into the
    'Greenpeace Affair'.
    1. Rainbow Warrior (*ship*)—History
    2. Harbors—New Zealand—Auckland—
    History—20th Century
    I. Title   2. Fitchett, Joseph
    363.1'23'0993122   G530.R3/

    ISBN 0-575-03856-X

Photoset in Great Britain by
Rowland Phototypesetting Ltd, Bury St Edmunds, Suffolk
and printed by Billing & Sons Ltd, Worcester

CONTENTS

MAPS AND DIAGRAMS

A section of photographs follows page 128

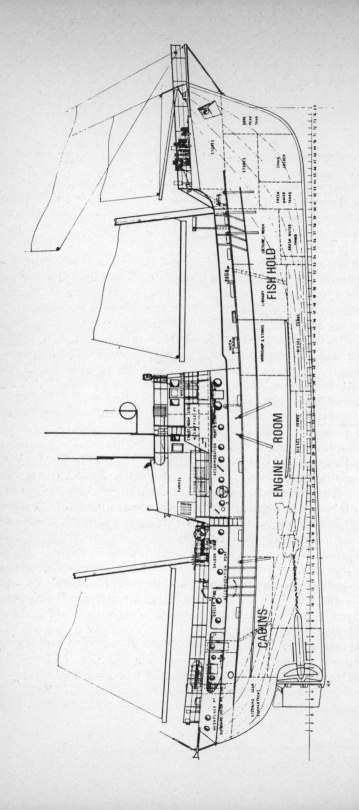

1

RAINBOW'S END

Attack was the last thing on anybody's mind in Auckland that night of Wednesday, July 10th, 1985.

The Greenpeace flagship *Rainbow Warrior* had been in port three days. There was still a feeling of quiet euphoria mixed with restrained excitement, even late at night as some crew members left the ship to sleep ashore and a few visitors remained to chat over a bottle of beer in the messroom.

In one sense it was journey's end. The long haul out from Florida and across the Pacific was concluded. The journalists and television crews who had sailed on the 'peace voyage' to observe the evacuation of Marshall Islanders radiated by nuclear fall-out had packed their cameras and left. The ship's new ketch rig, added so the engine could be shut down and sails hoisted to bowl her through the Pacific's brisk trade winds, had proved a grand success. There had been a hearty and heart-felt welcome. After three days the friendly Aucklanders were still streaming aboard to say 'G'day!' and leave offers of hospitality and help.

In another sense it was a new beginning. A new party of journalists and politicians would come on board. Like everyone else from the captain to the deckhands, they would find themselves on the ship-cleaning and dish-washing roster. Victuals were being laid in for another long voyage, engines and gear overhauled. In a few days the self-styled 'peace warriors' would slip their moorings and be ocean-bound on yet another adventure to capture world headlines. Their unremitting mission: to lever the superpowers into abandoning the environmentally destructive testing of nuclear bombs.

The waterfront of Auckland is not run-down, seedy and dangerous like that of most port cities. The wharves jutting like fingers into the blue-green waters of the Waitemata Harbour play a key role in the city's character. Great cruise liners and rusty freighters seem to nudge ITS shopping malls, bus station, airline offices and hotels. At the end of every street you can see water and ships.

Marsden Wharf, where *Rainbow Warrior* had berthed the previous Sunday afternoon, was the smallest of these commercial piers. Once used by small coasters and the vanished fleets of sailing scows plying the coast, it was now given over to yachts visiting from foreign parts, a handful of fishing boats and various government and harbour launches. There was no control on the wharf gate and no guard on the ship's gangway. Anybody could park under the overhanging eaves of the cargo sheds running the length of the wharf, then stroll aboard the ship. A few lights in the rafters, none much more powerful than domestic bulbs, threw a dim glow over the tarmac. The water beneath and around the wharf was in total shadow except for the wriggling silver worms of light cast over the surface from tall, powerful clusters of flood lights in the container terminal on the adjacent wharf.

The night was the answer to a commando's prayer. No moon until after midnight. Sky rather overcast. A bit of a lop on the water. The tides were nearly on neaps, when rise and fall was least, so currents were not strong. High water was due at 1.04am. Unless he surfaced and was silhouetted in a shaft of light from the other wharves a frogman would be perfectly concealed. But who was looking over the ship's side for military combat swimmers placing explosives? Who was peering under the wharf in case a rubber dinghy happened to be paddling among the mussel-clad timber piles?

New Zealand was not that sort of place. Never in its short history had the country been the victim of an attack, unless you counted the guerrilla wars between native Maori people and British settlers just over a century ago. It was a land blessed by peace. No bomb had ever dropped on it, no shot was ever fired at it in anger. *Rainbow Warrior* was secure in the lap of a country that was arguably the least tense and most peaceful on Earth.

In her cabin deep down in the ship, near the now silent screw, Margaret Mills stirred and awoke as a muffled thud carried through the ship's fabric. Something heavy had been dropped on deck, or the gangplank was being adjusted because the ship was beginning to rise against the wharf with the tide. A homely, grey-curled and limber woman of 56, Margaret had heard the noise before and put it down to just another shipboard racket that made sleep difficult.

A dedicated peace worker, Margaret had volunteered to be the relief cook on board *Rainbow Warrior* during the ship's stay. In her lively and motherly way she treated everyone like boy scouts and they loved her for it. As cook she was at the heart of things. Everybody stopped by for a chat. Fernando Pereira, the Portuguese-born Dutch photographer, had carefully escorted her into the freezer room to point out his packages of film that she should never touch. He talked of his children at home in Amsterdam, though he was separated from his wife, and told Margaret how, on the long voyage out, he had pined for fresh brown bread.

Margaret thought the twelve crew members from eight countries were a friendly lot, relaxed, easy-going, dedicated, mostly young.

8

She was struck by the way they talked to you as if you were a human being, not just as cook or employee. There was nothing of either the Captain Bligh or the eco-freak about any of them. They were hard working and professional, and had warm hearts. It was a treat to work with them.

Margaret's only problem was getting a good night's sleep. At her cottage on Waiheke, one of the lovely suburban islands just outside Auckland Harbour, she slept with her windows wide open and the curtains billowing in the breeze. Her cabin on *Rainbow Warrior* was on the lowest deck, below the waterline, and had no porthole. The hum of ventilation fans and the rumble of the generator and the noises of people moving round the ship made sleep fitful at best. Worn out by two restless nights she had fallen deeply asleep until woken by the thud on deck. She thought back over the events of the busy day, hoping to drop off again.

Greenpeace directors had flown in from the Pacific-rim countries for a regional meeting to discuss the upcoming protest voyage. Patrick Moore and Jim Bohlan arrived from Canada, Michelle Sheather and Mike Bossley from Australia, and American Steve Sawyer, co-ordinator of the 'Pacific Peace Voyage', from Washington DC. Peter Bahouth of the US was arriving next morning. With New Zealand Greenpeace directors Elaine Shaw and Carol Stewart, they had planned to sleep and hold their meetings on board *Rainbow Warrior*. To get some peace and quiet they decided at the last minute to put up at a surf club – deserted because July is mid-winter in the southern hemisphere – on a wild black-sand beach called Piha, 25 miles (40 km) out of town. First, they had a special engagement on board.

At about eight o'clock, after a reunion dinner in a nearby café, they returned to the ship. It was Steve's birthday and Margaret had baked him a big chocolate cake. The crew, many of whom had been busy all day refreshing the vibrant colours of the rainbow arching over the dove of peace on the ship's bows, packed into the messroom with their friends. There were also some visitors, including a nattily dressed young French businessman who had poked around the ship. Nobody paid him much attention. He was friendly and expressed admiration for the Greenpeace campaign for a cleaner, unpolluted planet. To cheers and congratulations, Steve unwrapped a gift. It was a large brass bolt from the ship's old winch. All sang 'Happy Birthday' and toasted him with a glass of wine.

The celebration made the evening's all-important meeting late in starting. *Rainbow Warrior* was to sail as mother-ship to a flotilla of four yachts picketing the coral atoll of Moruroa, in French Polynesia, where the French were conducting a series of underground nuclear tests. Now, all the key people in the little squadron were to meet in the lecture theatre built in what had been the fish hold when the ship sailed the North Sea as a research trawler.

The Greenpeace leaders explained to the yacht skippers that stiff resistance – if not direct interference – was expected from French naval patrols, as had happened before. Any protest vessel that strayed over the 12-mile (20 km) boundary of the prohibited zone that the French had drawn around the atoll would risk instant arrest and confiscation. Alternatives were agreed in case radio frequencies were jammed by the French. The atoll was in one of the remotest parts of the Pacific and the nearest ports, in French Polynesia, would be officially hostile to any of the Greenpeace fleet, so systems were established for *Rainbow Warrior* to re-provision the yachts and provide them with fresh water from her water-making plant. The rendezvous off Moruroa was decided for August 15th. The yachts would make the 4,000-mile (6,500 km) passage direct. The mother-ship would divert to Rarotonga, in the Cook Islands, and anchor outside the reef to lobby the meeting of the South Pacific Forum. On August 6th, the fortieth anniversary of the Hiroshima nuclear bomb, this assembly of 14 nations was to vote on whether to declare the South Pacific a nuclear-free zone.

Though low-key and friendly in the typical Greenpeace way the meeting had the key elements of a briefing for a military assault. There was an edge of excitement in the stuffy air. Steve Sawyer reminded the skippers of the aims of the operation: to remain on station as long as possible, especially through September when the Non-Proliferation Treaty was being discussed in Geneva. The Greenpeace flotilla, with *Rainbow Warrior*'s direct picture trans-mission links to international media, would help focus public atten-tion on the reality of nuclear testing. The idea was to build tension so other countries would be provoked into making statements that exposed their feelings. If any of the fleet was harassed by the French Navy, black and white photographs could be radioed from *Rainbow Warrior* to leading news agencies. It was hoped the ship would sail with members of parliament from Sweden, Denmark, New Zealand and Vanuatu on board, so it might even have enough political clout to risk going into Tahiti.

But it was stressed that any decision to sail inside the prohibited zone around Moruroa and risk the consequences was up to individual skippers. Russell Munro, 32, a long-striding New Zealander whose steel yawl *Django* was tied up alongside the ship, his fiancée sleeping on board, was quite prepared to risk losing his boat, his NZ$8,000 investment, and the two years of loving care he had lavished on building the yacht with his own hands.

Little did anyone suspect that while these military-like plans were being finalised in the fish hold, a military operation of a quite different and more sinister kind had been taking place just a few feet away, on the outer side of the rivetted steel plates forming the ship's hull. With loud generator noise from the engine room and the intensity of the discussions, nobody would have noticed any strange sound made by a saboteur.

All were tired and some were jet-lagged. Soon after eleven o'clock, after those waiting on deck had sent 'Let's get going!' notes down to the fish hold, the meeting broke up. Some of the directors not involved in the skippers' meeting had already left for the surf club at Piha. Elaine Shaw rounded up the rest and followed in a rental car.

Others had already left for the night. Dutchman Henk Haazen, 31, and his girlfriend Bunny McDiarmid, 28, had helped to refit *Rainbow Warrior* in Florida then signed on as third engineer and deckhand. Although their cabin, formerly a scientific laboratory, was one of the largest in the ship they decided not to sleep on board. Instead they would stay with Bunny's parents who lived in Auckland. She had just been re-united with them after a seven-year absence and wanted to be at home as much as possible before she sailed off again. Henk lifted his big old BMW 750 motorbike off the maindeck and they rode away. Natalie Maestre, 19, was having a rest from the ship and sleeping at Margaret Mills' cottage on Waiheke Island. Grace O'Sullivan, 23, a deckhand from Ireland, had gone for a short break to Great Barrier Island. Bene Hoffman, the second mate from West Germany, was away on a tramping trip. Peter Willcox, 32, the American skipper, turned into his bunk. Radio operator Lloyd Anderson, another American, fell asleep while reading, still wearing his glasses. Andy Biedermann, the Swiss doctor, was in his cabin.

As *Rainbow Warrior* settled down for the night, second engineer Hanna Sorensen unaccountably felt an urge to go for a walk and get some chilly air into her lungs. Thinking her friend Martin Gotje, 26, was asleep she went ashore without telling him and walked the length of the gloomy, dusty wharf towards the city lights.

Martin, first mate of the ship, was in fact one of the eight men sitting around the two narrow tables in the cosy messroom next to the galley. The tall, curly-haired Dutchman, always known as 'Martini', perched on a padded seat at the end of the table nearest the door. Nobody had the energy for a yahoo party. They were winding down, thinking of going to bed but too weary to make the effort. Also round the table sat Fernando Pereira, who had joined the ship in Hawaii, and Richard Rae, 18, then planning to skipper a small catamaran in the peace flotilla. At the head of the table

11

sprawled Russell Munro, whose yacht was tied up alongside, and Rien Achterberg, 36, another big Dutchman who lived on Waiheke, who was working in the Greenpeace office by day to co-ordinate the logistics of the protest flotilla and sleeping on board by night. Australian Chris Robinson, 32, was to skipper *Vega* on what would be the Greenpeace yacht's fifth protest voyage to Moruroa.

There was not much to drink, only a couple of bottles of beer to share among eight. Yorkshireman Davey Edward, 32, the ship's engineer, made a crack about it. Hans Guyt, 33, a former Dutch seaman who founded Greenpeace in Holland and sailed in *Rainbow Warrior* across the Pacific, looked at the clock on the bulkhead to see if the pubs were still open. He was surprised at how late it was. The hands of the cabin clock stood at 11.38pm.

A shattering explosion blasted *Rainbow Warrior*.

The lights went out. The steady drone of the generator stopped abruptly. There was a sound of breaking glass. In their ringing ears people heard the sound of running water: not a trickle but a roar.

In the same instant the entire ship lurched, thrown upwards and sideways. She did not straighten again. They sensed her going down, not fast but relentlessly.

Davey Edward hurled himself out of the messroom. He reached the engine room door along the passageway in about eight seconds. As he jerked it open the sound of roaring water filled his ears. The engine room was already well submerged. The sea was hurtling into the ship through a vast hole in her side, filling her at a rate afterwards calculated to have been around six tons a second.

Fast asleep until the explosion, skipper Peter Willcox first thought they had collided with a ship at sea. Then he looked out of the porthole, saw the lights on the wharf, and thought the generator must have blown up. Naked, he ran down the passageway and looked over Davey's shoulder. The emergency lights flickered on. In the dim illumination he could see water boiling around the ladders leading down to the engine, and steam from water hitting hot pipes. The lights flickered out as the rising water covered the batteries. The noise of the cataract was immense. Davey slammed the door. 'We'd better get everyone off,' the skipper said.

The messroom was left in total darkness but for the glimmer of the container-terminal lights coming through the four portholes. Somebody said, 'Christ, a tug's hit us!'

Russell Munro thought not. The generator had stopped too quickly. It could only have been a bomb. He worked his way clear of the table and put his hands on somebody's shoulders. 'Come on, let's get out!' he said.

Out in the passageway Rien Achterberg made for his cabin, only

12

a few feet away. He thought he would grab his working files, camera and sleeping bag. But there was an acidy, burning, metallic smell in the air. Don't, he told himself. He sensed the ship going slowly down, and listing more sharply. A former chef and baker who had sailed in Dutch coasters, Rien had once been in a ship that suffered an engine room explosion. He thought the same thing must have happened again. He abandoned his belongings.

While the others groped their way forward along the central passage towards the pale light over the maindeck, from which they could get ashore, five went aft. Russell Munro headed for his yacht, his one thought to get her clear before the ship sank and dragged her down. Russell's girlfriend Terisa, woken by the blast, was standing in the cockpit in her nightie wondering what had happened.

Hans Guyt found himself at the aft end of the side-deck with Martin and Fernando. Water was already licking through the scuppers and wetting the planks. Fernando shouted in English, 'She's sinking isn't she?'

Near the aft end of the passageway was a steep stairway leading down to the lower accommodation. At the foot of the stairs the doors of five cabins opened into a small lobby, now in pitch darkness. Three men slid down the stairway. Martin had obtained a flashlight and was desperately searching for Hanna whom he thought was in her cabin below. Dr Biedermann went down to help, and check the other cabins. And Fernando, who had something of a reputation in the ship for being last-man ready, never went anywhere without his precious Cannons. The cameras were on the bunk in his cabin.

Margaret Mills was just dropping off again when the loud bang shook her awake. Her first thought was that *Rainbow Warrior* had been hit by a ship. Then she heard running water and wondered if a tap had been left on. More curious than bothered, and not a bit alarmed, she quickly dressed. She was so unflustered that she took the time to tie her shoelaces. She didn't know the power had failed because she hadn't tried to switch on the light.

Fumbling towards the door she arrived in the wardrobe and thought it would be better to find her glasses. Without them she was a cripple. At the same moment she opened the door and realised a man was standing in the darkness. She didn't recognise him until he spoke. 'Come on, Margaret, we've got to get out,' Dr Biedermann told her.

'Wait . . . my glasses!'

'Don't be silly, the ship's sinking!'

On the basis (she related later) that boy scouts helped little old ladies across the street whether they wanted to go or not, Margaret decided to do what she was told. She still thought it all a bit ridiculous. Ships didn't sink in port. Then she saw the water pouring down the stairway.

At the top of the steps Hans Guyt, wondering whether to nip down to collect belongings from his cabin, saw Martin with the flashlight. At that moment the ship listed sharply. Hans returned to the side-deck where Margaret was splashing forward towards the ladder, up to her calves in water. As Martin turned to go up the stairs he glimpsed Fernando packing his cameras into a bag. Water was jetting into the compartment through wire runs, under great pressure. He ran up the steps thinking Fernando was right behind him.

In that instant a second explosion erupted beneath the stern of *Rainbow Warrior*.

From the yacht's cockpit Terisa saw a flash of light streak through the cloudy water, just beneath the surface. The aft part of the ship lurched as if struck from below by a giant hammer. The lower accommodation must have flooded instantly. Those on deck scrambled up the ladder or took flying leaps to the wharf. Peter Willcox shouted, 'Abandon ship!' Then the skipper went forward, checking the cabins along the passageway to ensure everyone was out. Intending to check that the fish hold was clear he found the stairway compartment giving access to it was already full of water. He headed for his cabin to collect his glasses and some clothes but there was no time. The ship was going down. Still naked, he waded out, climbed to the boat deck and jumped ashore.

'Look out, she's tipping!' Everyone scattered back from the edge of the wharf. Just four minutes after the first explosion, two minutes after the second, the twin steel masts tilted suddenly towards the wharf as *Rainbow Warrior* listed and settled on the bottom. To the dismayed survivors it seemed almost miraculous that she neither capsized nor disappeared. The ship lay on her starboard side, not quite submerged, her masts nearly touching the gutter of the wharf-shed roof.

Russell pushed his yacht clear with a spinnaker pole. It had no engine so he hoisted sail and ghosted across to the opposite wharf. Then he raced back by dinghy to salvage what he could of the objects floating around on the dark water.

Forlornly the numbed survivors gathered on the edge of the wharf, staring down at the ship. The first sirens were in the distance, getting louder. Several nearby ships had transmitted alarms to Auckland Marine Radio which had alerted police. The small passenger ship *Gulf Explorer*, once the Penzance to Scilly Isles ferry in Cornwall, England, had been thrown heavily against the pilings by the second blast. The two explosions were heard throughout the lower part of

14

the city, sending roosting seagulls screaming like white shrapnel into the night sky.

Martin was in shock. 'I think Hanna's in there,' he muttered bleakly. Rien escorted him with Margaret to a Dutch yacht whose skipper had run along the wharf offering aid. They were given blankets and coffee.

Peter Willcox, wearing only Davey Edward's shirt to cover what was necessary, tried to discover who was missing. On the long voyage out there had been routine lifeboat and fire drills but this was a contingency never catered for. It was hard to think exactly who of the crew should have been aboard and who was ashore. And what about the visitors? Peter worked out a list of names then called them out. Two were not accounted for. Where was Fernando? Did anyone see Hanna?

A few minutes later, expecting to go to bed, Hanna returned from her walk. Instead, she found the wharf closed off, blue flashing lights sparking in the darkness, and the ship she had left in peace and security barely half an hour before now a hulk on the bottom of the harbour.

Fernando was still missing. Skipper Peter Willcox and chief engineer Davey Edward climbed on board and peered down the engine room stack cover in case there was some way of searching for him. But the ship was full of water. The situation was hopeless.

Again and again they went over the possible causes of a double explosion big enough to blow their ship apart. The engines were all diesel, so it couldn't have been a fuel problem. In any case, the only engine running was a small generator. The oxygen and acetylene cylinders were stowed in a special compartment in the forepeak, near the bow. The cooking stove was electric. The amount of gas carried on board was negligible.

Meanwhile, after the 45-minute drive on the dark roads twisting over the bushy ranges outside Auckland to deliver the others to Piha Surf Club, Elaine Shaw arrived home to find the telephone ringing. It was a newspaper reporter. 'I want to talk about *Rainbow Warrior*.'

'It's after one in the morning, what do you mean?'

'Didn't you know? Your boat's been sunk.'

Elaine slammed down the phone. It rang again at once. Now a radio station was asking the same question. She telephoned the surf club. Still only half believing – and praying – it was all a joke, Elaine explained to Steve Sawyer what little she knew. They had only just left *Rainbow Warrior*. How could she be at the bottom of the harbour?

The little waterfront police station opposite Marsden Wharf, closed down for the night at 11pm as usual with only a direct

15

telephone link to central control, had been opened up by police at the scene. When Steve arrived after a frantic dash from Piha he found the appalled survivors gathered like refugees. Fernando had not been found. Martin reported seeing him in his cabin in the lowest part of the ship moments before the second explosion. With heavy hearts they feared the worst.

A team of divers from a police sub aqua club in Henderson, an outer suburb, was scrambled to the scene. But a submerged ship in murky waters at night was no place for sport divers. At 2am Lieutenant Hugh Aitken, staff diving officer of the Royal New Zealand Navy, was roused from his bed at home near the base at Devonport, just across the harbour. Since recent Defence cuts had limited their resources, navy divers were no longer expected to do police work. But there was no time to mess about. A ship had sunk and a man was missing, possibly fighting for breath in an air pocket. Within the hour Aitken's team of five divers had mustered their gear, crossed the harbour, and were on board the police launch alongside *Rainbow Warrior* preparing to dive.

The water was covered with a scum of diesel, oil and debris. After eight days of rain it was also full of suspended silt. Visibility underwater was zero. Only the weakest glimmer could be seen from a powerful torch pointed towards the face at arm's length. Four navy divers kitted up. Two would carry out the operation using the kind of penetration diving techniques developed for exploring caves, and two would stand by to deal with any emergency. The divers slid into the water. One stayed outside the ship to ensure the safety line did not snag. The other fumbled his way down into the lower accommodation. Within seven minutes he had surfaced with the body.

Fernando Pereira was found lying face-down on the floor of the cabin next to his own. The plywood partition between the two cabins was shattered. The floor beneath him had bulged upwards from the force of the explosion, the steel belted into a long ridge several inches high. An autopsy later revealed that the victim's body was unmarked and he had died of drowning.

Had his fateful rush to retrieve his cameras caused him to be trapped by a sudden inrush of water moments after Martin went up the ladder? Had the force of the explosion left him stunned and disoriented in the darkness with tons of water pouring down on his head, so he lost his way out? Exactly what happened to Fernando will never be known.

With all crew members and visitors accounted for, there was now a new priority. What had caused the explosions? As an expert in underwater demolition and military mine clearance, it had never been far from Lt Aitken's mind that the destruction was no accident. This impression was strengthened when he closely questioned the chief engineer. Gas or fuel explosions could be ruled out if only because there had been not one but two distinctly different blasts, two minutes apart. Also, the second explosion at the ship's extreme aft end was itself suspicious. Nothing explosive was stored there. Propellers and rudders did not normally blow up.

Aitken's immediate concern was that if *Rainbow Warrior* were the victim of deliberate sabotage, and the two charges had been triggered by some sort of timing device, more time-bombs could be ticking away beneath her even now. They could explode at any moment.

The lieutenant told his men to carry out a complete clearance check of the ship and nearby wharf pilings. Even the yawl *Django* was checked to ensure a charge had not been placed on her keel.

Dawn revealed *Rainbow Warrior* lying on her starboard side in a scummy pool of debris. A floating oil boom was laid to contain any seepage from her bunkers. Most of her dark green hull and white superstructure was submerged, along with the maindeck and Davey Edward's motorbike. Only a wing of the bridge, draped with a large banner proclaiming 'Nuclear Free Pacific', and behind it the white funnel with its North American Indian motif, were high and dry. The newly painted rainbow seemed to arch like a real rainbow from the murky harbour waters. Beneath it, seemingly skimming the waves like a gigantic seagull, the white dove of peace dipped a wing and trailed its olive branch in the sea.

It was in the middle of the morning, while a larger and fresh team of naval divers was surveying the wreck more thoroughly, that the vast hole was found in the side of the hull. It measured 6½ feet (2 m) by eight (2·4 m), as big as a garage door. It was positioned almost exactly in the centre of the engine room, the ship's largest compartment.

Furthermore, when the navy frogmen made an investigatory dive inside the ship, they found the steel hull plates had been petalled *inwards* by the blast. This told the whole story. 'There was no doubt in our minds then that the ship had been sunk by explosive charges attached to the outside of the hull,' said Aitken. 'It was a professional sabotage job – we couldn't have done it better ourselves.'

But the police took some convincing that terrorism had indeed struck at Marsden Wharf. And the police, in turn, had trouble convincing others. To prove they were right, and to assist the police case, the naval team shot an underwater video film of damage to the stern, showing popped rivets, cracked plates, the bent prop-shaft and distorted blades of the screw. It was clear that the first blast had been intended to sink *Rainbow Warrior*, the second to ensure that if the peace ship were raised she would never sail again.

The rest of New Zealand woke up to a sinister realisation. For the first time in history their pleasant land had been violated by an act of terrorism. Margaret Mills might have expressed the horror of the whole country when, deeply shocked by the news, she exclaimed: 'But we don't have bombs here!'

For the moment, while the world demanded answers, Margaret Mills sat at the windows of her cottage on Waiheke Island and composed a memory:

> I didn't know him,
> I met him on the ship
> And talked of bread.
> The bread he liked was brown,
> Close textured,
> Soft on crust.
> I searched the city,
> Found his bread.
> He ate it with the soup,
> Said it was good.
> The loaf was never finished.

It was only good fortune, and certainly nothing to do with the skills of the saboteurs, that Margaret was not penning requiems in blank verse to others among her new friends. She was lucky not to have been the subject of one herself. Any person in the engine room when the first explosion occurred would have been killed instantly. Henk and Bunny paled when they saw the shrapnel holes ripped in the floor of the cabin where they would have been sleeping had they not decided to stay with Bunny's parents. In the floor of the main passageway were shrapnel holes as big as Henk's fist, the steel pushed upwards like jagged volcanoes.

Had the second explosion detonated a few seconds earlier it would have trapped not one person in the lower accommodation but five.

Only the grace of God, it seemed, had saved the ship from turning turtle, possibly trapping and drowning all on board.

Soon the shock waves of the twin explosions that sank the peace ship were ricocheting far beyond the remote and peaceful bounds of 'God's own country'. *Rainbow Warrior*, it seemed, still had time-bombs on board but they were the political kind.

The first questions were the obvious ones. Who had clamped the explosive charges on the ship's hull? Who was so frightened of the so-called voyage of peace – or its owners, the environmental-protection group whose symbol was a rainbow – that an elaborate sabotage mission was conducted to blow the ship and rainbow clean out of the water?

The Greenpeace affair, as the papers tagged it, flowered into an epic international scandal. Ironically, it would achieve in grand measure every single one of the results the bombs had been intended to prevent.

It propelled the small band of 'direct action' environmental guardians to the centre of the world stage. It cast a brilliant media spotlight on French nuclear testing in the South Pacific. It enhanced New Zealand's controversial determination to opt out of military defence by means of nuclear weapons. And, evoking President Nixon, the scandal rocked the socialist government of France to the top of the tree.

Who was responsible for the appalling order, 'Sink the *Rainbow Warrior*'?

The whole story may never be known. But the seamy picture of incompetence, arrogance and evil intent that emerges from the available facts reveals the depths to which a supposedly honourable government of a superpower will stoop to pursue its own ends. At the very least it gives a sinister new lease to an old adage: with friends like these, who needs enemies?

Like many a good adventure yarn it's a David and Goliath story. It opens with a clash between the navy of a superpower and a small yacht. And the setting is an island in paradise.

2

BOOM-TIME IN PARADISE

A voyager's first sight of a coral atoll is a faint bristly line flat on the horizon. Binoculars reveal nothing but a row of feathery tufts, like cabbages. Bending in the brisk tradewind that fills your sails, the coconut palms become taller as you approach, seemingly growing straight out of the sea on slender leaning stalks. Now a navigator must be very cautious. Somewhere between the inviting palms and the great blue oceanic swells rolling under your keel lies the reef, a platform of fissured, razor-sharp rock rising sheer from the ocean floor until its upper surface is just awash. At night or in stormy weather it can be invisible. The effect of a ship running headlong into a reef is akin to an aircraft hitting a mountain. Perched on the crosstrees high up the mast in the sunshine, however, you can see the line of surf thundering into the coral, and the gap of smooth water where the rich blue waves of the ocean run into the brilliant pale turquoise of the shallow lagoon.

From the air you would see the reef as only a slender ribbon of land, little more than a skidmark on a field of blue, making a crumpled sort of circle. The lagoon it encloses could be as much as sixty miles (100 km) in diameter. But the reef itself is only a few hundred yards wide at most and barely ten feet (3 m) above sea level. Along its outer edge the ocean swells thunder against a bulwark of living coral where multitudes of tiny organisms are tirelessly constructing cement-like houses around themselves, by minuscule amounts advancing the reef into the deep ocean. Some of the reef is bare, some is covered in scrub, a lot may be submerged. But threaded along its perimeter are groves of coconut palms rooted in the brilliant white sand lapped by the warm lagoon.

In the window-clear water massive clumps of coral seem to reach up to the keel as you feel your way into the lagoon. Brilliant parrot fish dart away in the shallows as the anchor splashes down. When you swim ashore the water is as languorously warm as the air. This green lake in a blue ocean, walled in by sand, surf and a few tossing palms, is a pocket of paradise – the very soul of Pacific romance.

Among the world's most detached parts, atolls of this sort comprise the majority of the 130 inhabited islands, grouped in five archipelagos, of French Polynesia. The other islands, like Tahiti itself, are stunningly different. They are tall, rugged, lava peaks clothed in dense green jungle falling steeply into the lagoons that surround them. Where rivers cut down the ravines the reef is broken so the surf rolls right into the lagoon and bursts upon black-sand beaches. In the noonday heat the craggy pinnacles, as much as 7,000 feet high, stream plumes of cloud. When seen from afar the island seems to be speeding through the waves like a great passenger liner.

Tahiti, largest of the islands in French Polynesia, lies about mid-way between Australia and Chile; it is well south of the equator but north of the Tropic of Capricorn. The islands of its oceanic outback cover a geography of grand scale. If Tahiti were positioned in Paris, French Polynesia would embrace the Pyrénées, the English Channel, Stockholm, Bucharest and stretch nearly to Sicily. The Tuamotu archipelago would form a milky way of pristine atolls through central Europe from the North Sea nearly to the Black Sea. Though the area they cover is vast on the map the total amount of dry land, if all the islands were pushed together, is half the size of Corsica. And the population of 166,000 – well over half living in the capital of Papeete on Tahiti – would hardly fill a European market town.

The lightly coloured native Polynesians (I shall refer to them as Tahitians) are an intelligent, handsome, easy-going, gleeful and once war-like people whose ancestors long ago voyaged all over the Pacific in sailing canoes to settle lands as far distant as Hawaii and New Zealand. The men are tall, big-framed, powerful; the women lithe, smooth-skinned with flashing dark eyes and long jet black hair. Beauty ages early in the tropical sun but from middle age the Tahitians are statuesque people of regal demeanour.

In the two centuries since Captain Cook lost his breeches to a dusky maiden of the night the vision of Tahiti as an earthly paradise has captivated the minds of writers, philosophers and travellers. Not only were fish and fruit so abundant in these beautiful islands that you hardly needed to stoop for them, but casual love games and sex encounters without the complexities of loyalty and commitment were a way of life. Sailing ships were sometimes greeted by hordes of lovely young women who swam out to meet them pushing bundles of fruit, their skimpy paper-bark garments melting in the water. Small wonder that discoverers, whaling captains and no doubt a missionary or two hung their morals on Cape Horn as they sailed by.

Up to about 1961 the islands remained in a dream time, hardly touched by the real world. Though colonised by France they had nothing to exploit. The islands offered nothing to sell but their beauty when the weather was nice; in Tahiti the weather was always nice. The few tons of copra and pearl-shell harvested from the coconut groves and lagoons were sufficient to balance the finances because consumer needs were negligible. Living was free and easy and you hardly needed money. If it rained you plucked a leaf for an umbrella. Fish queued up for your table. For a cool drink you shinned up a coconut palm and cracked open a nut, or fermented it to make a lethal toddy. When fish or coconuts had to be carried home you plaited a leaf to make a basket. For entertainment there were dancing and singing and feasting. Standards of living weren't high in Western terms but you didn't have to work very hard, there was total security because social life was based on the extended family, and there were no such things as social security, welfare, mortgages, insurances, taxes or even electricity bills.

The number of French in Tahiti was hardly one thousand. In the small administration, officials were resigned to the fact that ultimately the small number of educated islanders (Tahitians, those with mixed blood known as 'demis', and Chinese) would step into their shoes – one of these days.

Tahiti was the very image of self sufficiency, contentment and bright high-handed adventure. I saw it myself as a young man. Travelling from New Zealand to Europe, my ship glided into the lagoon at Papeete one glossy morning in 1959. A sea of smiles in brown faces crowded the wharf as if ours was the first ship in months. Hordes of small boys gambolled on the mooring warps and dived for coins in the bottle-clear water. Schooners and a handful of sun-faded cruising yachts lay stern-to the quay beneath scarlet flamboyants. The eager tourist, I swam in the lagoon and swigged from freshly cut green coconuts and strolled beneath the wind-rattled palms. In the soft sweet-smelling evening I watched the sun go down over Moorea, the craggy island ten miles distant. Then to Quinn's, a waterfront shack with a tin roof and walls of woven cane, one of the most disreputable and romantic dives in the Pacific. Amplified guitars and hollow-log drums beat out a *tamure*, the fast-pulsing traditional dance that tingles the blood and fills the air with a thunder of kisses. In every booth, girls with flowers behind their ears and bright *pareu* dresses sprawled languidly with dazzling smiles upon the knees of sailors and tourists.

Beyond the sun-faded little reef town with its wide verandahs, paint-cracked timbers, red rooftops and dusty streets lay a world of far-flung islands connected by cockroach-infested old sailing schooners that lurched into the lagoons with laughing riff-raff crews and colourfully gin-sodden skippers. Only two events of any significance had ever occurred in French Polynesia. One was the mutiny aboard HMS *Bounty*, in 1787, which set the so-called civilised world dreaming of bountiful islands where men had unforgivably dared to throw off the yoke of authority to try their luck with Nature in her most appetising image. The second, in 1961, was the making of the MGM film of the mutiny that starred Marlon Brando. For it projected those images of paradise on the Cinemascope screens of the world and happened to coincide with the opening of a jet airport blasted out of the reef in Papeete.

The new airport brought tourists. Big hotels sprang up. Tahitians had their first taste of American dollars and the consumer delights they could buy, and liked it. Their days of happy isolation were ended. Had it been only a consumer revolution that they faced, as did other native races like the Inuit (eskimos) of Greenland and North America who were similarly reeling from the impact of a murderously benign Western lifestyle, it is likely the Tahitians would have adapted with comparative ease and developed a national character in light of their own aspirations and the resources of their islands. There was reason to think they would be helped deferentially towards independence like other Pacific Island communities who were then shaking off their colonial regimes and edging towards nationhood. Instead, what happened in French Polynesia was the exact reverse.

In the North African desert, far distant from the heavenly scents of the *tiare* flower, Algerian bullets and bombs were wreaking bloody carnage in the fight for independence from France. And France, in the meanwhile, had decided that never again would she run the risk of being occupied by a foreign power, as she had been in two successive world wars. President Charles de Gaulle had put in train the development of a nuclear bomb. France would henceforth have her own nuclear arsenal. Her nuclear armoury would not be as massively large or as sophisticated as those of the superpowers, but it would be the third most powerful in the world, more than sufficient to discourage an enemy from coveting her territories or assets.It was called the *force de frappe* (literally: 'striking force').

For research and development of her own nuclear weapons France required an area where devices could be test-fired. A testing ground was established in a remote part of the Sahara Desert, in Algeria. Four bombs were tested in the atmosphere (they were suspended above the ground and exploded so the blast formed a mushroom cloud and dispersed into the sky) and 13 more were tested underground.

Many African states strongly objected to the tests. Nigeria broke off diplomatic relations. The UN General Assembly resolved that the continent of Africa should be respected by all as a nuclear-free zone.

Algeria won her bloody fight for independence in 1962 but France was able to continue testing for five more years. Another testing

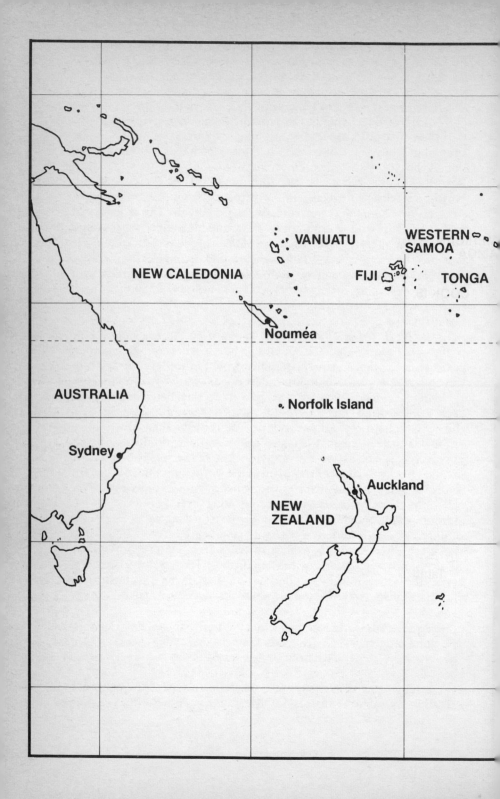

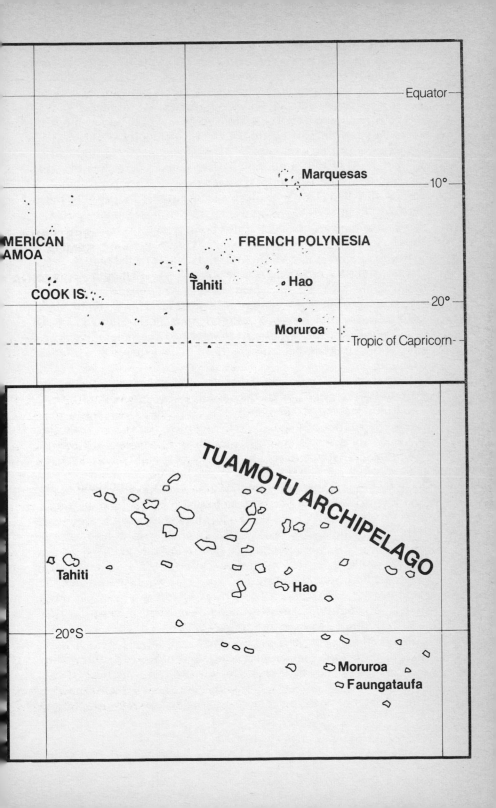

laboratory was required, and swiftly. Moreover it had to be a site that was not only environmentally safe, as far as the French were concerned, but one that enjoyed reasonable political stability. It would be inconvenient to have to make yet one more retreat under fire from expensive and critically important test facilities.

The sites chosen were three atolls, only one of them inhabited, in the south-eastern part of the Tuamotu archipelago. The nuclear devices were to be exploded in the atmosphere above the reef of Moruroa. A second atoll called Faungataufa, 25 miles (40 km) distant, would be kept in reserve and used as a forward base. A third atoll called Hao, 560 miles (900 km) from Tahiti and 280 miles (450 km) from Moruroa, would serve as rear base, staging post and the site to which personnel could be evacuated when detonation took place.

For the French the overwhelming advantage of the plan was that the test site was some 10,000 miles (16,000 km) distant from Paris. Yet it was handy to a French colony with a ready-made labour force. The promise of rest and recreation facilities in Tahiti no doubt made their hearts pump with joy. And the French never doubted that the bomb business with its fall-out of francs by the million would be regarded as nothing but a wonderful gift. No time was wasted in asking them.

Indeed, in 1963 a delegation of local political leaders travelled to Paris to urge a revision of the whole colonial system of government. Far from listening to their requests, let alone conceding to their demands, Charles de Gaulle told them loftily that he was rewarding them for their long-standing loyalty and patriotism: 'I have not forgotten all that you have done [for France] and this is one of the reasons why I have chosen to install this base in Polynesia.'

There was nothing new about testing nuclear devices on atolls. The British and the Americans had done just the same on islands under their control in the Pacific north of the equator. Now they were testing under the desert in Nevada, only 75 miles from Las Vegas. In a 310-mile (500 km) circle around the site lived no less than 15 million people. When accidental 'venting' of radioactive materials occurred, following an explosion, winds had carried the fall-out as far as Canada. The Soviet Union was not that much better, with the city of Omsk (population one million) just 350 miles (560 km) from its test site at Semipalatinsk.

Put a 310-mile (500 km) circle round Moruroa, on the other hand, and you enclosed a population of only 2,300, the nearest only a tiny community 75 miles (120 km) over the horizon from the test site. Seen from the French perspective the site was a dream. The atoll was about as close as you could get to the end of the world without

26

falling off. It was surrounded by a boundless ocean sprinkled only with tiny islands. On the scale of political clout which might be exerted by meagre populations to interfere with the test programme, the islands hardly rated a zero. From Moruroa these islands lay mainly beyond the west, north and east sectors of the horizon. To the south there was nothing but open ocean for 3,000 miles (4,800 km) to Antarctica. The atoll was nowhere near any sea lanes or air routes. All the major cities of the South Pacific were at least 4,000 miles (6,500 km) away, more distant than New York is from Nevada. Moruroa, moreover, was not only the ideal site but one that happened to be handy to a little paradise to which every red-blooded Frenchman dreamed of escaping without his wife.

In launching its test programme the government of France therefore stood no nonsense. There was no question of condescending to ask any opinion, local or otherwise. Repeated United Nations resolutions to stop the testing were ignored. Repeated requests by the local Territorial Assembly for an international commission to review the safety of the testing were rejected. At no point were the Tahitian people consulted.

Instead of being stood on their own national feet by a benign administration, Tahitians found themselves under the thumbs of a high-handed colonial autocracy.

The consequences of contact between native island societies and technological man, hauntingly captured by author Alan Moorehead in the phrase 'the fatal impact', were initially epidemics and tyrannical missionary regimes. Now the French were administering the 'coup de grâce'. It was achieved through the simple expedient of flooding the place with soldiers, settlers – and French francs.

An umbrella organisation of all the many agencies involved in the massive project was set up under the name *Centre d'Expérimentation du Pacifique* (CEP) with a headquarters in Papeete. The scientists of the Atomic Energy Commission (CEA), the army, the Foreign Legion engineers and the Navy also built headquarters and barracks in Tahiti. Within a year the island (then with a population of 60,000) was accommodating as many as 7,000 military men and technicians, half of them permanently, half on rotation. Most were bachelors, none paid tax, all earned much more than they did in France, and all – having seen how Marlon Brando in the guise of Fletcher Christian had entertained himself in the *Mutiny on the Bounty* – were hot for the favours of a dusky *wahine* and carried the cash in their pockets to be certain of success.

Soldiers were warned to walk facing the traffic so Tahitian men, understandably overwhelmed, couldn't sneak up behind on bikes or scooters and club them on the back of the head. When the military were allowed to wear civilian clothes, tourists were mistaken for soldiers or sailors and attacked in the street. Then, although it had been illegal to operate a brothel in France for years, it was decided the law did not apply during military campaigns and that it would be a useful solution to the 'outlet problem' if 'relief stations' were established on charming little vessels anchored in discreet corners of the lagoon, with hostesses supplied from the Orient. The idea fizzled out only when high school students got wind of the plan and, with support from the local media, drummed up a powerful protest.

Meanwhile, military men voyaging around the islands had nailed recruiting posters to the trunks of palm trees. Within about half a year five thousand Polynesians had exchanged their tranquil island-based existence as occasional copra producers, farmers and fishermen for that of salaried construction workers on shift. In their terms the earnings were fabulous but with hindsight it's hard not to weep at the irony of it. Where subsistence was probably easier and more comfortable than anywhere in the world, the taxpayers of Mother France were lavishing sums of cash the equivalent of thousands of dollars per head per year. And the Tahitians, putting up little resistance, fell easy prey to the monsoon of francs. Tempted with the consumer delights of the outside world, it was only a short step to the realisation that as Tahitians they must die if Tahiti were to live.

Thousands more islanders streamed into Papeete. In the Polynesian tradition of the extended family, uncles, aunts and distant cousins shared in the good fortunes of a man with a high-paying job. Slums spread up the beautiful valleys. The native people now had money to spend but food was no longer virtually free; prices spiralled. With the depopulation of the islands agriculture slumped. Instead of picking a handful of limes outside your hut, with which to cure your fish and make that most Tahitian of dishes, *poisson cru*, limes had become so scarce they were imported from California at a high price. Fresh fish became so expensive that only the rich could afford it. Even a small tin of fish – tuna that might have been caught in Tahitian waters by a Japanese boat, canned in American Samoa, and exported to Tahiti from California – cost around US$5. Now most could afford only smoked mackerel.

At the same time Tahitians had to compete against a massive influx of 25,000 new settlers from metropolitan France and former colonies in Africa. Still arriving at the rate of about one thousand a year, the flood shows no sign of abating even now. The Chinese and the demi people, too, opted heart and soul for the new boom-time economy and a policy of Tahiti for the French. The work ethic of the Chinese, as the traditional storekeepers of the islands, had never been much affected by South Seas languor. And the large and voluble demi population was able to achieve a smooth and eager transition from the easy-going Polynesian ambience into the challenging, competitive and rewarding French one. Commercial opportunities came in the form of the new airport and big hotels that put Tahiti on the map as a tourist destination. New enterprises sprang up in every direction, requiring the inspiration, investment, management and skilled labour that only the French, the demis and the Chinese could supply.

Papeete has become a peppy, noisy, glossy South Seas city in miniature with malls of chic boutiques, lively restaurants, hugely expensive rents, no direct taxation and nowhere to park. Its character is completely French, not Tahitian, except in the colourful pre-dawn market where island pineapples, coconuts, mangos, bananas and giant water melons are heaped in fragrant mountains. Quinn's Bar has long since disappeared under a tide of high-rise concrete and the bars of Papeete are of the neon and space-invader variety that grace Skid Row everywhere. But the blue Pacific fronting the tree-lined Pomare Boulevard still sparkles its invitation to adventure. The marvellously craggy outline of Moorea still sits like a real Bali Hai on the horizon. The blue-water yachts with baggywrinkle in their rigging, to prevent the chafe of sails on long passages, still rock on the last breaths of the surf rolling over the reef, though there is talk of moving them to a marina.

The rack of bananas is no longer carried on a wide muscular shoulder but in a hulking Toyota 4WD with cross-country tyres. The lunchtime joggers pounding along Pomare Boulevard, carrying outrigger paddles and wearing headbands and running shorts as colourful as the bougainvillaea, are French office workers and businessmen training for pirogue racing. In June 1985 so many French people and school children wanted to travel back to France for summer vacations that Air France had to lay on no less than 12 extra jumbo jets.

But one element of Papeete life remains delightfully Tahitian. What locals call 'le truck' is to the municipal bus what the sailing schooner is to the jumbo jet. To the cab and chassis of a light lorry is bolted a home-made wooden shack with hard seats. You stoop under the low flat ceiling as you mount from the rear, wincing from the impact of disco or Country & Western music belted from twin 12-inch speakers. In their delightful Polynesian way the people smile and slither along to make room. Trucks parade constantly along the island's perimeter road, tooting at everyone in sight in case they want to jump aboard. To hail one you just wave. It's like travelling on a flying verandah.

How do the Tahitians figure in this old-style colonial set-up of 'Tahiti for the French'? It doesn't take long for the feeling to dawn that the French people think Tahiti is a really beautiful place which would be a lot nicer without the Tahitians; but then who would do the menial work, who would dance and sing for the tourists filling the foreign-chain hotels?

Nearly all the 20 flights passing through Tahiti every week seem to come and go in the early hours of the morning and as you pass through Immigration it's three yawning Tahitians dressed in orange *pareus* who strum guitars and serenade your arrival. It's Tahitians who crew the sleek bonito fishing launches that line the waterfront, cleaning down the decks every evening then directing the hose inside their trousers to cool the blood. It's lovely Tahitian girls with glum expressions who serve in hotel restaurants, often criticised by tourists because they have yet to cultivate the knack of smiling in order to earn a tip (though tipping is not expected in Tahiti). It was a slender, long-haired, perfumed Tahitian maiden, of a beauty you'd willingly mutiny for, who, when I ordered a coconut-flavoured ice cream at her neon-lit kiosk, made no effort to restrain or even avoid the cockroach trotting across the tub of ice cream from which she was scooping my purchase. She rolled it up inside the scoop of ice cream then pressed it into a sugar-cone and passed it to me with a melting smile. This was the old Tahiti.

At night it's Tahitians you see polishing the floors behind the windows of brightly lit banks, stores and offices in town. It's Tahitians who thread thousands of tiny dyed shells on nylon to make necklaces for tourists, and weave marvellous crowns of flowers; in the evening they sit under the thatched stalls lining the boulevard where the cruise ships dock, murky Gauguin figures picking their feet in the gloom.

These days the Tahitian people have difficulty reaching the lagoon to pursue their age-old custom of gleaning for shellfish, octopus and fish. The way is barred by fences and gates with notices saying *tapu* (forbidden). All the prime coastal land has been cornered by the highly paid administrators and businessmen. The grassy swards beneath the shady palms, where the only grass huts shelter BMWs and Renaults, are loud with the scream of lawn mowers. The same is true of the island of Moorea, ten miles (16 km) distant, where the more beautiful white-sand beaches and unspoiled valleys have become Tahiti's principal tourist playground with a Club Med, several large hotels, and weekend houses for well-off Tahiti residents. To enjoy their lagoons now, Tahitians must return to the atolls.

The transformation of Tahiti in the image of metropolitan France is complete in every respect. Newspapers, radio and television are pro-French, pro-development, and the Polynesian viewpoint is feebly represented. Both the French administration and the military breathe heavily down reporters' telephones when they are writing about contentious issues.

The education system is entirely French. Children of all races are educated in French as if they were in France. No effort is made to make use of the textbooks developed by neighbouring Polynesian countries. Tahitian children are therefore disadvantaged from the beginning because they are not taught in their mother tongue; those who attend kindergarten from the age of two may become proficient in French but it is not the language spoken by their parents. Moreover, well over half the Tahitian population is under the age of eighteen. They are still in school where, thanks to an inappropriate education in a foreign language, they are totally unprepared to compete against French, demi and Chinese graduates.

With 2–3,000 youths flooding on the labour market every year the unemployment problem is soaring and there are no jobs in sight. The standard of living in Tahiti is by far the highest in the South Pacific, ten times the level of neighbouring countries like Western Samoa and comparable with that of over-developed countries. But the economy is entirely artificial. As M. Bernard Gerard, French High Commissioner in Tahiti, eloquently put it to me: 'The fuel of the Polynesian engine comes from the expenses of the administration and civil servants' salaries.'

This civil service is immense with no less than 15,000 bureaucrats in a country whose total population is only 166,000. The 2,200 top jobs are held by expatriates. With allowances, they make twice what they earn in France, have generous holidays and home leaves, and pay no tax. The minimum wage is about £350 a month, as in France. A local person who has graduated from high school can earn about £400 a month working in a hotel, but more than £1,000 as a lowly clerk in the administration. A trainee teacher on the first day of employment is paid the same as a French teacher who had been qualified for two years.

But living is costly. Instead of direct taxation there are stiff import taxes. On the price of a new car, for example, you pay an import tax of 50 percent. Every year a special tax is negotiated for the value of military and nuclear hardware. Overall, France's total import into French Polynesia is around £280 million (US$400 million) a year of which a little less than ten percent is received in the form of Customs dues for the bomb. Once self-sufficient in food, French Polynesia now imports all but five percent of its needs. Exports are negligible – still some copra, a new Japanese-backed industry cultivating black

31

pearls in the atoll lagoons, and earnings from ten thousand tourists a month – and there is small hope of the economic base growing stronger.

In short, the bomb business has brought to Tahiti a boom-time economy but the price Tahitians are paying is a high one. They are being brain-washed by French culture, bought out by artificially high wage rates, bribed by the promise of Western consumer goods and swamped by ever-increasing numbers of better-educated foreigners more capable of making the most of the new dynamic lifestyle of the place.

But they are not physically oppressed. They enjoy all the rights of citizenship of France. Any Tahitian who moves his gear lever into 'Drive' can enter the race on equal terms; the few who have avoided flunking out at school have been warmly welcomed. The French argue that the boom-time is hardly a fate worse than death. What is happening to the Tahitians, one might observe, is hardly different from the fate of the Maoris in New Zealand and the Aboriginals in Australia more than a century ago.

But the rampant colonialism corrupting the old and romantically carefree Tahiti, polluting its island culture and buying out its people, is regarded with profound suspicion and distrust by other countries as well as those who protest against the development of nuclear weapons. What has happened to Tahiti, they assert, is typical of the heartlessness of the nuclear arms race. France has deliberately used the Tahitians to serve her military convenience. The innocent Tahitians have no chance of resisting the hurricane of consumerism poisoning their delightful lifestyle. Isn't France behaving like the drug-pushers who tempt our teenagers with pot and LSD on the streets?

The deeply felt resentment of the French in the South Pacific is rooted as much in the high-handed and autocratic way they have achieved their ends as in the effect. While empires were being dismantled everywhere else, while colonised countries were being groomed for independence and stood on their own feet, while Charles de Gaulle himself was stirring the pot in Quebec with his inflammatory message that independence was the desirable aim of all 'subjected' peoples, the French in Tahiti were doing the exact reverse. Today their image as obsessed colonists imposing an inappropriate lifestyle on a 'subjected' people – in order to build a secure social foundation beneath their nuclear laboratory – is not readily understood by the French. As they see it, French Polynesia is legally an overseas territory of France. The beautiful islands in the South Seas are as much part of France, they say, as Brittany. Tahitians enjoy the rights and benefits of all French citizens (though this means they have no control over the French coming to live in their islands). This status and attitude of mind accounts for the blank looks that Australians and New Zealanders encounter when laying charges of colonialism: 'Ah, but this is already France – how can we be colonists?'

It is also somewhat irksome for those trying to whip up a scandal that the French blitz has upset outsiders rather more than it has the native Tahitians. Seemingly it's only outsiders who worry about the loss of the famous Tahitian smile.

Through the 1970s there was ample evidence of political repression. The few local leaders seeking a modest degree of autonomy were exiled or locked up on dubious grounds. At elections they were refused use of government facilities such as radio stations and inter-island transport for electioneering. A French businessman shot dead in his bed was the victim of a political killing, and a bomb exploded in the Post Office, but it was hard to be a guerrilla in Tahiti and the perpetrators were rapidly brought to book. Then the Territorial Assembly was occupied for many months until a shift of power in Paris promised a new constitution. Today, all affairs but finance, defence, broadcasting, justice, secondary education and foreign relations are controlled locally and the potentially explosive situation is in fact rather calm. This might be due to what M. Gerard suggests is a combination of the languid climate, the Polynesian state of mind, and what he defined (drawing pictures of clouds in the air with both hands) as 'a trend towards optimism'.

The independence movement does not, at present, play a significant role in the legislature. Its strength is hard to gauge because of the fragmentation of political parties. Numbers in the annual peace and anti-nuclear marches vary between a few hundred and a couple of thousand. Some observers say an independence movement is poised to sweep into power; others believe it's virtually moribund though it has a dynamic spokesman in Oscar Temaru, Mayor of Fa'a, a large municipality on the outskirts of Papeete.

In 1982, after long and agonising deliberations, the Synod of the Evangelical Church of French Polynesia (the Protestant Church to which 55 percent of the population belong, only one of its 80 parishes using the French language), wrote a letter to President Mitterrand asking him to stop the nuclear tests. The Church received no answer. A second letter the following year was fobbed off with the answer that there was nothing to be concerned about. A third letter was not answered. Now the majority of church leaders are realising the only way to be completely reassured of the people's safety is to work for political independence – 'It could be the birth of a new grass-roots movement,' says John Doom, secretary-general of the Church.

Independence is one thing and the bomb business is another but it's difficult in Tahiti to speak out against one without also seeming to be opposed to the other. France *is* the bomb. To protest against the tests is to oppose France. After all, the bomb is being developed to ensure the defence of an independent France – and Tahiti is part of that France.

Moreover, everybody in Tahiti has at least one family member whose income and welfare depends directly on the bomb business. Do you really want to kill the goose that lays the golden egg?

Besides, it hardly escapes the notice of local political leaders that France long ago separated the three bomb-test atolls of Moruroa, Faungataufa and Hao from the sovereignty of French Polynesia. From a legal point of view these islands are as much a part of France as the Elysée Palace and no longer have anything to do with French Polynesia. Should French Polynesia succeed in cutting the colonial apron strings the testing programme – with little inconvenience to the authorities – will carry on. And it will then impinge little on the way of life, or the livelihoods, of Tahitians.

Thus the burning political issue in French Polynesia is not independence, but dependence. And when so many depend on the fruits of the bomb business, who dares (or can be bothered) to question the fundamental morality of nuclear politics?

'Truly,' confided one local newspaperman, 'we're more concerned here about the lack of zoning laws, and the construction sites that allow mud to wash into the lagoon with every downpour, dirtying the beaches and killing the coral, than with what goes "Bang!" on Moruroa.'

But outsiders are much concerned with what goes 'Bang!' on Moruroa.

Resentment at the exploitation of Tahiti to serve French interests explains only part of their rage. Equally important is their frustration at the haughty indifference with which French authorities treat perfectly reasonable fears about the effects of the nuclear tests on the environment and the health of local people. The government of France does not concern itself with any obligation to assuage doubts. And this high-handed secrecy, its critics claim, is the most pernicious kind of colonialism of all. An army of scientists, engineers and soldiers descends upon a remote Garden of Eden, repeatedly triggers off the fires of Hell, then adopts a policy of say nothing, answer no questions, reveal no data. 'Everything,' France has always claimed, 'is perfectly safe.'

For those with the nerve to doubt that this could really be true, and who try to discuss with the French the scientific basis of their assurances, what could be more maddening than the bland Gallic shrug? Incredibly, the fact that a test has taken place is not even announced. People in Tahiti hear about it either through the 'coconut telegraph' from friends and relatives working on Moruroa, or by way of news reports from New Zealand whose seismic laboratory in the Cook Islands, about 1,000 miles (1,600 km) to the west of Tahiti, registers the shock waves and provides experts with sufficient data to calculate the strength of the blast.

Typical of France's offhand response to deep local anxieties is the cancer scare. It goes back to the earliest days of the tests.

Despite the fighting in Algeria, French testing continued in the desert throughout the construction of new facilities on the atolls. Then they rapidly moved house. The last desert test was in February 1966, the first on a barge floating on the Moruroa lagoon on July 2nd of that year. The Partial Test Ban Treaty of 1963, which banned nuclear tests in the atmosphere, was ignored. France refused to sign on the grounds that for technological reasons it was no longer possible to conduct tests underground as she had been doing in North Africa.

Up to 1966 officials in the administration had been regularly publishing public health statistics. Shortly before the first blast this was stopped and requests from the Territorial Assembly to resume were ignored. The CEP renewed its bland assurances that the tests posed no threats to the environment or to public health. It announced that regular checks would be made of the radioactivity in fish, the basis of the islanders' diet, but all figures were withheld.

In September of 1966 Charles de Gaulle, President of France, made a trip to observe one of the inaugural explosions. On arrival at the atoll he embarked on the cruiser *De Grasse*. Next day was cloudy with a strong wind blowing from the wrong direction and the test was delayed because any fallout would be carried westwards towards Tahiti, the Cook Islands, the Samoas and Fiji. Next day the weather was unchanged. The president had a busy schedule and apparently let it be known that he could not cruise around the Pacific for ever.

Dangling like a small refrigerator from a helium-filled balloon in the sky over Moruroa, the 120-kiloton nuclear device was triggered. 'Ah . . . c'est magnifique!' the president reportedly commented.

Radioactive fallout drifted over the Pacific Island countries and 'alarming levels' were measured in rainwater catchment tanks. The levels of fallout on Tahiti and other inhabited islands of French Polynesia were never published.

One who saw an explosion at that time was John Doom, then running a radio station. He had gone to Moruroa to act as interpreter for the official party and was evacuated to Mangareva, 260 miles

(420 km) to the east, to watch the blast. 'Until then I had always accepted French assurances that the blasts were harmless,' he says. 'But when I heard the explosion and its echoes, saw the mushroom cloud boiling up into the sky, I felt so ashamed at what we were doing. It was even worse when fallout began to drift over the island, though it didn't reach critical levels. The doctors felt it was important enough to treat the 580 people on the island, hosing them down to wash off the fallout and giving them some sort of medicine. But treatment was prevented by political advisers. It would make the people too alarmed.'

From that moment John Doom realised the value of French assurances that no fallout would ever land on inhabited islands and that the tests posed no risks. For nearly two decades all requests for detailed information, even when made formally by the Territorial Assembly, were stonewalled. The public health service was almost entirely directed by the armed services. In 1984, of the 111 public health doctors in the colony, 83 were military. Death certificates were required only to furnish legal proof that a patient had died and notification of cause of death was not required. Autopsies were in any case difficult due to the practical problems of coping with corpses on remote tropical islands, and were seldom carried out also for religious reasons.

But pressure on the authorities mounted and in July 1983, through the embassy in Australia, the French at last issued statistics. They showed that incidence of cancer per 100,000 people was 50 in French Polynesia, 106 in Australia, 175 in metropolitan France and 264 in New Zealand. Moreover, not only had the actual numbers of cancer cases per year remained more or less steady, but the proportion of cancers likely to have been caused by radiation (those affecting the blood, thyroid gland and internal organs) were no more frequent than other types of cancer caused by smoking, alcohol or diet.

Far from allaying suspicions, the figures stirred even deeper doubts. Weren't the figures related only to deaths in the main hospitals in Tahiti? What about those who died and were buried with no autopsy in the islands? And those evacuated for treatment to Australia, New Zealand, New Caledonia, the United States and France (entire hospital wards of cancer-stricken Tahitians were rumoured in Paris)? And those treated in the CEP's own hospital for its workforce on Moruroa?

For all these reasons there is a strong gut-feeling among those active in the anti-nuclear movement that the figures lie. In summer 1985 Marie-Therese Danielsson, wife of the distinguished anthropologist Bengt Danielsson who has lived in Polynesia since he arrived on board the *Kon Tiki* raft in 1948, had seen four or five friends and neighbours, all in their early forties, struck down by leukaemia and other cancers that might have been radiation-induced. The Danielssons' own daughter, who saw the flash in the sky made by a distant test and reported seeing a white dust falling on the grass, later died of leukaemia; she, too, would have been in that age group. 'We simply cannot believe that the figures are not being distorted to conceal the awful truth that fallout from the early tests is causing cancer,' says Mrs Danielsson.

Meanwhile, New Zealand film men have been secretly filming cancer victims and typically mange-ridden island dogs to 'prove' that nuclear fallout is killing the islanders, and this kind of unsubstantiated reporting will be readily believed. The authorities have recommenced the publication of health statistics and insisted that cause of death be noted on death certificates. In view of the small populations in the remote islands, and the publicised figures of those evacuated abroad for medical treatment, it's possible that the fears are grossly exaggerated. But if the figures have nothing to hide, the authorities have a funny way of putting across their case. As long as they try to allay genuine fears with half-truths and glaring omissions the truth will inevitably be perceived as propaganda – a truth laundered to suit French military interests.

Today John Doom, a thick-set and jovial demi whose quaint name was derived from an ancestor who was a German adventurer called Dohom, rips round Papeete in a VW bus with a radiation detector bleeping on the dash. It has sounded an alarm only once, when he drove into the gates of the CEP headquarters, though he never discovered what had set it off and doesn't believe it was a malfunction. 'Can you imagine the French admiral in charge of the CEP telling me – Yes, we have a radiation leak in Papeete?' he asks with a rumbling laugh.

What we have to remember about the nuclear testing on Moruroa is the meaning of the name, he asserts. *Moru* means secret (or fishing line) and *roa* means big. Moruroa is the atoll of the big secret – and France intends it to stay that way.

3

ATOLL OF THE BIG SECRET

In the picture on the brochure front cover, palm trees lean over a bone-white beach lapped by an azure lagoon. A handful of people laze in the warm water. It could be the Club Med. In fact it's the French nuclear laboratory in the South Seas: Moruroa, 'the atoll of the big secret'. Never could a remote coral island have been more aptly named.

At least twice a day Caravelle jet airliners of the French Air Force whistle out of the cloud-fleeced blue sky and set down on this loneliest of atolls after flying two hours 25 minutes east-south-east from Tahiti (the equivalent of Zagreb from Paris). But nobody can buy a ticket to Moruroa. Only those with very special permission are invited.

Try to make a landfall here in your own little ship and – twelve miles (20 km) off – you are intercepted by a patrolling warship. You never get close enough for more than a distant glimpse of the strange lattice towers, thick with antennae, jutting above the palm trees. Or the burned-out remnants of the mock-up of a naval frigate. Or the immense blockhouses constructed of thousands of tons of steel and concrete, their walls reportedly 20 feet (6 m) thick and showing the black scorchmarks of a hurricane of fire.

If, as a frigate bird soaring on the warm tradewind, you were to make your own freewheeling approach over the forbidden shore, what you saw would be a puzzle. For this paradise isle is something between a Foreign Legion military camp and a sprawling, ugly construction site. Barely half a mile (800 m) wide, much of the reef is sealed beneath concrete or tarmac. Thin dusty roads of crushed coral wending along the top of the reef link a mysterious assortment of blockhouses, level concrete pads and smoothed areas of sand and shingle. These are the spots where the unimaginable forces of nuclear cataclysm have been released, each one a 'point zero'. Up to July 1985 France had triggered 112 explosions, 41 in the atmosphere and 74 deep beneath the reef or below the shimmering lagoon.

Not all of the atoll Moruroa could be described as God's gift to paradise. Much of the reef is barren or near desert. In fact it's one of the least attractive and hospitable atolls of the archipelago. It was discovered in 1767 by the British navigator Philip Carteret who named it Bishop of Osnaburg Island after George III's second son.

In 1792 the American whaling ship *Matilda* was wrecked on the reef. Survivors who managed to construct a boat and get back to Tahiti – a lucky escape because many of the Tuamotu atolls were inhabited by cannibals – reported its position and the atoll was later mapped as Matilda's Reef.

The atoll was never inhabited by more than a handful of people. Attempts to harvest the copra (dried flesh of coconuts) during the latter part of the last century were frustrated by cyclones that swept the meagre land on the low-lying reef. Towards the end of the Second World War three Polynesians living on the island – a man, a woman and her lover – furnished the French writer André Roussin with inspiration for his South Seas novel, *The Small Hut*. When French naval hydrographers charted the island in the early 1950s there were only two Polynesian couples living there, next to a thatched shed for storing the copra which was collected – probably as infrequently as once every year or two – by a trading schooner.

From the air the meandering reef, 39 miles (63 km) round, makes an outline that resembles, if anything, a wide-brimmed sun hat or sou'wester. The area of lagoon it encloses is about the same as Paris. The atoll is 13½ miles (22 km) at its broadest east-west extent and 6·2 miles (10 km) from north to south. In many places the reef comes near to being breached by the sea and a lot of it is submerged. The surface is mostly bare with patches of scraggly low scrubs and only one or two groves of palms. Unless the legionnaires have eaten them all the biggest wild animals are massive slow-moving coconut crabs climbing the palms by night to pry open coconuts with pincers big and powerful enough to nip off your hand. In damp corners of greenery creep the giant African snails, now a Pacific Island pest. It's only regrettable, the military brochure points out, that their size and appearance do not make them very tempting to eat.

The main entrance to the lagoon is three miles wide but the navigation channel threaded by the grey military landing ships bringing equipment and supplies is narrow and tortuous. The lagoon is thick with fish, especially the brightly coloured parrot fish, small reef sharks and pearl-bearing mussels.

At the eastern end where the reef is broad and crooked like an arm around a white sandy cove, there is a dense grove of palms and pandanus. This is the *zone de vie* (literally: zone of life) for as many as 4,000 people. These days the work-force comprises about 1,200 Tahitian labourers, 400 French civilian technicians, scientists and engineers, and about 1,500 military men of whom 600 are legionnaires. Women technicians often work on Moruroa for short periods but the total number of females is seldom higher than twenty.

Beneath the palms is a shanty town of lack-lustre utilitarian buildings, from little accommodation units resembling cargo containers with windows to office buildings, scientific laboratories, and mess halls. The Cinéma Martine shows movies twice a night. In the 'Foyer Martine' you can have a drink, play ping pong, buy newspapers, borrow books, watch videos, get photographs developed and telegraph flowers. You can also make travel and hotel reservations for leave periods which fall every two weeks for civilians and six weeks for soldiers. Sea-water is desalinated for domestic use but bottled mineral water imported from Tahiti is preferred for drinking and is consumed by the thirsty soldiers, workers and scientists at the rate of 6,000 litres a day. The church is shared by both Catholics and Protestants. There's a soccer field, volleyball court, hospital, two banks and an officers' club.

Adjoining the living area to the north is a long straggling industrial zone of cargo wharves, immense storage yards and warehouses, stone crushers with heaps of aggregate for mixing concrete, piles and stacks and rows of construction equipment, garages, an electricity generating plant, fuel dump, garbage piles and the jet-landing strip where a carved wooden sign says 'Welcome to Moruroa' in French and Tahitian.

Together, the two zones make a strip of reef barely four miles (6·5 km) long. The rest of the atoll is a prohibited zone.

Strangest of all, on the seaward side of the inhabited part of the atoll workmen toil in the hot sun over the construction of an immense double wall. Running in two parallel rows about fifty yards (45 m) apart, the barricade comprises vast concrete blocks, each weighing seven tonnes and standing nearly 14 feet (4·25 m) high. Placed shoulder to shoulder for six miles (10 km), their purpose is to prevent the low-lying atoll from being swept unexpectedly by a *tsunami*, or tidal wave. On all Pacific atolls the danger of storm surges and tidal waves originating from distant earthquakes is always present. For this reason raised refuge platforms, each big enough to hold about 120 people, stand every few hundred yards. On the atoll of the big secret, however, the tidal waves are sometimes man made.

There is nothing of the laid-back South Seas lifestyle about this atoll, though both sea and air temperatures are more or less even and equal through the year, averaging around 23 to 25 degrees C. It's more like a slave camp. Work continues round the clock. Air Force planes fly in and out, carrying personnel and sometimes sinister-looking secret cylinders. Helicopters clatter around the perimeter of the reef. Trucks big and small are constantly on the move. After lunch and on Sundays a few people might sun themselves on the strip of beach or take a sailboard out on the lagoon, but fishing is prohibited for the simple reason that if you eat the fish or shellfish

40

that are so abundant in this beautiful lagoon you run the risk of a horrifying and lingering death.

The perimeter of the reef is divided into sectors given the names of females, flowers and birds. It must have been a bright idea to start at the northern tip and, working clockwise, name every feature on the reef alphabetically. But what started out with Aline, Brigitte, Colette and Danielle got to point Zoë when only halfway round so additional names like Eider, Faucon and Dindon were added. In some places the reef is fissured by deep, narrow clefts. The whole thing has been cracked, as if by a great earthquake, and parts of it are slumping beneath the surface of the waves.

Out in the lagoon a jack-up rig, of the sort commonly found in the North Sea or the Gulf of Mexico, is constantly at work drilling wide-diameter holes deep into the coral sea-bed lying about 80 feet (25 m) under the water. Helicopters ferry workers and scientists to and fro. When the hole is completed, just over six feet (2 m) wide and as much as 3,280 feet (1 km) deep, the rig raises its legs, is towed by a tug to a new precise location, and begins again.

Then a big barge is towed to the completed hole. On it stands a covered building with a high tower attached. For several days there is intensive activity on the barge. A grey-painted watertight cylinder some fifty feet (15 m) long is delicately eased into the water. Frogmen guide it into a tulip-shaped funnel at the top of the shaft. When the cylinder is lowered to the bottom of the shaft it is plugged with concrete.

Finally the barge is replaced by another which is connected to the top of the shaft with thick bundles of electric cables and wires. Then you begin to feel an air of edgy anticipation about the place. One evening – nearly always around 5pm – loud sirens send workers scurrying to the large platforms built on stilts above the coral. The song-happy Tahitians drop their shovels and come with guitars. Frenchmen bring books and bottles of sun-tan lotion. Names are checked off to ensure every person on the atoll is accounted for. Safety supervisors check in by telephone or radio.

Meanwhile, in a concrete blockhouse scientists are intent on a countdown reckoned to be at least as complex and tricky as the launching of a space rocket. Flickering screens provide simultaneous camera views of point zero (the top of the shaft), the lagoon, the surrounding reef and the barge of sophisticated electronic instruments. A reef shark is seen nonchalantly swimming past a camera in the clear water. A helicopter patrols the area with more cameras. Ships and aircraft have been warned to keep away. Only the frigate birds haunting the reef-edge seem unaware of the cataclysm about to strike.

With the relentless and thorough care that comes of shredding US$8 million into thin air, controllers in the operational nerve centre complete final checks. 'Three . . . Two . . . One . . .'

Three keys are turned.

A nuclear bomb explodes beneath the lagoon of Moruroa Atoll.

In the swiftest imaginable fraction of a millisecond the optical fibres leading up to the barge convey data about the effects and efficiency of the explosion before they are themselves destroyed. The basalt rock around the device is assailed by a temperature of well over one million degrees Centigrade, hotter than the surface of the sun. The surrounding rock vaporises instantly, creating pressures of one million atmospheres. The blast forms a chamber some 1·5 million cubic metres in volume. Further out, the rock vitrifies then drops into the chamber as a form of molten glass. Even further out, for an incredible distance, the rock shatters. The roof of the chamber falls in, leaving a chimney of open space which does not – assuming the experts have calculated right – extend all the way to the surface. A 10-kiloton blast at a depth of 3,280 feet (1 km) is thought to create a chimney extending to a height of about 1,000 feet (304 m). Once a small 5-megaton test blast at a depth of 5,900 feet (1,800 m) in Alaska did shatter the rock all the way up to the surface.

On land little is felt of the immense jolt: only the faintest tremble through the soles of the feet. The shock wave is so gentle it neither shakes down a stack of delicately balanced fuel drums nor collapses a precarious pyramid of wine glasses. The shock wave ripples through the seabed but quickly dies out. But on the surface of the lagoon the effects of the concussion are spectacular.

Fountains of white water spout thirty feet (10 m) in the air. Over an area some 2,000 feet (600 m) broad – oddly enough, not always immediately above point zero – the lagoon appears to boil. For thirty seconds it's a maelstrom of frothing, dancing pinnacles as reverberations hammer the shallow lagoon-bed. Television screens in the control room show the barge of instruments leaping and rocking madly, tossed by violent waves.

The scientific and engineering teams make rapid safety checks. Has radioactive gas leaked into the air, venting by way of some new crack in the reef? Did the airborne observers spot unusual fountains of spray or gas from the lagoon or open sea? Has the explosion shaken down any sections of reef, causing a tidal wave that could sweep the atoll? Not for nothing do helicopters continuously sweep the area while nearly 3,000 people remain on the safety platforms. Then sirens give the all-clear.

Another nuclear test has been concluded by the government of

France. In the tropical evening the scientists and engineers drink a cool beer no doubt feeling that they have earned it. The data is whisked off to laboratories in France for detailed analysis by computer. But that's not the end of it.

The incredible, unimaginable heat created by the explosion beneath the lagoon remains stored in the rock for decades, even centuries. The vast chamber of molten rock filled with rubble is reckoned by French experts to lock in all the fearful and immensely dangerous radiation generated by the blast, sealing it for thousands of years. When it does eventually seep out into the ocean they say its effects will be harmless.

But considerable doubt has been cast on the safety and integrity of the tests which the French fire off with such Gallic self-assurance. When they claim the environment will not be harmed, the French may well be correct. But they have not been able to prove it. The case they have to answer is that the entire atoll, now blasted with so many holes that it resembles a Swiss cheese, is so cracked and crumbling that radiation could already be seeping into the open ocean.

In general the early nuclear tests conducted by the French were less 'dirty' and less harmful than those of other superpowers. But it has never been a French priority to surrender information and hard data merely to bolster other peoples' confidence in what they are doing. It has never been a French habit to make a clean breast of accidents on the atoll. The French deploy nothing but bland assurances to relieve anxieties over the fundamental question: is the fragile and brittle basalt bedrock of the atoll – with its 71 vast underground chambers of radioactivity surrounded by hot shattered rock – being blown to bits?

The first 41 nuclear devices detonated on the atoll were slung from balloons, dropped from aircraft or placed on barges. When triggered they vaporised everything within several cubic miles. They sent great mushroom clouds spewing into the heavens, unleashing massive amounts of radioactive material that fluttered down like poisonous ashes over vast areas of ocean dotted with inhabited islands. France refused to join other nuclear powers – the United States, Great Britain and the Soviet Union – in a Partial Test Ban Treaty to put all nuclear test explosions underground because she claimed atmospheric tests were essential to the development of her nuclear armoury. This continuation of dreadful atmosphere-polluting nuclear tests by France (and China), when the other nuclear powers had stopped, provoked intense international hostility. It was especially high-handed because the horrifying and long-lasting effects of nuclear explosions on man and the environment, not fully understood during earlier tests by other countries, were now well known.

In New Zealand, 4,000 miles (6,500 km) from Moruroa, Strontium 90 levels in milk caused by French nuclear fallout steadily increased. One could only shudder at the likely radiation effects building up in the drinking water of the Pacific island communities where, because there are no rivers, rainwater is collected from rooftops and stored for drinking in large tanks. Though the French insisted there was no fallout they released no data from their radiation checks. While remote islanders could do little about it, least of all in French Polynesia itself, it was a different story in New Zealand. Hundreds of organisations from the Milk Vendors' Association to town councils and the Southland Oyster Openers' Union, protested. Students took up the cause and demanded that New Zealand send a warship. The protests were echoed and reinforced in Australia. When the testing programme began to detonate immensely more powerful H-bombs the effect was like stirring a wasp nest with a stick. But the government of France imperviously pursued its steadfast course. Until April 1972, when it was confronted by a totally unexpected and original phenomenon of protest.

Just as an important new series of tests was about to begin, naval ships patrolling the 100-mile (160 km) 'no-go' area around the atoll spotted on their radar screens a mysterious blip. It was too fuzzy and slow to be a freighter or fishing vessel in this lonely part of the world's loneliest ocean, yet was too distinct to be a giant wave whipped up by several days of storms. What they found, creaming through the tumbling seas with her reefed sails punched full of wind, was a small white sailing ketch. Her stern bore the name *Vega*. On her mainsail was the familiar symbol of the Campaign for Nuclear Disarmament, and the Omega symbol of the ecology movement, and in large black letters the name Greenpeace III. The faded red and white maple leaf flag of Canada flew at her stern.

Battered by storms and sea-weary after the five-week voyage from New Zealand, the 38-foot (11·6 m) *Vega* was crewed by an Englishman, a New Zealander and an Australian. Her skipper and owner was David McTaggart, a Canadian who had elected to celebrate his 40th birthday by sailing into the shadow of the hydrogen bomb. His rage was directed not at the bomb itself but at the French action in effectively cordoning off 100,000 square miles of ocean. McTaggart aimed to sail inside the danger zone proclaimed by France and, always staying within international waters, to approach within twelve miles of Moruroa Atoll. If the French towed him away it would be piracy. If they detonated a nuclear bomb over his head it would be murder.

The lone protest ended nearly in disaster (see next chapter) when a French warship rammed the yacht. A second protest voyage the following year ended even more spectacularly, and photographs of French commandos boarding the yacht and beating up the crew made front page news all over the world. Whether the voyages were courageous or foolhardy, they established a means of active interference with French testing. They focused publicity on the tests and were seen as a kind of strike force representing a broad spectrum of horrified but helpless protest groups. More organisations and groups were stimulated into action. French aircraft and ships were blacked by New Zealand labour unions, French goods boycotted. Demanding government action to stop the French tests, a petition organised by Radio Hauraki in Auckland collected 100,000 names. More vessels sailed to the bomb zone. Australia and New Zealand were granted an interim injunction by the International Court of Justice in The Hague on the grounds that nuclear testing in the atmosphere was inconsistent with international law. France denied any violation and dismissed the Court's ruling, claiming that nuclear testing was a matter of national defence and was therefore outside its jurisdiction.

Incensed, the New Zealand government sent the frigate HMNZS *Otago* into the bomb zone with cabinet minister Fraser Colman on board. Ignoring France's 62-mile (100 km) no-go zone proclaimed around the atoll, the warship was just 21 miles (6·5 km) from the reef when a small nuclear device, probably an H-bomb trigger, was exploded. Later a second warship, HMNZS *Canterbury*, took over the vigil and witnessed a bigger blast. Their voyages were supported by a supply ship of the Australian navy.

By the end of the 1973 testing programme France had been forced into a corner. Protests were no longer a matter of hot air. The yacht *Vega* had shown the effectiveness of direct action. David McTaggart himself, having nearly lost an eye at the hands of French commandos, was suing France for piracy and assault. Yachts might be ignored but not the naval ships of two neighbouring countries.

In 1974 the new president of France, Valéry Giscard d'Estaing, announced France's nuclear scientists had attained a new level of technology. Tests in the atmosphere were no longer required. Henceforth all nuclear explosions on Moruroa Atoll would be detonated beneath the reef. The French scientists claimed their seismic and geological tests had shown that the volcanic basalt below the atoll was an ideal environment for testing nuclear bombs. There would be no more atmospheric fallout, no pollution of the environment: all the radiation generated by the blasts would be sealed within the chambers created by the explosions.

45

It seemed the perfect solution to France but it allayed few doubts elsewhere. France continued to reject repeated demands from the local Territorial Assembly for an independent evaluation of the suitability of the site and the effect of nuclear tests on public health.

But with the switch to underground explosions much of the international hostility was defused and the logistics of testing operations were altered. The test programme now required a smaller workforce. Scientists, soldiers and labourers could be accommodated on Moruroa itself instead of in Tahiti. France had bought a breathing space but it did not last for long. Doubts about the safety of the tests were reinforced by a series of alarming incidents on the atoll.

An explosion in a concrete bunker on July 6th, 1979 killed two men and seriously injured three others. The French claimed it was an industrial accident resulting from an explosion of chemicals and was not nuclear in origin. Other reports suggested the CEP had decided to re-use a contaminated and sealed concrete bunker. The interior walls had been covered with paper soaked with acetone, a chemical that dissolved the lethal plutonium clinging to the cement. A spark ignited by a worker drilling a hole in a metal plate caused the acetone gas emitted by the paper to explode, scattering plutonium over the vicinity.

Less than three weeks later, immediately following a visit by President Giscard d'Estaing, the atoll came close to disaster. A nuclear bomb being lowered down a shaft in the reef became irretrievably stuck. Scientists decided to trigger it anyway. The detonation had a shattering effect. It caused an earthquake of 6·85 on the Richter scale. Workers later reported a crack 15 inches (38 cm) wide and more than a mile (1,600 m) long in the surface of the reef. Worse, a great chunk of the reef-edge was shaken loose and plummeted down the sheer underwater cliff fringing the atoll. This created a tidal wave between six and nine feet (2–3 m) high that swept over parts of the atoll. It overturned vehicles, smashed buildings and injured five people, two seriously. The authorities at first insisted the freak wave had nothing to do with the testing. Even when forced to admit the facts they archly maintained their usual assurances that although the explosion had split the rock through to the sea, no radioactivity could possibly have leaked out.

Concerned for the safety of its 3,000 civilian workers on Moruroa the powerful Socialist-allied trade union *Confédération Française Démocratique du Travail* lodged its documentary evidence in a Swiss vault for safety and alleged that the atoll, shaken to bits by the effects of more than sixty blasts, was sinking. It reported underwater cracks, one nearly twenty inches (50 cm) wide and half a mile (800 m) long, could be leaking radioactivity into the sea. A long section of the reef had slumped as much as five feet (1·5 m) due to successive explosions, not insignificant when the coral ring barely cleared the waves.

Also, there had been a problem disposing of the many tons of radioactive debris from the days of atmospheric testing. It could not be dumped into the sea because it contained large amounts of plutonium, a lethal cancer-causing substance with a half-life of 24,000 years. Instead, the polluted materials were spread over a large section of the northern part of the reef and sealed beneath a blanket of tarmac. In March 1981 a storm sent breakers crashing over the reef. They ripped up the tarmac and washed the radioactive materials with the plutonium into the lagoon. Anti-nuclear campaigners claim the pollution must have been swept out into the waters of the open Pacific where it entered the marine food chain. The lagoon was closed for a clean-up for a few days but CEP workers were soon resuming their daily swims.

The presidency of socialist François Mitterrand from May 1981 did nothing to budge France's long-standing commitment to the *force de frappe* (see Chapter 6). But it did usher in an era of more frank and straightforward dealing. Selected journalists were invited to the atoll on carefully orchestrated visits. Officials admitted that fallout had affected the islands during the atmospheric tests. It was generally acknowledged that serious leaks of radioactivity had occurred. But there was still nothing to worry about, the French said, and to prove it they took the amazing step – unheard-of when the Gaullists were in power – of allowing independent scientists to investigate the atoll's secrets. The visitors would be given just enough leeway, the government hoped, to pacify critics and satisfy concerns over the accidents.

First to arrive, in June 1982, was a team of eight French scientists led by Hazoun Tazieff, a vulcanologist. Allowed just three days on Moruroa and three days in Tahiti, the team decided the slumping of the atoll could have been part of its natural evolution and was not necessarily connected with the tests, but *some* of the subsidences were indeed the result of explosions. The report published a year later concluded there was little risk of radioactive contamination from the underground tests and fallout from the past atmospheric tests was harmless throughout the area, but it presented no substantiating figures. The report added that leaks of radioactivity from the underground chambers were unlikely in the short term, but if cracks in the basement of the atoll connected the test chambers with the open sea there was a real risk of pollution in the long term. The scientists complained that some information provided by local official monitoring groups was unsatisfactory, that no studies had been made

47

into the impact of the pollution washed into the sea by the 1981 storm, and strongly urged that more scientific information be released to bolster general confidence.

Far from abating, criticism became increasingly hostile and strident, especially from nearby countries then coming close to declaring the whole of the South Pacific a nuclear-free zone. Australia announced it would halt exports of uranium to France as long as the tests continued. In an attempt to allay fears, France boldly invited an international mission of scientists to inspect the test site.

The inspection team set out in October 1983. Led by Professor H. R. Atkinson, head of the New Zealand National Radiological Laboratory, it included another radiation expert from New Zealand, a marine geologist from Australia and a biologist from Papua New Guinea. Every aspect of its investigation programme had been the subject of intensive negotiations. Some thought the constraints imposed by France were so severe that any legitimate verification of her scientific claims would be impossible. The scientists would stay four days on the atoll and four days in Tahiti. Sampling would be permitted only in certain areas. There was never any question of *carte blanche*.

Their report published in July 1984 had the effect of lifting the lid from a can of worms. Arguments raged over the significance of some of its findings. The French extracted direct quotations that appeared to vindicate their procedures and bless everything they were doing, and gleefully gave them maximum publicity around the world. And anti-test campaigners, besides exploiting material that seemed ample justification of their serious concerns for the safety of the environment, quickly established what they claimed to be serious scientific shortcomings in the report.

Just one of the many key and complex questions in the controversy is the fundamental one of what happens to the massive heat and radioactive wastes generated in the test chambers by nuclear explosions? They do not go away and have a cold beer under the palm trees, as the scientists do, but remain as a problem likely to haunt Mankind for centuries.

The French contend that the report vindicated their choice of the atoll as an ideal test site because the harmful radioactivity was locked up in the test chambers deep under the atoll for thousands of years. In its oft-quoted Summary Conclusions, the report states that submarine leakage of radioactivity from the detonation chambers could occur in a time period of 500 to 1,000 years. Elsewhere, however, the report finds that radioactive wastes *could* filter through the rocks into the ocean as soon as five years from now, if the rocks were cracked by further testing.

But other scientists in New Zealand who wrote a critique of the report for Greenpeace admit that the best-case scenario of 500 years might in fact be feasible *if* water seeped through the rocks at the rate of only one metre a year (this figure was accepted by the authors of the report from the French) and *if* there were no further shattering and cracking of the rocks due to more testing.

In fact the flow-rate of contaminated water through the rocks may be very much faster than one metre (3ft 3ins) per year.

Professor Manfred Hochstein, director of the New Zealand Geothermal Institute, claims it is the presence of water that makes Moruroa anything but the ideal test site which the French would like to claim. Every explosion sets up a miniature geothermal system in the test chamber. Under great heat and intense pressure the water seeping into the chamber converts to steam and sets up a convection system. The radioactive gases are condensed and drop to the bottom of the chamber, falling into water which, due to the high pressure, becomes an exceptionally corrosive brine likely to eat through the glass-like rock. The concentrated radioactive wastes would then be likely to seep out, perhaps ten times faster than the investigating scientists had allowed for. At such high pressures the volcanic rock is in any case far from impermeable. The leaching process could well be hastened by cracks and fissures created by the explosions. With more tests planned, the cracking will increase.

Hochstein believes it likely that hot contaminated brine from various explosion cavities mingles as it flows from one chamber to another. The brine might, in fact, be moving through the shattered rock at the rate of 50–100 metres (164–328ft) a year. Unlike Nevada and Siberia where there is no doubt that radioactive wastes are locked in for ever because there is no water to transport them, the volcanic atoll is in fact – Hochstein and other geothermal experts contend – a far from 'perfect' container for nuclear explosions. 'The French have quoted the report out of context and been caught out in a lie,' says the professor.

What of the pollution likely to wash out into the lagoon and open ocean? In one sense it will be so diluted by the vastness of the deep oceanic waters that it will be environmentally insignificant. Yet it will inevitably contaminate small living organisms which in turn will be eaten by larger creatures. At every step the radioactivity will become more highly concentrated. The bigger the fish the further it swims. If studies of the food chain have in fact been made, as France claims, they have not been published. French authorities say their radiation experts make comprehensive scientific checks on tuna and other fish landed for human consumption but do not release the figures.

The report is also challenged on a gamut of other important points. There is no basis, its critics say, for the French to claim 'total absence of pollution', that venting does not release radioactivity into the atmosphere during tests, that fissures in the atoll are not worrying, that underwater landslides have not impaired the outer rim of the atoll, that it has been 'proved' that the tests have had no effect on the health of Polynesians. The report has made a lot of new information available but we can still only speculate on whether the atoll is falling apart and sinking, whether radioactivity is escaping from the test chambers and whether the tests are harmful. Well reasoned speculation, however, points to very serious causes for concern.

Despite such challenges Dr Andrew MacEwan, a member of the report team who has since succeeded Atkinson as chief of New Zealand's Radiological Laboratory, has stated that the testing of nuclear devices on Moruroa will be safe for at least ten years. 'I would cheerfully take my wife and children there for a holiday,' he told newsmen.

As they lazed in the lagoon at Moruroa in early 1985 the master-minds of the French testing programme thought they were sitting pretty. France was the only nuclear power to have allowed foreign scientists to investigate a test site. The Atkinson Report showed radioactive doses from fallout were less than one twentieth the world average. The ambient radiation levels in the *zone de vie* were lower than elsewhere in the world and traces of fallout from the atmospheric tests were insignificant (according to French figures, radiation levels at Moruroa are one-seventh those of France). More-over, their statistics revealed not the slightest degree of risk to public health. To obviate the risk of damage to the perimeter reef, tests were now taking place beneath the lagoon. There was no reason therefore why France shouldn't continue her programme of nuclear tests to the end of the century and this was announced to the world.

Yet deep unease remained on vital questions such as the integrity of the atoll, the likelihood of environmental contamination due to seepage, and the risk of cancer.

It fuelled the deep resentment and hostility that South Pacific countries and anti-nuclear campaigners continued to feel towards France for her colonial exploitation of French Polynesia, for her systematic destruction of a lovely atoll that will remain 'hot' for ever, and because France was alone among the nuclear powers in not testing her weapons at home.

Also, the Atkinson Report was regarded by anti-test campaigners and Greenpeace as a 'seriously flawed' document. Until properly independent and complete studies and sampling were conducted, they said, one must assume the worst – that French testing at Moruroa was polluting the environment and causing health problems for the people of French Polynesia.

Despite the great French public relations exercise to sell an image of perfect safety to the outside world, Moruroa remained as much as ever the atoll of the big secret. For this reason, another fleet of protest vessels – including the old *Vega* and led by a mother ship called *Rainbow Warrior* – was in early 1985 being prepared to sail for Moruroa.

And the French government was reviewing its plans to resist them. For it had learned since its first brush with the *Vega* in 1972 that when Greenpeace sails appeared in the sunset off Moruroa, the fair face of France could be made to look very red.

4

WARRIORS OF THE RAINBOW

When the sea-battered 38-foot (11·6 m) ketch *Vega* hove-to off the atoll of Moruroa in 1972 it caused the hugely expensive postponement of nuclear tests and ultimately forced the government of France to think again. The tests went underground and skipper David McTaggart could claim his action had directly influenced the Goliath of the world's third largest nuclear power. This was admitted when a Paris Appeal Court pronounced judgement on McTaggart's long fight to win Cdn$128,000 recompense for damages caused by the French Navy's acts of 'piracy' against his yacht. Though the verdict went against him, McTaggart was astonished when the government *procureur* made a special point of giving him much of the credit for bringing a halt to the atmospheric tests.

Direct action by half a dozen resolute and courageous people in a small sailing yacht had succeeded in deflecting the political and military might of a powerful state. And the lesson was not lost on the small bands of deeply committed people intent upon reversing what they saw as the world's slide towards ecological disaster. It was from about the time of this court judgement in 1976, and with the leadership of David McTaggart, that the environment protectionists loosely allied under the Greenpeace banner were transformed into a tightly run, stripped-down fighting organisation with a fleet of ships. The name of the game was direct action.

Its story begins in Vancouver in 1970 when the US Atomic Energy Commission was planning to trigger an underground nuclear explosion on Amchitka Island in the Aleutians which trail far out into the Bering Sea from the south-west of Alaska. A bunch of friends, some of them hippies and US draft dodgers, decided to form a protest group quaintly named The Don't Make A Wave Committee. It decided the only way to make ordinary people aware of the environmental disaster which the blast might cause was to sail a small boat 2,400 miles (3,800 km) to the island and drop anchor next to the bomb.

The famous name was coined – some say at a planning meeting, others recall it was on board their boat – when a member made a V-sign saying, 'Peace, peace!'

'Make it a green peace!' another added.

'What a great name – let's call it the Greenpeace voyage.'

The dilapidated 20-year-old halibut seiner *Phyllis Cormack*, eighty feet (24 m) long, set sail with 13 crew in autumn 1971. Hampered by rough seas and inexperience, the expedition never reached the island. The US Coast Guard turned it back because some of the crew had apparently gone ashore in a remote part of Alaska without checking in with Customs officials. A second voyage called Greenpeace II, in a converted 150-foot (45 m) minesweeper, also failed in its mission.

But the issue caught the public imagination. Thousands of people demonstrated their hostility to the tests by plugging the US and Canadian border, the first time it had been closed since the War of 1812. The bomb was duly triggered on Amchitka but the rest of the test programme was transferred to a new site in Nevada. The island became a bird sanctuary. For eco-freaks, greenies and serious ecologists alike, the discovery of such power at their fingertips was a revelation. The place to exercise it next was obvious, but they had no boat capable of making the ambitious and demanding voyage as far as Moruroa in distant French Polynesia.

At this time David McTaggart was falling in love in New Zealand after cruising the Pacific in his yacht *Vega* and intended to circumnavigate the globe. A lively, quick-footed Canadian, he was a world-ranked badminton player, had quit high school and never looked back. He made and lost a million in the construction business, was divorced three times, and exchanged the rat race for the South Seas when his ski lodge in the Sierra Nevadas was demolished by a gas explosion. He had avoided politics all his life. Ecology, he thought, was something tied to aesthetics; in his business aesthetics added up to profits.

When McTaggart read in a newspaper that a Vancouver protest group he had never heard of was seeking a yacht to make a protest at Moruroa, the only significant link was that Vancouver was his home town. But this was enough to set him wondering. The violation of his rights as a yachtsman by a country trying to cordon off 100,000 square miles of ocean in clear defiance of international law made him sore. He had a boat capable of the 8,000-mile (12,800 km) round voyage from New Zealand. It was, he decided, a situation in which he wanted to get involved.

After settling a small local difficulty with the local Customs (he was fined NZ$700 for smuggling 104 watches into the country) McTaggart hoisted his mainsail which now bore the words 'Greenpeace III' and set a course for the French bomb zone.

For more than a month the little *Vega* played nip and tuck with a cruiser, a minesweeper and a tug of the French Navy. Stiff notes were carried back and forth by sailors in inflatables. Sometimes

David and his three crew lowered the yacht's radar reflector and stole away into mist or darkness. So low to the water that she was swallowed in the troughs between large swells, her fabric sails eluding the pulsing electronic beams of searching radars, *Vega* challenged the French Navy with the difficult and thoroughly maddening task of locating her again.

When a helium balloon was seen dangling from a sinister black box in the sky over the reef, David and his crew made wedges with which to block fallout from the cabin ventilators. If the bomb detonated, they decided, they would draw straws to choose who would dress in oilskins and remain on deck exposed to the fallout to work the yacht. Later two blasts did occur but they were small enough to be inaudible; the fallout drifted in the opposite direction.

Repeatedly the yacht was harassed by naval ships. Once they made a sandwich of the *Vega*, steaming so close on either side that the yacht's frightened crew felt certain they would be squashed. The tactics were intended to terrorise and they did. David stuck to his guns. He was outside the 12-mile limit, an innocent yachtsman in international waters.

Then, apparently trying to deflect the yacht from sailing towards a fallout cloud, the minesweeper smashed her bow into the *Vega*'s bulwarks. Part of her rigging was caught up in the warship's bows as it backed away. Mast, sails and hull were seriously damaged. None of the crew was injured though it had been a narrow escape.

The yacht was towed into the dockyard at Moruroa itself for quick and partial repairs then sent on her way. With pictures of the protesters happily dining with the French admiral, news reports reflected an image of a benevolent navy extending a patient helping hand to a protest crew wnose navigation error had led to damage of their yacht. With a heavy heart David realised he had lost the propaganda war.

But the voyage awoke something in the hearts and minds of people everywhere. Individuals, groups, organisations, trade unions and even governments were moved to make a stand against the nuclear tests. The following year, 1973, New Zealand and Australia sent warships to the bomb zone. Scores of yachts were planning to sail in *Vega*'s wake but only two made it. The 100-foot (30 m) former Baltic trader *Fri*, with 13 crew including a French clergyman, was boarded in mid-ocean by commandos and towed into the base on the atoll of Hao. When the second yacht *Spirit of Peace* was out of the way collecting provisions at Rarotonga, and the frigate HMNZS *Otago* was at a safe distance, a large H-bomb was triggered. The warship relayed pictures of the mushroom cloud to the rest of the world. It provoked an international outcry.

When David McTaggart sailed again for Moruroa that year, his crew now one man and two women, it was with a heightened sense of the desperation of our times. The sight of the bright yellow balloon with its atomic bundle high in Moruroa's blue skies had burned in his soul 'an inextinguishable impression of the diabolical presence of atomic power . . . of the guillotine drawn high over our necks and over mankind.' He had failed to win recompense for damages to his yacht. His own country had not only refused to back him but had more or less disowned him. This time he knew the French Navy would be even more hard-nosed than before. As expected, it wasted no time.

An inflatable boat zoomed alongside and commandos armed with truncheons stormed aboard. The two men were severely beaten. A blow pulped David's right eye. Again the yacht was taken in tow while David was evacuated for urgent medical treatment. But the attack had been photographed by the girls. Their video camera was hurled overboard but they had succeeded in concealing the 35mm still camera, leaving a decoy on the cabin table which the commandos had seized. When the crew was later flown to Tahiti the film escaped repeated searches because one of the girls had concealed it in her body. In the blaze of publicity the French claimed that David had stumbled and hit his eye on a deck winch. Then the pictures were released. The affair stoked up the furore over the testing. The implacable, impassioned opposition to the atmospheric tests finally stung the government of France into detonating her bombs underground.

The astonishing success of this courageous and effective direct action brought Greenpeace into full flower. Its seeds of environmental idealism were sown far and wide. Everywhere people formed protest groups and called themselves Greenpeace. Spectacular media coverage had pushed membership up to 10,000 but there was no formal organisation.

An imaginative and irresistible Greenpeace credo evolved, rooted in a legend of the Cree Indians:

'When the Earth is sick and the animals have disappeared, there will come a tribe of peoples from all creeds, colours and cultures who believe in deeds not words and who will restore the Earth to its former beauty. This tribe will be called the Warriors of the Rainbow.'

Even legendary Indian tribes had a hierarchy of chieftains who decided which battles to fight and how to win them, but Greenpeace did not. By February 1976 its fifty different branches and offshoots, all hustling for money and demanding control of how it was spent, were arguing like squaws. The grass roots organisations scattered through America saw no reason to cream off hard-won funds to support a so-called head office in Vancouver. Canada's bid for control was countered by David McTaggart who quietly set up legitimate Greenpeace organisations in Great Britain, France and the Netherlands; others had sprung up in Australia and New Zealand. All allied themselves with US branches under the umbrella of Greenpeace International, with McTaggart as chairman, and the Canadians fell into line. Out of the long period of haggling over housekeeping was born a streamlined international environmental strike force.

While the tribal tepee was being put straight the Warriors of the Rainbow were out there getting on with the job of saving the planet. Direct actions by Greenpeace – spectacular, risky, outrageous, brave – blazed into the headlines and made the world stop and think.

First targets were the Russian, Japanese and Norwegian fleets decimating the last remnants of whale populations in the oceans. The United Nations had called for a moratorium on whaling but whales were still being slaughtered by the thousand. Every species but the small Minke was endangered. Protest groups trying to stop the slaughter abounded. In San Francisco alone more than two dozen whale-saving groups drummed up hoards of money by doing little more than organising boycotts of Japanese goods. In summer 1975 Greenpeace planned something a little different.

After two months at sea in the faithful old halibut boat *Phyllis Cormack*, by tracking radio conversations the Greenpeace team finally located a Russian whaling fleet 60 miles (100 km) off the coast of California. The fleet comprised the 450-foot (137 m) factory ship *Dalyni Vostok* and nine 150-foot (45 m) whale-chasers with harpoons on platforms high in their bows. At first, when Greenpeace men landed on the carcass of a baby whale floating nearby, they were taken for rustlers and a chaser sped straight for them with fire hoses being made ready.

Greenpeace dogged the Soviets until a pod of sperm whales was sighted. Three inflatable rubber boats with powerful outboard engines were launched. One sped for the bows of the whale-hunter to place itself in the harpoon's line of fire and attempt to protect the whales. The others took up station with cameras rolling.

There was consternation in the lead boat when its engine coughed out just as the high steel bow of the Russian ship was scything down. Robert Hunter and Paul Watson prepared to leap for their lives but Paul tried one despairing pull on the starter rope, the engine kicked over, and the inflatable was spun along the ship's side so close that the men could have touched it.

Speeding back into position ahead of the bows they saw the harpooner take aim as the whales broke the surface, coming up to breathe. Bouncing over the waves they steered directly between the harpoon and the whales. The gun fired with a crack and a cloud of smoke. Trailing its cable the brightly barbed 250-pound (113 kg) missile armed with an explosive head passed only a few feet above their heads. It arrowed deep into the glossy back of a whale surfacing to breathe and exploded. The cable splashed into the water just five feet (1·5 m) from the inflatable's side. The whale screamed and thrashed in the water.

The brave – perhaps foolhardy – venture saved no whales directly. The Soviets had been within their rights. But the dramatic film was rushed to San Francisco. Walter Cronkite was first on air with it. Then it brought the horror of the whale slaughter into living rooms all over the world. Also, the footage showed under-sized sperm whales being dragged up the ramp at the stern of the giant factory ship. That year the Soviet Union, along with Canada and Japan, had voted to increase the whale catch quotas. When the International Whaling Commission met in London the Soviets were seriously embarrassed. For long afterwards ordinary people disgusted by the spectacle of whale killing were still writing to the US president about it.

The first confrontation with giant whaling ships set the pattern for others in succeeding years. Officials sniffily dismissed them as undiplomatic but the tactics were as effective against whale-killers as they had been against French atomic blasts. In one action Greenpeacers drove an inflatable boat straight up the stern-ramp of a factory ship then stepped out and distributed leaflets. To dovetail with this headline-catching daring they ran campaigns such as an American boycott of Norwegian fish products to pressure the Norwegians into halting the purchase of whale meat. With other wildlife organisations they also persistently lobbied the International Whaling Commission. Result: whale catch quotas have been steadily reduced and in 1986 the huge commercial slaughter was to be phased out.

Abuse of the environment, Greenpeace believes, is sliding the world into ecological suicide. The planet is being ravaged in piece-meal fashion by short-sighted exploitation of resources. We face the possibility of wholesale environmental destruction by the holocaust of a nuclear exchange. Let's wake up to it; let's do something to stop it.

Greenpeace direct actions – non-violent, putting nobody in danger but themselves – are intended to shake governments out of their apathy. The rape of the planet might already be unstoppable. The urgency is explained in a British Greenpeace brochure headed *Paradise Lost – Countdown to Destruction*:

> Planet Earth is 4,600,000,000 years old. If we condense this inconceivable time span into an understandable concept, we can liken Earth to a person of 46 years of age. Nothing is known about the first seven years of this person's life, and while only scattered information exists about the middle span, we know that only at the age of 42 did the Earth begin to flower. Dinosaurs and the great reptiles did not appear until one year ago when the planet was 45. Mammals arrived only eight months ago and in the middle of last week, man-like apes evolved into ape-like men and at the weekend the last ice age enveloped the Earth.
>
> Modern Man has been around for four hours. During the last hour Man discovered agriculture. The industrial revolution began a minute ago. During those sixty seconds of biological time modern Man has made a rubbish tip of paradise. He has multiplied his numbers to plague proportions, caused the extinction of 500 species of animals, ransacked the planet for fuels and now stands, like a brutish infant, gloating over his meteoric rise to ascendancy, on the brink of a war to end all wars and of effectively destroying this oasis of life in the solar system.

Most environmental groups first sit down among themselves to work out what they think a government will accept. What you argue about in Washington, according to US Greenpeace campaign co-ordinator Stephen McAllister, is how quickly things are going to hell – the slope of destruction. Other groups say, 'Let's slow it.' Greenpeace says: 'Let's stop it – right now!'

'This,' adds McAllister, 'is what gives Greenpeace a little bit of zeal.'

In one campaign after another Greenpeace deployed direct action teams in a guerrilla war against governments, multinational corporations and powerful pressure groups. In 15 years they were involved in 47 major campaigns around the world. Drawing on their experience against the French tests and the whaling fleets, the strategy was to choose the most dramatic, visual issues and fight them through publicity. Explained Robert Hunter of Vancouver: 'We fire images rather than missiles – mind bombs delivered by the world media.'

Tactics centred on a small fleet of ships – the green navy. First came the North Sea research trawler, re-named *Rainbow Warrior* (see next chapter) and sent into action in 1977. Greenpeace in the Netherlands bought the *Sirius*, a 440-tonne former pilot cutter, in 1980. An ocean-going tugboat re-named *Greenpeace* was given to the organisation by the Maryland Pilots' Association in April 1985 (though a finder's fee of US$500,000 had to be paid). In West Germany the organisation bought the 75-foot (22 m) river boat *Beluga* to look for illegal discharges of toxic materials in the Rhine and the Elbe. The Baltic trader *Fri*, veteran of the Moruroa campaign, completed a long 'peace voyage' to China, South East Asia, Europe and Nicaragua then was chartered by Greenpeace to fight pollution in the Great Lakes. And still making regular voyages to protest against the continued nuclear tests on Moruroa was the faithful old ketch *Vega*. From time to time other vessels allied themselves to the 'eco-navy'.

There was never any risk that the warriors of the Rainbow would be stumped for lack of issues.

Every year Great Britain, the Netherlands, Belgium and Switzerland were dumping close to 100,000 tonnes of radioactive waste at an 'approved' site in the Atlantic, 500 miles (800 km) south-west of Land's End. With scientific backing Greenpeace contended the concrete-sheathed drums could be cracked and crushed on hitting the bottom 2½ miles (4 km) down and radioactivity would leak into the ocean. Again with frail but zappy little inflatables launched from a mother ship, Greenpeace went into battle.

They blockaded the harbours at Cherbourg in France and Barrow in England to prevent the poison-carriers from moving; in France they were resisted with tear gas. The dump-ships were dogged in narrow waterways by high-speed boats weaving in front of them. At sea, puny inflatables sped alongside the British ship *Gem* to place themselves beneath the barrels splashing down chutes into the sea. The ship's crew tried to swamp them with fire hoses and lashed at the inflatables with grappling hooks. One falling drum landed on an outboard motor and upended the inflatable. The dramatic photographs of the unprotected rubber boats bursting through jets of water told their own story. Said Peter Wilkinson, a director of Greenpeace in Britain: 'Someone, somewhere, has to take these risks to bring home to people what's going on.'

When a British court ordered Greenpeace not to interfere with *Gem* on pain of £20,000-a-day fines, Dutch Greenpeacers took up the cause.

With Spanish ecologists and politicians on board to bear witness, the *Sirius* hounded the Dutch dump-ship *Scheldeborg*, harassing operations with four rubber boats. A heavy drum dropped on the bow of an inflatable, catapulting its driver into the sea. He landed near the ship's propeller and was quickly scooped up unhurt by other boats. The ship's captain radioed an apology and stopped the dumping.

Two Greenpeacers equipped with air mattresses and wetsuits

camped in a cargo of toxic sludge filling the hold of a French dump-ship. The captain ordered the dumping to go ahead and when the doors opened in the bottom of the ship to empty the load the protesters barely escaped being swept out. Other protesters blockaded the West German acid-carrier *Kronos-Titan* by chaining themselves to its anchors.

The Dutch dump-ship *Rijnborg* was boarded at sea and the cabins of its cranes occupied by protesters until they were arrested by the captain. Soon afterwards a protester suffered a head injury when a barrel fell into an inflatable; the protest was called off but Greenpeacers received a rapturous welcome when the *Sirius* sailed into the port of Vigo where the Spanish fishermen and local people had been deeply concerned about the 'atomic graveyard' being created on their doorstep. Later the *Gem*, too, was boarded by six protesters who chained themselves to the dumping platforms. In Cherbourg the *Sirius* was bombarded with tear gas by French police as it tried to blockade a ship arriving with radioactive waste from Japan.

These spirited campaigns reduced the powerful atomic energy authorities of several countries to a helpless fury. But their most profound effect was on public opinion. When the British built a special new dump-ship with outrigger cages to frustrate Greenpeace tactics it was blacked by the National Union of Seamen.

Meanwhile similar battles were going on in the Great Lakes, North American rivers, and in the North Sea which – accumulating 80 million tonnes of toxic wastes a year – had been dubbed the sewer of Europe. Wearing only wetsuits, four protesters sat under a pipe that was spouting an industrial effluent of diluted acid into the River Humber. Another four jumped into the water ahead of a West German chemical carrier to prevent her disgorging acid into the North Sea. The ship steamed through them, dumping acid.

'Our divers are entitled to bathe in a clean North Sea,' Greenpeace radioed from the *Sirius*.

'Get out of my way – you are completely mad!' the dump-ship's captain is said to have retorted. But when the protesters again dived into the water under his bows he gave up and returned to port with tanks still only half emptied.

In 1983 the dumping nations placed a moratorium (extended in 1985) on the whole dirty business. But the campaigns continue against dumping in rivers and lakes.

Another prime target was the routine – almost daily – discharging of waste water from the giant nuclear reprocessing plant at Windscale (later re-named Sellafield) on the north-west coast of England. Greenpeace claimed this was rendering the Irish Sea the most radioactive sea in the world and was causing scores of deaths through consumption of contaminated fish. One Greenpeace report contended that highly toxic plutonium could be breathed in from sea spray, and the tiniest amounts caused fatal lung cancer. Right or wrong (the issue is still being furiously debated) it caused a furore.

First attempts by Greenpeace divers to plug the discharge 70 feet (21 m) under the sea were foiled when they discovered it had been secretly modified so their carefully designed 'cap' was useless. Then they had to grapple for the pipe because marker buoys had been removed. Success came only in open defiance of a court order. Greenpeace was fined £50,000 for contempt. When Greenpeace researchers located a slick of contaminated materials on a nearby beach, British Nuclear Fuels was fined £7,500 for negligence. It was only after the affair had filled the headlines and outraged public opinion that the British government agreed to work towards the elimination of discharges into the sea.

On other fronts Greenpeacers scaled industrial chimneys to protest against acid rain, campaigned against the keeping of dolphins and killer whales in aquariums and zoos, tried to save the slaughter of dolphins in Japan and of pilot whales in the Faroe Islands, uncovered pirate whalers in Spain and illegal whale catches in Chile, chained themselves to navigation buoys in the River Rhine and fought for the protection of endangered wildlife such as turtles. In British Columbia protesters disrupted trophy hunting in the Spatsizi Plateau Wilderness Park, were assaulted in their camp by guide outfitters flying in by helicopter, and initiated a court case that kept the whole problem in the spotlight for seven years.

Undeniably effective, the campaigns did not always score a bull's-eye. The Greenpeace contribution to the ending of the controversial baby-seal hunt in Newfoundland, involving direct actions such as the spraying of seal pelts with green dye to make them commercially useless, was justified on the notion that the harp seal was in danger of extinction. Biological surveys showed this to be untrue. As a result of the campaign hundreds of Inuit (eskimo) hunters living in remote areas of the Arctic with no alternative livelihoods found themselves surviving on welfare.

When Greenpeace turned on the fur industry with the aim of stopping the cruelty of the trap it found thousands of Indian families in the Canadian backwoods were likely to suffer the same fate as the Inuit. To its credit, Greenpeace halted its potentially damaging campaign.

Peace pirates? Eco-guerrillas? Monkey-wrenchers? Anti-nuclear musketeers? Knights of the Biodynamic Round Table? Robin Hoods tricking the technocrats to spur people out of their moods of resignation? By 1985 Greenpeace had been called a lot of things, not all of them polite. But it had come a long way from the 'hippy navy' of its earliest ventures.

Greenpeace was viewed with mixed feelings. You mightn't agree with everything the protesters did in the line of direct action. But you had to admire their intrepid spirit and you couldn't fault their aim. By 1985 about 1¼ million people around the world were impressed enough to send small membership donations totalling a tidy US$14 million a year. Only rarely did a benefactor such as a pop group step in with a gift exceeding three figures. There was no other significant income, apart from the sale of T-shirts and campaign buttons, and Greenpeace has always claimed its books are completely open.

Out of these slender means the organisation funds its direct action campaigns, a fleet of ships with the rainbow blazing on their bows, and 32 offices in 15 countries (Great Britain, Netherlands, West Germany, France, Belgium, Luxembourg, Austria, Switzerland, Denmark, Sweden, Spain, New Zealand, Australia, Canada and USA). Also, a photo division is based in Paris, a film department in London, and the ships are run from a base in London docks. Finances and campaigns are co-ordinated through Greenpeace International. It is registered in the Netherlands but operates from two floors of a modern office in Lewes, a country town in Sussex, England. The five-member Greenpeace International board comprises David McTaggart and directors from Canada, the US, Great Britain and West Germany.

Virtually a multinational, the secret of the organisation's survival on such meagre resources is simple. It works on a shoestring. The 250 staffers around the world are paid a bare living wage. This is adjusted according to the size of family, travel costs and other sources of income they might have. Deckhands collect £45 a week with their keep; David McTaggart is paid about £15,000 a year, directors up to £13,000.

Moreover, the core of staffers are selected for their high level of professional competence and range of capabilities, and they draw on a large army of eager volunteers. They are not wage slaves but passionate idealists. But dedication isn't enough. Only those who achieve results work for Greenpeace. There's no room for free-loaders. You have to do a lot more than just your job; it's a way of life. In the ships everybody from journalists to the captain does a fair share of cleaning and washing up.

To run such a big organisation and accomplish so much on so little astounds Greenpeace critics. Many contend Greenpeace must receive financial support on the sly, even from the KGB. 'But those who make such accusations have no idea how we really operate,' explains Peter Wilkinson. 'All of us work for next to nothing and many work for nothing at all. Our business doesn't have to show a profit margin at the end of the day. What we do is expose the raw nerve.'

Overall, the emphasis has always been on 'green' rather than 'peace'. About half Greenpeace campaigns involve wildlife (whales, seals, etc) and ocean ecology; a quarter are directed at the problem of toxic wastes. The remainder concern the nuclear fuel cycle (including uranium mining, transport of nuclear materials) and disarmament, with the focus on nuclear testing. 'The tests,' says David McTaggart, 'are nuclear war by inches.'

Greenpeace claims to be genuinely non-political. The whale, they say, doesn't care whether it's a Capitalist or a Communist harpoon that kills it. But the anti-nuclear and disarmament campaigns, though conducted on environmental grounds, do overlap with devoutly political peace movements. Though not a pacifist organisation Greenpeace has pacifists in it, especially in New Zealand where the peace movement is strong. It also has vegetarians. Greenpeace does not advocate unilateral disarmament but seeks a comprehensive and verifiable test ban treaty. Its slogan under a picture of a mushroom cloud: 'In 1945 they found they could destroy the world – almost 40 years later they are still trying to prove it.'

Though it protests against all nuclear powers Greenpeace's anti-French campaign has been particularly unrelenting, first because of French intransigence in continuing atmospheric pollution and more recently because of their persistent 'environmental aggression'. This furnishes critics with ammunition to allege that Greenpeace is anti-West and communist-inspired. Why doesn't Greenpeace protest against the tests in Russia and China?

Greenpeace has been a fully international organisation only since 1981, Wilkinson explains. Already in 15 countries, it's moving into the Third World with a branch soon starting in Argentina. The Eastern bloc is difficult for all the obvious reasons. Greenpeace has staged one action in Czechoslovakia, when a chimney was climbed to protest against acid rain. A hot-air balloon was sailed over Berlin into East Germany as a disarmament protest.

In 1982 the *Sirius*, with 28 people on board, sailed boldly into the Soviet port of Leningrad and dropped anchor. Crew members wearing T-shirts with the text 'USSR Stop Nuclear Testing Now' written in Russian handed out leaflets and posters in the streets but were hustled away. While guards patrolled the ship's deck the crew inflated 2,000 gas-filled balloons bearing an anti-nuclear message and released them suddenly from the hold. Then Soviet tugs towed the ship out to sea. Later a French newspaper asserted the visit proved Greenpeace had important KGB backing. How else could the protest ship have been allowed within sight of the place if it were not in the KGB's pocket?

This sort of remark generates a frustrated Greenpeace sigh. Says Wilkinson: 'When we occupied the American nuclear test site in the Nevada desert they branded us commic spies. When we tried to stop Norwegians from killing seals we were said to be in the pay of rival Canadian fishermen. When we protested against nuclear power stations we were apparently in league with the oil industry. When we tried to stop the horrendous cruelty of leg-hold traps we were accused of working for makers of artificial fur . . . What more can I say?'

Also, everything 'greenies' do is not necessarily connected with Greenpeace. An organisation called Greenpeace London, for example, is an anarchist collective that became involved in a vandalistic 'Stop London' action.

With its insistence that the planet Earth clean up its act, however, Greenpeace made plenty of enemies. You can't humble governments and powerful industrial corporations without making waves. In London a direct action was pipped when protesters aiming to climb Big Ben to hang an anti-nuclear banner over the face of the famous clock arrived by boat on the Thames to find police officers waiting to warn them off. The unexpected modifications to the Sellafield waste pipe also pointed to a mole in the organisation, or at least a breach of Greenpeace's own security. A professional security firm was called in to sweep the Islington offices for bugs. In the US, too, Greenpeace workers reported unusual clicks on their telephone lines and anonymous sedans that fired up their engines and followed when they left for home.

For Greenpeace, the non-violence of its direct actions – 'We put no individuals in danger except ourselves' – had always been a point of honour. Though the organisation had been bitterly criticised, heavily fined and openly derided at many levels of government and big business, it had never been the victim of attack.

But nobody could imagine what aggressive direct action would be encountered when Greenpeace International directors agreed to send their flagship *Rainbow Warrior* on an ambitious new mission. She would carry the rainbow through the Pacific, drawing attention to the growing scale of 'nuclearisation' of the area.

What could be more harmless than a 'Pacific Peace Voyage'?

5

LAST VOYAGE OF *RAINBOW WARRIOR*

When Greenpeace first sprouted branches in Europe in 1977 it operated in a borrowed office, used a borrowed telephone line, and its small team of four funded its activities with their own meagre savings. But the picture changed with a grant of £38,000 from the Dutch branch of the World Wildlife Fund. Characteristically, Greenpeace did not spend the money on setting up an administration in a cosy office with its own telephone. Instead it blew the entire sum on the one item vital to its planned programme of campaigns to save the oceans. It bought a ship.

The vessel Greenpeace chose was neither a doughty little cruising ketch in which to cruise around in the sunshine, nor a snappy powerboat in which to cut a dash. She was a rust bucket languishing at a fish-dock wall, deserted, dirty and derelict. Beneath her salt-crusted paint and oily decks they saw an old girl wise in the ways of the sea. A stalwart, sea-kindly and capacious veteran of many a North Sea storm, the ship had been built in Aberdeen, Scotland, as a typical side-trawler, one of scores designed specifically for ten to 14-day fishing voyages in the 'middle' waters in the North Sea, the Norwegian Sea, and towards Iceland. But when she went down the slips in 1955 there was a difference about her.

Christened *Sir William Hardy* after a scientist who became Britain's premier marine ecologist, the ship was built by the Ministry of Fisheries and Agriculture as a fishery research vessel. For more than twenty years she ploughed the fishing banks of the North Sea, shooting her trawl for science rather than profit. The data obtained from counting, analysing and tagging the slippery harvest that dropped on her deck when the cod-end of the trawl-net was opened provided marine biologists with their first proper understanding of the North Sea's rich fish stocks. In her laboratory, scientists plotted the drastic decline of those stocks due to over-fishing which in turn had resulted from political bickering and apathy.

An appropriate choice of ship to do battle against the poisoning of the world's oceans, the former research trawler was also ideal for practical reasons. With a length of 160 feet (48 m) and a beam of 27½ feet (8 m), the ship was big and strong enough for any foreseeable task. She could carry a couple of dozen people on long voyages in reasonable comfort. She had ample deck space for cargo, and for transporting small boats such as inflatables. The fish hold offered a large internal space that could be adapted for a variety of roles. Her tanks gave a cruising range of about 10,000 miles (16,000 km), enough to get her nearly halfway round the globe.

Moreover, her hull lines had evolved over hundreds of years of nautical experience. A trawler was more than just a fishing boat. It was a submarine hunter, seeking schools of fish beneath the waves. It was a cargo ship, unique in finding its cargo from the sea, at sea, going out with empty holds and full bunkers, returning with full holds and empty bunkers. A trawler spent more time than any other vessel stopped at sea so it had the sea-keeping qualities of a lightship. To drag a heavy trawl along the sea-bed the trawler was as powerful and manœuvrable as a tug, yet to rush its cargo to market it was also a high-speed vessel, comparable in terms of length/speed ratio with the cruise liner *QE2*. In weather so dangerous that other vessels fled to the shelter of a safe port, a trawler put to sea and stayed there, doing a job of work. A trawler was reliable, because nine-tenths of its life was spent on the job. Above all, a trawler was a lifeboat: the lives of its fisherman-crew depended on its ability to 'keep' the sea.

A team of volunteers descended on the derelict hulk and the ship was transformed. The fish hold was converted into a theatre, with tiered seats for lectures, displays and meetings, and a section was partitioned off as a library. The laboratory became an extra cabin. With the cabins provided for scientists as well as the ship's officers and her fishermen, the ship had berths for 23. The costs of insuring her hull and machinery, and bringing them up to the standard required by insurers, were prohibitive so the vessel was insured only for public liability and was registered under the British flag as a yacht. A Cree Indian motif was painted on her white funnel; another decorated her stern. Large white letters spelled out the name Greenpeace along the side of her dark green hull. A rainbow arched proudly around her bow. A white dove of peace, trailing an olive branch, was painted on either side of her stem. Re-named *Rainbow Warrior*, she sailed into battle for the protection of the oceans.

In her first year of operations *Rainbow Warrior* hassled whalers in Iceland and was arrested by a gunboat for interference. Then she had a go at Spanish whalers, carried Greenpeace on its first confrontation with the dump-ship *Gem*, and sailed to the Orkney Islands to thwart attempts by Norwegian hunters to cull grey seals on behalf of British authorities. In 1979 Icelandic whale hunters fired five harpoons over Greenpeace inflatables which had been launched from *Rainbow Warrior*. Again the mother-ship was arrested and Icelandic authorities confiscated the inflatables. But the world-wide campaign to save whales was beginning to bite, for

Great Britain banned the import of all whale products. Defying an order banning her from French territorial waters, *Rainbow Warrior* intercepted the dump-ship *Pacific Swan* arriving from Japan with a cargo of spent nuclear fuel and hounded her into the port of Cherbourg. Greenpeace inflatables squeezed between the ship's hull and the dock in an attempt to stop the unloading. Six protesters were arrested and riot police turned fire hoses on demonstrators. *Rainbow Warrior* was impounded and her captain arrested. Only after 3,000 local trade unionists staged a strike in her support were the ship and captain released.

A few months later, in June 1980, *Rainbow Warrior* tried to interrupt the fin-whale hunt by Spanish whale-chasers and was arrested by a patrol vessel. Though the ship was impounded in the port of El Ferrol, in north-east Spain, Greenpeace refused to pay a bond of £62,000. The authorities removed vital parts of the engine so the ship was immobilised and charged her captain, 29-year-old Jonathan Castle, of the Channel Islands, with 'obstructing ships in Spanish waters'. To be heard by Court Martial, the offence carried a minimum penalty of six months in prison. But it never came to court. After five months of languishing in the Spanish harbour *Rainbow Warrior* made a daring escape. Greenpeace volunteers smuggled replacement engine parts on board and they were fitted by the ship's own engineers. In the dead of night the crew cast off the moorings. Before the Spanish police had woken up to what was happening *Rainbow Warrior* was charging out into the open Atlantic and the safety of international waters.

Meanwhile Greenpeace had been stepping up its campaign to stop the clubbing of baby harp seals on the ice off Newfoundland. The same two Greenpeacers who were first to see a whale-harpoon shoot over their heads had made headlines by blockading a ship filled with sealers as it crashed through the ice. Others had sprayed baby seals with green dye to destroy the value of their pelts. *Rainbow Warrior* crossed the Atlantic in February 1981 to lead the spring campaign and was seized by Canadian Mounties for illegal interference with the hunt. Seven protesters were arrested and fined. After her release the ship sailed to Boston to protest against oil and gas development on the rich fishing grounds off the New England coast, then joined in a campaign to stop the dumping of toxic wastes in the New York bight. While battling through ice floes once more to reach the seal hunt, in March 1982, Greenpeace heard the news that the European Parliament would ban the import of seal-pup pelts. It was the death-knell of commercial sealing.

After sailing through the Panama Canal *Rainbow Warrior* campaigned to save dolphins from drowning in the huge nets used by tuna fishermen. Off South America some of her crew boarded a Peruvian whale-hunter and chained themselves to its harpoon. In California the ship resisted offshore oil and gas developments, and frustrated a US Navy plan to dispose of superannuated nuclear submarines by sinking them in the ocean deeps. Then came the daring escapade that made the eco-navy's name a household word. Greenpeace invaded Siberia.

In the half-light of a murky Arctic dawn, in July 1983, *Rainbow Warrior* steamed out of a fog bank and approached to within a hundred yards of the coast of Russia. During the night the ship had crossed Bering Strait, which separates Alaska from the Soviet Union. Now she was coming into a small settlement called Lorino on the Chukchi Peninsula, the Soviet Union's most eastern point of land. As expected, the 22 anxious and excited Greenpeacers noted the busy factory on the shore where whale carcasses were being processed. And on the hillside above the village they saw row upon row of wire cages containing fur-bearing animals, probably mink. Far away in Brighton, England, the 40 nations of the International Whaling Commission were meeting to discuss a moratorium on whaling, to begin in 1986. Greenpeace had invaded Siberia to prove that the whales slaughtered by the Soviet Union were not for the subsistence of its indigenous people, as the regulations allowed, but were being used illegally to fatten animals in a state fur ranch.

Three inflatables with six people sped in to the beach. The five Americans and a Canadian, two of them women, photographed the whaling station and the fur farms while calmly pressing leaflets into the palms of sleepy and nonplussed Soviet workers. Within ten minutes two dark-green trucks roared up. Armed soldiers surrounded the protesters, forced them to stand in a circle, and confiscated cameras and films.

Watching it all from *Rainbow Warrior*, skipper Peter Willcox decided it was time to beat a tactical retreat with the film that had been shot through telephoto lenses from on board. Then Soviet ships materialised out of the murk and gave chase. At full speed *Rainbow Warrior* raced for American waters, about forty miles (64 km) distant. Two armed Soviet gunboats, a merchant ship and a couple of speedboats came after her. Helicopters buzzed low over the Greenpeace ship and dropped canisters containing messages saying in English: 'Stop at once'. The gunboats, much larger than the old trawler, came up on either side and officers shouted through loud hailers, 'You are under arrest, stop your engines!'

When the merchant ship cut across their bows to box *Rainbow Warrior* between three vessels, Peter Willcox avoided the trap by quickly stopping his engine then turning away. Had the Soviets fired a shot across his bows he would have stopped. As usual, Greenpeace was determined to put no lives at risk. At worst the ship would have been towed into a Soviet port, all their film would have been confiscated and Greenpeace would probably have been lucky to get its ship back.

Expecting to be stopped and arrested at any moment, Greenpeace decided to try getting the all-important films home to Alaska by another means. First mate Jim Henry volunteered to make a break for it. The reels of 16mm movie film and still pictures were wrapped in plastic. Extra fuel tanks were loaded in a 16-foot (5 m) Zodiac inflatable. Jim Henry cast off from the ship's side and zoomed away into a fog bank, hoping to reach Alaska. But the fog did not conceal him for long. A helicopter followed, hovering a few feet above his head. Realising he wasn't going to make it the American hurled himself into the icy water, leaving the inflatable to race ahead with the film.

As *Rainbow Warrior* steamed out of the fog the mate was seen being lifted to safety by the helicopter while the empty inflatable sped round and round in tight circles. Judging his moment, Bruce Abraham leapt into the inflatable but broke his left ankle. *Rainbow Warrior* recovered the dinghy with its cargo of precious film, and the injured man, then resumed her race to safety. Though Soviet patrol ships came to within about twenty feet (6 m) of her bulwarks they took no action more threatening than the firing of flares. As *Rainbow Warrior* reached American waters the Soviets gave up the chase.

More a voyage of publicity than discovery, because another organisation had been to Lorino two years before, the Greenpeace action caused a media sensation. Was there a newspaper or a news broadcast in the Free World that didn't cover the story? Even the Moscow papers mentioned it, though in less glowing terms.

Held for five days in spartan barracks with the windows papered over and only a chess set and a Rubik's cube for entertainment, the seven arrested protesters were taken by Soviet ship to a rendezvous on the international dateline and handed over to Leo Rasmussen, mayor of the Alaskan town of Nome, whom the State Department deputised to take delivery of the prisoners. There had been no time to do paper work and when the Soviets asked him for identification the best he could produce was his volunteer fireman's card. It did the trick and the Greenpeace protesters returned to heroes' welcomes.

By now Greenpeace had achieved world-wide notoriety. Its direct action campaigns had played an important role in stopping the seal hunt, bringing a moratorium on whale slaughter, and initiating another moratorium on the dumping of wastes in the sea. The 'green navy' had grown to five vessels (another former trawler, the *Cedarlea*, had been bought by Greenpeace in Great Britain for the Sellafield campaign but was later sold again). It was time to focus yet again on the big one – the environmental catastrophe that could kill all life on the planet.

Rainbow Warrior was ordered to Jacksonville, Florida, to be fitted out for a special mission. She would double the Pacific Ocean on a 20,000-mile (32,000 km) peace voyage.

The aim of the 'Pacific Peace Voyage' was to focus public attention on the realities of the nuclear arms race, nub of the long-standing Greenpeace campaign for a Comprehensive Test Ban Treaty. This was no mere pipe-dream of a bunch of ecology freaks. Every American administration from Eisenhower to Carter had worked for it. First negotiations between America and Russia had been cancelled when the Soviets shot down an American U-2 spy plane over their territory. Kennedy achieved the Limited Test Ban Treaty which banned all but underground tests (though France and China did not sign). Two other treaties restricted the size of underground tests. The Carter administration had been intent on concluding a comprehensive test ban when the Soviets invaded Afghanistan. Then Reagan suspended all negotiations and was the first president not to support United Nations resolutions in favour of a comprehensive ban. His administration did not believe such a treaty could reduce the threat of nuclear weapons or maintain the stability of the nuclear balance.

The continual testing of bombs, Greenpeace contended, did nothing but fuel the nuclear arms race. One superpower made a technical advance then the others had to catch up, and so on, with no end in sight. Inevitably, nuclear weapons would spread to other countries. Thus the dangers of nuclear war increased and the chances of human survival diminished.

In any case, Greenpeace reasoned, even a limited nuclear war involving less than ten percent of the superpowers' nuclear arsenals would destroy all life on Earth because the 'nuclear winter' phenomenon would put the world's forests to the torch, fill the sky with dust and ashes and change the climate. Didn't this make nuclear weapons and the concept of nuclear warfare obsolete? At the very least it eliminated any need that might have existed for testing more and more new nuclear weapons.

The whole question was critically urgent because the Nuclear Non-Proliferation Treaty was coming up for renewal in September 1985 and could be in serious trouble. The 124 nations that signed the Treaty did so on the clear understanding that the superpowers, as set out in Article Six, would make progress towards nuclear and general disarmament. Seventeen years and thousands of nuclear weapons later, what progress had been made? While the 124 partners had kept their side of the bargain the superpower signatories (United States, Soviet Union, Great Britain) had consistently broken their promises. With nuclear explosions continuing to take place somewhere in the world on average once a week, what case could the superpowers make to prevent smaller and more volatile nations from entering the race?

To bring maximum pressure to bear, Greenpeace directors decided to direct a media spotlight on the 'nuclearisation' of the Pacific Ocean. At the centre of the spotlight, fitted with new electronic equipment to transmit photographs around the world, would be *Rainbow Warrior*.

The Pacific Ocean was arguably the most 'nuclearised' zone in the world. It was the one place where nuclear weapons had been used in anger. Its people in some areas still suffered the terrible effects of radioactive contamination by fallout from earlier explosions. Nuclear tests were still being conducted there. Plans were well advanced to use the ocean as a dump for nuclear waste. And much of this nuclearisation of the Pacific was being achieved through the means of colonisation, not only in French Polynesia but – in a particularly repressive form – in the Marshall Islands by the United States. Although America had stopped nuclear tests in the Pacific in 1958 she continued to fire unarmed intercontinental missiles at Kwajalein Atoll, a US$1 billion firing range considered one of her most crucial military facilities.

At the other end of the Pacific the anti-nuclear issue was raising a political storm. New Zealand's new Labour Government had refused to admit nuclear-armed or nuclear-powered American warships into the country's ports (see next chapter). As America refused to say whether her warships were armed with nuclear weapons, all US Navy vessels were effectively barred. The long-standing ANZUS (Australia, New Zealand, United States) Treaty was falling apart.

Significantly the 14 member countries of the South Pacific Forum, including Australia, New Zealand, and all the small island nations (with the obvious exception of French Polynesia) were on the point of declaring the entire South Pacific a Nuclear Free Zone. The crucial vote would be taken at a meeting of the Forum in Rarotonga in August 1985. It was intended to ban the manufacture, stationing or testing of nuclear weapons in the region but allow the transit of nuclear-powered or nuclear-armed ships and leave the question of port visits up to individual countries.

At the same time France was embarking on yet another cycle of nuclear tests on Moruroa Atoll. Pressure from Greenpeace had been unremitting. The *Vega* had made four voyages to Moruroa and been arrested by naval ships three times. An Australian protest yacht, *Pacific Peacemaker*, had been rammed and also arrested. Now there was added concern over radiation leaks, incidence of cancer in French Polynesia, and the integrity of the atoll itself, as revealed in the furore over the Atkinson Report (see Chapter 3). Among the devices planned for detonation during the southern summer of 1985, Greenpeace learned, was a new neutron bomb.

Other explosions would test the reinforcement of nuclear missile heads that could be dangerously exposed to counter-measures operated from space defence weapons. As usual France gave a Gallic fist to her furiously objecting neighbours in the South Pacific and in May 1985 blew her biggest underground bomb to date – a 150-kiloton blast (equivalent to 150,000 tonnes of TNT) felt 4,000 miles away in New Zealand.

The *Rainbow Warrior*'s Pacific Peace Voyage was planned to thread together all these distantly scattered elements of nuclear activity in the Pacific. Carrying reporters and film crews, she would first draw attention to the nuclear legacy of the American tests on Bikini Atoll in the Marshall Islands of the North Pacific, where land was contaminated and native people suffered such horrible ill-effects that some had died. The ship would make a protest at the missile testing range of Kwajalein, drawing attention to the oppression of local people who had been kicked out of their homes and herded on to a tiny overcrowded island. In Vanuatu (formerly the New Hebrides) the ship would drum up support for the Greenpeace campaign to prevent the Japanese dumping nuclear waste in oceanic trenches nearby.

In New Zealand *Rainbow Warrior* would prepare for her role as 'mother ship' leading a flotilla of protest yachts to Moruroa, and en route drop anchor off Rarotonga, in the Cook Islands, where the South Pacific Forum (on the 40th anniversary of the devastation of Hiroshima by the world's first atom bomb) was voting on the question of a South Pacific nuclear-free zone. A campaign button best summed up the spirit of the voyage:

> If it's safe –
> Test it in Paris,
> Dump it in Tokyo,
> And keep our Pacific
> Nuclear Free

The campaign would hit the United States, Great Britain (for the legacy of its Christmas Island tests), Japan, and France. Though

France was not singled out for exceptional treatment she would be the only one to rise to the bait. Little could anyone guess at how effectively the name *Rainbow Warrior* would blaze in the headlines. Or imagine that the Pacific Peace Voyage would leave her a shattered hulk on the bottom of a New Zealand harbour.

The first leg of the ambitious 20,000-mile voyage would take her on a meandering route across the emptiest and remotest zones of the northern Pacific. The second would involve a prolonged stint of lying hove-to in remote open ocean of the South Pacific, off the atoll of Moruroa, far from a safe refuge or any kind of engineering assistance in a friendly port. To sail such long distances and hang about in the open ocean for long stretches *Rainbow Warrior* needed the most meticulous preparation.

Already she had been fitted with a new 600 horsepower General Motors diesel main engine. Now it was decided to rig her as a ketch with two steel masts and a complete set of white Dacron sails. In the latitudes of strong, steady and reliable tradewinds where she would spend much of the voyage her sails would bowl her along with the main engine switched off to save fuel. This was not only a matter of cost but of prolonging the ship's range and endurance off Moruroa. Even when the work was done by teams of volunteers the bill for the conversion job was US$100,000. A steel bowsprit was welded to her stem, giving *Rainbow Warrior* something of the dash of a clipper ship. The enclosed wings of her bridge were cut away to make room for the winches required to sheet in the big foresails. In the engine room a water-maker was fitted so the ship could maintain station as long as possible off Moruroa and supply water to the other protest vessels. A young German student on a hitch-hiking holiday stopped by the ship and asked if he could do something. A skilled cabinet-maker, he did a beautiful job of refurbishing the altered wheelhouse with wood panelling.

Meanwhile Steve Sawyer, a New Englander and director of Greenpeace International who was co-ordinating the voyage, received an unusual and irresistible request from the distant Marshall Islands. The people of Rongelap had been exposed to very high levels of radioactivity by the American nuclear tests. Their island was grossly contaminated. They had found an alternative home on an island 120 miles (193 km) away but the US Congress was dragging its feet over their claim for compensation. Officials refused to help with the move and meanwhile the people were sickening and dying. Would the *Rainbow Warrior* evacuate the people of Rongelap, ferrying them with all their belongings to a new and uncontaminated island home? Greenpeace didn't hesitate.

The Marshalls are part of Micronesia, tiny islands scattered over a vast area of ocean north of New Guinea and east of the Philippines. Along with Yap, Truk, Palau and other islands of Micronesia, they were the scene of fierce fighting during the Second World War. Since then, under United Nations mandate, Micronesia has been administered as a Trust Territory by the United States. Though given strategic and military use of Micronesia the US was obliged to protect the lands, resources, and health of the local people, and to help them towards economic self-sufficiency as well as independence or self-government. Of the 11 UN Trusteeships created after the war, Micronesia was the only one yet to shrug off its quasi-colonial regime and become independent. Like France in Polynesia, the US seemed to be doing everything possible to ensure a permanent economic dependence: colonialism for the sake of nuclearism (a degree of autonomy for the islands was agreed by the US Congress in December 1985).

Between 1948 and 1954 the United States exploded 66 nuclear bombs in the atmosphere over the atolls of Bikini and Enewatak in the Marshall Islands. Radioactive fallout hit 14 atolls in all. Inhabitants of the two test sites were evacuated to safety but others were less fortunate. On March 1st, 1954, the United States exploded a 15-megaton hydrogen bomb. Code-named Bravo, it was a thousand times larger than the atom bomb dropped on Hiroshima. On Ronge-lap, 55 miles (88 km) away, schoolmaster Billiet Edmond saw a huge and fiery sun-like object rise up in the western part of the lagoon. 'It was a sun . . . much bigger than our sun, illuminating and giving off heat like our sun, yet its intense heat was far greater and invincible and much brighter . . .'

Then came the mushroom clouds, the thunderous noise of the explosion, the terrible wind that twisted coconut palms and over-turned one house and blew people over. Soon afterwards came a snowstorm in paradise. Powder-like particles fell out of the sky. 'Children ran through it, playing with it, trying to catch the most . . .' With darkness came nausea, agonising itching of the skin, ears, nose, mouth and eyes. Within two weeks most had lost their hair.

According to officials it was an unpredicted wind shift that floated the radiation cloud over Rongelap and other inhabited islands. Greenpeace claims to have proof it was no wind-shift: the wind had been blowing straight at Rongelap for days.

The islanders were neither warned that the tests were taking place nor told what precautions to take in case of exposure to radiation. Fallout rained on the island within four hours of the test, blowing into drifts several inches deep. Belted by radiation levels estimated to have been 380 times higher than America permits for public safety, the people were not evacuated for three days. No clean-up was attempted. After three years the islanders were returned to their homes with assurances that there was absolutely no danger. But 22 years later they were advised that the northern islands of their atoll, which they had been using regularly for gathering food and firewood, were too radioactive to be visited. The residual radiation of Rongelap was in some places higher than Bikini itself, where 23 bombs had been detonated. Over the years the people suffered high rates of thyroid cancer, leukaemia, still births and miscarriages. Children had been born malformed or retarded. Three-quarters of the people under ten at the time of the Bravo blast had required surgery for thyroid cancers. One islander died of leukaemia, two died of radiation-induced diseases and two women had brain tumours also likely to have been caused by radiation.

Today the 320 people of Rongelap are convinced they have been used as guinea pigs by the American authorities. They say their return to the island was premature and that medical monitoring was conducted for research rather than for their own welfare. With bitterness they recall words reputedly from the wise mouth of Dr Henry Kissinger: 'There's only a few thousand people out there – who gives a damn?'

While the Marshall Islanders filed lawsuits in US courts seeking US$7 billion compensation for the damages (the US counter-offered $150 million) the people of Rongelap wanted nothing but a new home. Their own island, they said, was a nuclear coffin. Close relatives on the atoll of Kwajalein had offered them use of a jewel-like, uninhabited island called Mejato, one of 90 islets threaded on the coral reef of Kwajalein, the biggest atoll in the world. Intercontinental ballistic missiles fired from California splashed down in the centre of the lagoon, more than 30 miles (48 km) away. But they were not armed and the beautiful island's clean white sand and clear water had never been contaminated. Now the islanders needed only a mercy ship.

Appeals to the US for help were ignored or spurned. The authorities accused the islanders of grossly exaggerating the problem. They claimed that radiation at Rongelap was no higher than at Denver yet also advised the islanders to eat only tinned food. Then Jeton Anjain, the island's senator, heard of the forthcoming voyage of *Rainbow Warrior* and telephoned Greenpeace to ask for aid.

Welcomed by singing women and children, *Rainbow Warrior* dropped anchor in the lagoon at Rongelap in the middle of May, 1985, after the long voyage from Florida by way of the Bahamas and Panama. At Hawaii she had embarked journalists and film teams from London, Paris, and Auckland. She was also joined by

Greenpeace staff photographer Fernando Pereira, a Portuguese who had made his home in Holland. Her new sails had proved a great success, pushing her along at a steady ten knots with no engine.

Ashore, the entire population had turned out with garlands of flowers. But the job was to be much bigger than Greenpeace expected. Due to shallow reefs the ship couldn't get close to the beach to load. Piles of building materials and personal possessions were ferried out by 'boom-boom', a Marshallese name for any boat with an outboard motor. A line of people stood waist-deep in water, passing all their belongings over their heads, including the dismantled schoolhouse, out to the one boat. Transferring each load from the boat to the ship was dangerous in the heavy swell. A boy fell between the two and narrowly avoided being crushed. The oldest inhabitant, Muvenarik Kebenli, aged 68, agreed to leave only on condition her body would be returned to Rongelap's little cemetery after she died. Pigs and chickens could not be taken because they were contaminated. After prayers the first load of 76 people, sitting on the rolling deck under tarpaulins, made the 10-hour overnight trip to their new home.

Deckhand Bunny McDiarmid remembers it as an emotional and heart-rending business. 'All these people were in a ship they had never seen before with people they had never seen before taking them to an island they had never seen before, their belongings in boxes sealed up with masking tape – and it wasn't even their island that had been hit by the bomb, but 30 years later the effects were killing them.'

Over twelve hard-working days *Rainbow Warrior* made four ferry voyages. She transported 320 people, three generators and 15 tons of building supplies. Her foredeck was piled high with roofing iron, lumber, suitcases, pots and pans and crates of school books. Said Steve Sawyer: 'After the people of Hiroshima and Nagasaki, the people of Rongelap have been more severely contaminated than any other people in the nuclear age – the island is a microcosm of the aftermath of nuclear war.'

At Kwajalein *Rainbow Warrior*'s crew raised a flag on the reef to protest against use of the atoll as the target area for testing American MX and other strategic missiles. Here 3,000 American scientists and technicians live a tropical 'country club' existence in 900 acres (364 ha) of beautiful surroundings with cinemas, golf course, tennis court, bowling alley and yacht club. The atoll bristles with radar scanners and antennae. Its airstrip can handle the world's largest aircraft. But the 8,000 people cleared off the 90 small islets that dot the reef have been resettled on tiny Ebeye Island, just 67 acres (27 ha) in size. To achieve the same density, noted Harold Jackson, of the *Guardian*, one of the few journalists ever permitted to visit the top-secret atoll, the British Isles would have to accommodate twice the population of the whole world.

The islanders are crushed into squalid shanties on Ebeye with an unreliable water supply, inadequate schools, no proper medical care, no rights to land ownership, no telephones, and insufficient room to bury their dead. Only one in eight has a chance to earn cash, working as a maid or gardener, and there is one policeman for every five workers. Jackson added that the plight of the Marshall Islanders, had they been more firmly in the world's eye as are, say, Palestinian refugees, would be regarded as a world scandal.

As *Rainbow Warrior* headed south across the equator, steaming through the blistering doldrums, her twelve crew had become as close as any family. They were a lively, warm-hearted, disparate bunch from eight countries. There was no drug-taking and little alcohol; who could afford it on US$45 a week? The confidence that blazed in their eyes was striking. They had the happy look of people who had found their life's work.

Expecting an unruly group of spaced-out mystics, I had started my own research into Greenpeace sceptically. I had seen the results of the damaging Greenpeace anti-sealing campaign on Eskimo people in the remote Arctic. I was (and remain) concerned that persistent anti-nuclear campaigns, though courageous and laudable, subvert the will to maintain the means by which our freedom is defended. The freedom Greenpeace enjoys to stage gallant protests is also the most precious ingredient of our Western way of life. It's what our nuclear capability is intended to defend. The fact that Soviet citizens do not enjoy the same measure of freedom is exactly the reason why the West must maintain a nuclear deterrent. Nuclear war is always a risk but without a strong defence, Soviet blackmail and oppression is certain. Greenpeace could be abusing that freedom, even dangerously undermining it.

Some Greenpeacers have long hair, it's true. Some have rings in their ears, some wear CND badges, some are vegetarians. But some wear bush shirts and tramping boots and go hunting at weekends. Not many wear ties or business suits but some carry briefcases and have professional degrees in law, accountancy or marketing. At the top, Greenpeacers are highly accomplished in their fields and over-qualified for the jobs they do. Every telephone message I ever left at a Greenpeace office anywhere in the world was unfailingly returned promptly, courteously. And there was another factor, hard to describe. It was more surprising than their professionalism, deeper than their sense of commitment. It was the same quality that David McTaggart perceived in Greenpeacers after his first Moruroa voyage. They are people who emanate an extraordinary sense of *love* for the world, for natural wonders, for other people, but most of all for their friends and for their ship and its mission.

Reported Paul Brown of the *Guardian*, who sailed in *Rainbow Warrior* on her Rongelap mission: 'The crew had a deep-seated belief that however much they annoyed governments, their passport to safety was their non-violence. As long as no one was hurt by their actions, except perhaps financially, then they could challenge anyone on the high seas.'

Skipper Peter Willcox, 32, of Connecticut, had obtained most of his sea experience in ocean racing. For six years he skippered the yacht *Clearwater*, carrying passengers on environmental education cruises out of New York. He took *Rainbow Warrior* to Siberia and had been involved with Greenpeace ever since. Martin Gotje, the rangy Dutchman known as 'Martini' with a mass of black curly hair and a black beard, was first mate. For nearly ten years he had sailed in *Fri*, recently on a project taking seeds and agricultural tools to under-developed communities in the Caribbean and Central America. During the voyage he had become fond of Hanna Sorensen, a 25-year-old Dane with cheeks and long blonde pigtails like a souvenir doll; her ambition had always been to be a marine engineer but nobody took her seriously until she joined Greenpeace and was made second engineer. Her chief was Yorkshireman Davey Edward. Made redundant from his sea-going job he had taken part in the Greenpeace action to block the Sellafield pipeline; he was earning £300 a week working on North Sea gas platforms when Greenpeace asked him to go to the Pacific and 'it took only a split second to decide'.

Strong-man of the ship was Henk Haazen, 31, another tall blue-eyed Dutchman. His long blond hair was plaited at the back and tied with a bright tie-dyed silk ribbon. An *I-Ching* coin dangling from one ear gave him a piratical look. A trained carpenter, he had been in *Fri* for four years and was invited to join *Rainbow Warrior* after he had spent three months helping to do the conversion work in Florida. His girlfriend Bunny McDiarmid, 28, from Auckland, signed on as deckhand. Grace O'Sullivan, 23, a Greenpeace veteran from Ireland who had been in the front line of the Sellafield campaign, was the right person to be with in an emergency. Also a deckhand, she had been the first woman lifeboatman in Ireland, the first woman cliff rescue-team member and a lifeguard. She gave up accountancy to become the Irish surfboard champion in 1982. From Switzerland came the ship's doctor, Andy Biedermann, and from Austria the cook, Natalie Maestre. Red-bearded Bene Hoffman, of West Germany, served as second mate. American Lloyd Anderson was the radio operator. Also on board was Hans Guyt, 33, a former Dutch seaman who founded Greenpeace in the Netherlands and was international co-ordinator of the anti-nuclear campaign.

Like everybody on board from the skipper to travelling journalists, photographer Fernando Pereira, 33, helped out with any jobs that needed doing. At Rongelap he had shot a file of colour pictures showing every stage of the operation. Tall and dark with flashing eyes and a Latin way with women, he had fled the Salazar regime in Portugal and settled in Holland where he worked as a freelance, mainly for a small communist newspaper. He was divorced from his Dutch wife but deeply attached to his children, Marcelle, 8, and Paul, 5. In every port his one aim was to find gifts and souvenirs that he planned to mail home well ahead of Christmas because he knew he could be at sea for many months. He never went anywhere without his cameras. As *Rainbow Warrior* neared her landfall with her crew making plans for tramping trips, skiing holidays and motor-bike tours during their three-week stopover, nobody suspected such a professional habit could cost Fernando his life.

Rainbow Warrior steamed into Auckland on Sunday, July 7th. It was a sunny but cool winter's afternoon. Few of the many New Zealanders who sailed out to meet her in yachts and motor launches could deny a lump in the throat as the doughty little ship with her brilliant rainbow flag sounded a long and emotional salute on the fog horn. But the pilot gave the order 'Full ahead!' The ship left her friendly escort of about 30 vessels bobbing in her wake and headed for Marsden Wharf in the heart of the city.

On other fronts at that time Greenpeace was 'waging peace' with customary gusto. In Buffalo, New York, Greenpeacers were trying to plug a pipe discharging industrial wastes into the Niagara River. Under arrest in Antwerp, Belgium, for interfering with toxic waste-dumping operations, the crew of the other Greenpeace ship *Sirius* had sliced off her mainmast so she could pass under low bridges and fled down the Schelde-Rhine canal at dead of night. In Spokane, Washington, 15 Greenpeacers were planning to block a bridge over the Columbia River to halt trucks carrying radioactive wastes. In England, Greenpeace was needing £250,000 to save it from bankruptcy. Greenpeacers in Canada were making plans to hoist a net aloft with balloons to catch a Cruise missile. In New Zealand, Greenpeace was concerned about the sea lions being scooped up and killed in the nets of Japanese squid boats, but the main campaign centred on the manufacture of 2,4,5-T, a herbicide so dangerous to humans and the environment that it had been banned in the US since 1979. And Greenpeace International, with its new ship *Greenpeace* donated by the Maryland Pilots' Association, was preparing to land a year-long expedition of four people on the coast of Antarctica to draw attention to the frozen continent's exploitation.

As the crew of *Rainbow Warrior* heaved a line ashore and paid away their mooring lines, waving to a large welcoming crowd of old friends and wellwishers, who could have imagined that the Greenpeace organisation had already been penetrated by a secret service agent? Or that a team of military combat swimmers had already smuggled explosives into the country? Or believe that on the other side of the world a top-level government decision had been made and put into effect – 'Sink the *Rainbow Warrior*!'

From the moment of her triumphant arrival in Auckland, *Rainbow Warrior* had only three days to live.

6

SEND FOR CLOUSEAU

At the time *Rainbow Warrior* was being rigged with masts and sails for her Pacific crossing, a young French woman with a camera on her shoulder took a rattling elevator to the sixth floor of an old office building near the Magistrates' Court in the heart of Auckland. She saw a dark, cluttered suite of rooms, no larger than a small apartment. The walls and partitions of rippled glass were taped up with posters of whales and penguins, postcards from all over the world and campaign slogans. There was a shabby sofa and a Telex machine. High sash windows looked across the street at the trees and steep grass slope of Albert Park. It was the headquarters of Greenpeace New Zealand.

In fractured English the woman said she was Frédérique Bonlieu, a scientific consultant from France. She was spending a few weeks in New Zealand on the way to a geographers' conference on coral reefs in Tahiti. The country had always fascinated her and she was interested in the government's nuclear-free policy. Could she make herself useful in the Greenpeace office while she was here?

Somewhat surprised to hear a French accent in their offices, the six women who run the Greenpeace branch invited Frédérique in and offered her coffee. Elaine Shaw, co-ordinator of the anti-nuclear campaign, read the letter of introduction she had brought. Dated April 3, it was written by Jean-Marc Vidal whose acquaintance Elaine had made at an anti-nuclear meeting in Fiji a few years before. Vidal had an interest in ecology and was one of the group of Frenchmen whose ship had been arrested at Moruroa in 1973. Now a well-known ocean sailor, he runs a sailing school at Port Camargue, in the south of France. Elaine saw nothing unusual or suspicious about the letter. It was common for peace workers to be passed from one group to another in this way. When Frédérique said she would be happy to do translating and write letters about the campaign to French magazines, Elaine saw a way of making her useful. Greenpeace had a credibility problem when it wrote to French media and politicians about the fierce resentment felt in the South Pacific towards French nuclear and military policies. But the letters would hit harder if they were in the idiom.

In any case, Greenpeace needed all the help it could get. *Rainbow Warrior* would soon be on her way. Peace groups in Auckland were sponsoring yachts to sail with her to Moruroa. The whole purpose of the campaign was to raise public awareness of the effects of the testing, especially in France itself. 'You've come at the right time,' Elaine smiled.

The New Zealand branch of Greenpeace had always been a little different. It was founded in 1974 specifically to provide backing for the *Fri* on her 'Voyage For Peace' to China, eastern Russia, and the Far East. Ever since, nuclear testing and the arms race had always been its number one targets. Concentrating mainly on supporting and waging the paper war on behalf of *Vega* and other yachts heading for Moruroa, the branch's links with the peace movement had always been close.

In New Zealand, Greenpeace hardly needed to campaign against whaling because the government was on its side. But there were other environmental issues to keep the small team busy. With about 2,300 supporters, Greenpeace was worried about the sea-lions being caught in the nets of Japanese squid-fishing boats at Auckland Island, south of New Zealand, and had commissioned observers to collect baseline data on the health of the sea-lion population. It was fighting the pollution of the Tarawera River by paper mills. A direct action was planned against a chemical plant where the herbicide 2,4,5-T was manufactured. Once in wide use, banned in the US since 1979 and made nowhere else in the world because of its dangers, the herbicide contains Dioxin, one of the deadliest chemicals known. 'It's not soluble so it accumulates in your organs and never disperses,' explained Carol Stewart, 38, a Greenpeace director. 'You can walk through blackberries that have been sprayed with it, scratch your leg, and end up partly poisoned. Next time the poisoning will be worse. It's dreadful stuff.'

The new French recruit came into the office at irregular hours. Frédérique helped to open the morning mail and typed letters. The Greenpeace workers found her lacking in humour, a bit starchy, somewhat dogmatic. One likened her haughtiness to Valéry Giscard d'Estaing, the former president. But this was typical of a certain type of French character, they thought. Frédérique talked a lot, mostly in French, and held strong opinions that she didn't keep to herself. She spoke out in favour of the nuclear weapons because they gave France protection against Russia. New Zealand was remote from any enemies, she pointed out, while France was very close.

Frequently she defended France's right to be in the Pacific. When the question of independence for French overseas territories arose – notably that of New Caledonia where the native Kanaks (representing 43 percent of the population) were engaged in a bitter fight for independence from the colonial regime of French planters and mineral interests – Frédérique propounded the Gaullist view that New Caledonia, like Tahiti, was a part of France. In all of France the central government in Paris was detested, she explained. Other bits of the country like Brittany and Corsica also wanted to separate and run their own affairs. Most other regions resented interference. 'Doesn't everyone,' she would sigh, 'have trouble with Paris?'

Despite this lack of sympathy with their aims, the Greenpeacers accepted the French visitor with good grace. She was a professional geographer and wanted to learn the truth about what was happening in the Pacific. Fair enough. They invited her to move out of the youth hostel and stay in their homes. Carol and Elaine took her in for a week. Later she stayed in a house shared by a French-speaking Greenpeace volunteer and Auckland newspaper reporter Karen Mangnall. 'I didn't like her at first,' Carol admitted. 'I speak little French; her English was pretty bad and she didn't make much effort to use it. She made herself at home very quickly, as if she owned the place. When we learned the truth about her later, my only consolation was that the fold-up bed I gave her was horribly uncomfortable.'

Frédérique was a stocky, blue-eyed woman of medium height, aged 33. The shortish cut of her light brown hair, the spectacles and big light-coloured eyes, and the long aquiline nose reinforced her imperious image. She said she was a geomorphologist and archaeologist who worked all over the world as a freelance scientific consultant. She was the youngest of three children of an aristocratic Breton-Corsican family and lived in Pau, an isolated town in the Pyrénées.

To her new-found friends Frédérique explained that some dear friends in Paris were coming to New Zealand soon for a long holiday. There were lots of things she would like to find out for them. She needed some maps to send. Where could they rent scuba equipment and how much would it cost? Where could air tanks be refilled? Was it expensive to rent a boat for diving trips and where could they find one . . .?

Carol was kept busy on the telephone calling campervan rental firms and boat charterers on the French woman's behalf. In rental cars Frédérique herself went off on long trips to East Cape, Rotorua, the Coromandel Peninsula and – significantly – Northland. She was keen on photography and loved the coast. She took lots of pictures of the pretty beaches, inlets and harbours and packaged them up with all the maps, brochures and other information that she mailed to her friends in Paris.

Meanwhile the scruffy sixth-floor office in Courthouse Lane was alight with an air of excitement as plans were finalised for *Rainbow Warrior*'s arrival then her voyage to Moruroa.

The situation in New Caledonia was growing uglier by the day. Kanak freedom-fighters and French planters had been shot dead. Army reinforcements were flown in. Due to the troubles French authorities decided to switch the venue of the South Pacific Arts Festival from New Caledonia to Tahiti. Oscar Temaru, the Tahitian mayor of Fa'a who was a leading figure in the independence movement of French Polynesia, came to Auckland to drum up support for a boycott of the festival.

In Greenpeace lots of wild ideas were being proposed. One of them, discussed with Temaru, was the possibility of embarking Tahitians on board *Rainbow Warrior* with outrigger canoes. The ship would transport the canoes to a position twelve miles off Moruroa. Then the Tahitian invaders would paddle to the reef, making a landing through the surf and halt the tests by occupying part of the atoll. Another proposal was to sail *Rainbow Warrior* into Tahiti with a number of political figures from other countries on board; Greenpeace would be able to call on considerable political clout if the ship were impounded or turned away by force.

Frédérique Bonlieu – 'Our dear friend,' Elaine would say later, with the irony of the betrayed – had free access to any conversation and all documents. There were no confidential files or deep secrets in Greenpeace.

Firm instructions came from David McTaggart, in England, that the ship was not to sail inside the 12-mile (20 km) territorial limit and risk arrest. Her job was to keep station beyond the reach of the French Navy, mothering the protest yachts and transmitting pictures to keep the issue in the public eye, especially during September when the Non-Proliferation Treaty was being discussed in Geneva. The itinerary of the Pacific Peace Voyage was settled and mailed to Auckland on May 6. The letter arrived on May 15.

Just over one week later Frédérique made fond farewells, promised to return in September, and left for Tahiti.

In Papeete she attended the coral reef conference and was debriefed. She flew to Paris, then to an archaeological dig near Haifa, in Israel. Her real identity was Christine-Huguette Cabon, a French army lieutenant operating as a secret agent.

A career officer, Cabon had in 1977 become a member of *Le Cadre Spécial*, an élite corps similar to the British SAS. Injured in a parachuting accident in 1982, she was seconded for duty to the DGSE, the French external security service (see next chapter). Later, newspapers in France would allege she was a specialist in infiltration, and expert at laying the groundwork for operations, especially in the Middle East. Her controller now was said to be a captain in intelligence evaluation whose speciality was the infiltration of 'Green' movements in Europe.

In Paris, the intelligence gleaned by the mole from the Greenpeace office in Auckland confirmed their worst fears.

France had learned some tough lessons. You never got the best of any encounter with Greenpeace. Bullying tactics might work when the Greenpeace protesters were sailing a small yacht with feeble radio communications. But French minesweepers could hardly try the same tactics on a 417-ton ship. The only way to stop *Rainbow Warrior* would be to shoot her out of the water, and her satellite-relayed communications would transmit blow-by-blow pictures as well as a running commentary. The politicians and military chiefs must have shuddered at the frightening prospect of world front pages and prime-time TV news being filled with dramatic pictures of Tahitian canoes landing on the reef of the atoll of the big secret, raising flags, taking radiation measurements and making a big noise while the mother ship provided food, water, transport and – most unnerving of all – instantaneous media facilities.

More than the security of the testing programme was under threat. It was all bound up with the integrity of France's nuclear dissuasion, not to speak of national pride. And the threat was all the harder to handle for being non-military. The weapons being employed did not shoot bullets. They fired more wounding and effective ammunition – emotion, misinformation, ridicule.

No doubt realising that in the theatre of world front-page headlines a military machine could never win, the authorities decided on a pre-emptive strike. To understand the background to this decision, however, it is essential to realise the importance French people pin on their independent nuclear capability. The nuclear armoury enabling France to stand head-high among the superpowers – to deter attack yet remain unattached to the military apron strings of the United States and Great Britain – is more than self-esteem or pride. It is a question of the survival of an independent France.

According to the Stockholm International Peace Research Institute, France in 1984 had an arsenal of 80 ballistic missiles carried by five (now six) nuclear submarines and 18 intermediate-range ballistic missiles housed in silos. There were also about 50 launchers for short-range tactical missiles and just over 100 aircraft designated to carry nuclear weapons. President Mitterrand put the French capability in perspective when he pointed out (in Amsterdam in February 1984) that while France had 98 nuclear charges and Great Britain 64, the Soviet Union and the United States had about 9,000 *each*.

In 1985 France launched the first submarine of a new generation carrying multi-warhead missiles. When the rest of the fleet is retro-fitted France will have 900 warheads, more than ample to call the bluff of an enemy superpower with 9,000. France would shoot back with not just one weapon but a strategic 'triad' of sea-, air- and land-based missiles. They might not be sufficient to resist attack and therefore win a nuclear war against the Soviets. But all were targeted on Russian cities. This is the crux of France's national security.

Initially, the *force de frappe* was intended merely to deter. The policy was born out of the realisation that it would be difficult for any nation, even the United States, to risk its ultimate survival for the sake of its allies. In the mid-1960s President de Gaulle coined the notion that in a nuclear war with the Soviet Union the Americans would hardly be willing to trade Hamburg for New York. To defend herself in the modern era France therefore needed an independent nuclear force. It needn't be as massive as those of the superpowers. Let it be just big enough for the Soviet Union to be in no doubt that any attack on France would spell suicide.

Now more politely called the *force de dissuasion* but still essentially Gaullist in spirit, it involves a more flexible strategy. France realises she must be prepared to resist attack on Western Europe jointly with her allies and is increasingly developing more tactical or battlefield weapons. A new generation of weapons and updating of old ones has been demanded. In April 1983 the French Cabinet approved a five-year military spending programme giving priority to nuclear forces and their modernisation.

The S2 missiles carrying single large warheads and based in silos in Haute Provence, near Marseilles, were to be upgraded with a multiplicity of warheads which, like a shotgun, would ensure a target's destruction with lots of smaller but overlapping explosions. The Submarine-Launched Ballistic Missile known as the M20, also with one large warhead, is being replaced with a new version called the M4 carrying six multiple re-entry vehicles with smaller warheads. The air force's Mirage IV aircraft carrying single nuclear bombs were to be augmented or replaced by new nuclear air-surface stand-off missiles which could be launched from long distance, outside the range of Soviet air defence.

In the tactical sector the army's surface-to-surface Pluton nuclear missile would be replaced by the bigger and better Hades with three times the range. It was likely to be deployed over the border with neutron warheads so French nuclear weapons could be closely integrated into the forward defence of West Germany. The air force would get new Jaguar and Mirage IIIE aircraft wired for nuclear weapons. For the navy, new aircraft to carry nuclear bombs and nuclear depth charges.

Interestingly, both Britain and France set out to acquire independent nuclear arsenals at about the same time and both spend roughly the same amount of money. But there are pronounced differences. Britain's strategic defence is based on the four-boat Polaris submarine fleet, each launching 16 triple-warhead missiles. This fleet is being replaced by new, larger submarines with hugely expensive Trident missiles. Britain's tactical weapons are operated only under a 'dual key' with the US.

Though France spends a greater share of her military budget on nuclear weapons she gets more for her money. Her nuclear arsenal is substantially larger with a greater variety of weapons. All French nuclear weapons have been developed in France by French industry. British Polaris and Trident missiles are bought from the US though the warheads are made under licence at home. Because she has just one big egg in her strategic basket, Britain can update her weapons only with cataclysmic changes while the French are able to update first one leg of the triad then another. Britain's weapons are committed to NATO. France's strategy has been to defend only her own interests, though she is coming round to the view that by sheer force of geography no country can go it alone in Western Europe.

Another remarkable difference is public attitudes to nuclear deterrence. In Britain the consensus has been completely broken down by anti-nuclear campaigns in which Greenpeace played a part. In France there is little or no trouble with public opinion. In early 1985 an opinion poll concluded that 72 percent of all French people backed their nuclear defence, up from 67 percent the previous year. Greenpeace, with only 6,000 paid-up supporters in France, enjoys very little support for its anti-nuclear stand. Its persistent protests against Moruroa tests are seen as blatant anti-French bias. The Soviets and Americans tested as many as 42 bombs (in 1984) so why single out France for exploding only seven? Overall, France is responsible for only eight percent of all nuclear tests.

The French people themselves have grown to like living in a nuclear shadow. They are even proud of it. In the early 1950s they decided to turn to 'the friendly atom' for generation of electricity and the wisdom of their choice was endorsed by the oil crises of the 1970s. Now, two houses in every three are supplied with electricity from atomic power stations. Also, the French have the moral satisfaction of knowing that alone among the nuclear powers they have allowed a team of foreign scientists to investigate and take samples from their test site. The scientists reported that radiation on Moruroa is a great deal less than in mainland France.

In other important respects, too, France could claim a clean operation. Unlike the American and Soviet explosions, and probably the Chinese ones which still took place in the atmosphere, the French tests were far removed from people. Only a few scores of islanders lived within hundreds of miles. The rival superpowers could hardly shout about their own history of nuclear testing. Look at what the Americans had done to Bikini and Rongelap. Even at Nevada the underground tests had vented radioactivity into the atmosphere and high-level winds had dispersed fallout as far as Vancouver. In 1982 one blast made a crater big enough to swallow a skyscraper. Great Britain's testing in Australia seemed to have been carried out with callous disregard for the aboriginal people or the welfare of her troops; now she faced massive costs to clean up her legacy of contamination in the desert. The 'scorched earth' policy of the Soviet Union towards the protection of the environment was well known. The tests conducted in China were so dirty that fallout had collected on rooftops in England.

Twice in living memory France has been invaded by aggressors. Her people have no intention of letting it happen again. They know that the improvement, sophistication and reliability of their chosen weapon systems depend completely on continued testing. You can test the triggers. You can put individual components through trials. You can test the theories by computer modelling. But there's only one way to test the shelf life of weapons, only one way to obtain direct data, and only one way to be completely certain the device will work when you push the button to fire it. You have to assemble the thing in a remote place and try it out. Also, the rockets that deliver the bombs are test-fired every year into the Atlantic near Bordeaux so the assembled fleet of 'trawlers' from many nations can see they 'work'.

As a Frenchman you would regard the *force de dissuasion* on which your security rested as efficient, cost-effective, cleanly run, and tested in a way that was an example to other countries. As President Mitterrand described it to Mr Gorbachev of the Soviet Union, France's nuclear arsenal was just big enough to keep France in the game yet so small it hardly counted as part of the arms race. Moreover, the nuclear deterrence is a symbol of your national stature, your independence from Washington and Moscow. Lose it and you lose France, as even the political Left have realised. All four political parties in France support the maintenance of a nuclear capability, all four would resist the idea of supporting an anti-nuclear movement in any way. From the Catholic Church (though it has taken a firmer line on the trading of conventional armaments) there has been only the occasional protest of an isolated bishop against France's nuclear arms.

Against this determined and resolute commitment New Zealand's attitude to nuclear defence could hardly be in starker contrast. Her outlook on world problems is greatly influenced by the beauty and peacefulness of the country tucked away in its isolated corner of the Pacific Ocean. Apart from a tiny bit of Siberia there's nothing else but New Zealand between the North Pole and the South Pole. Even Antarctica is closer to Europe than New Zealand. Nuclear war is therefore perceived as something that might happen between super-powers like the United States and the Soviet Union but in a different hemisphere – 'Why do we have to get involved in any of that stuff?'

New Zealanders see no likelihood of their country being attacked for its own sake; the extensive coastline is in any case undefendable. Nor is it likely to be attacked as a staging post because it's not on the road to anywhere. Dr Henry Kissinger once scathingly remarked on the country's strategic significance: 'New Zealand is a dagger pointed at the heart of Antarctica.'

New Zealand has a proud tradition of leaping to the defence of her 'mother' country. None of the Allies committed a greater share of her manhood to both world wars. But global politics are now perceived in a different light. If the Soviet threat did not exist it would be essential to American military and armament interests to invent it. If the American threat did not exist the Soviet Union would not be able to justify its build-up of massive military strength and keep a convenient excuse for its low standards of living. So this arms race, New Zealand can say, is nothing to do with us. A conflict between the superpowers is a greater risk to our welfare than any attack on our territory. Our association with the United States seems to endanger the nation rather than protect it. We're still friends. We just want to go our own way. Stresses the prime minister, David Lange: 'It's inconceivable that we could be anti the United States, lunatic to think we are pro Moscow.'

Though New Zealand ranks among the Third World War's least likely nuclear targets, the fear of being caught up in it has spawned unusually strong anti-nuclear feeling. Disquiet extends far beyond political radicals. It lies deep in the traditionally conservative middle class. Legions of ordinary people leading blessedly peaceful and uninvolved lives simply feel that, as helpless bystanders of the destructive policies of the great powers, the best thing they can do is not get involved. The peace movement, provoked and sustained by continued French testing in New Zealand's neighbourhood, nourished by the hope that the country's remoteness will protect them from the nuclear holocaust to come, is therefore a political force of a potency that few French people understand, let alone sympathise with.

Numerous small communities and organisations, from individual suburbs to the Auckland Harbour Board, have declared themselves 'nuclear-free zones'. The Auckland Peace Office has 90 branches. Peace groups operate in every sector of society, even sailing clubs. Yachtsmen formed a 'peace flotilla' of up to 150 yachts and motor launches to demonstrate against nuclear-armed warships. The flotilla surrounded and tried to blockade American naval vessels coming into port. Protesters threw paint bombs at their hulls, dropped divers in front of their bows, and tried to block them with manoeuvres called 'pattern sailing'. The ship visits prompted union walkouts, stopped the ferry service between the country's two main islands and closed the port of Wellington.

Yet even the New Zealanders who opposed ship visits were – and remain – personally pro-American. The nuclear-powered guided missile carrier USS *Texas* had to go into full reverse when protesters threw themselves under her bows as she entered Auckland. But once she was docked the number of calls from Aucklanders offering hospitality to the crew was sufficient to entertain the entire ship's company.

When the Labour Party swept into power in July 1984 the new prime minister, David Lange, wasted no time living up to his election promises. He declared New Zealand a nuclear-free zone and made it clear that warships carrying nuclear weapons were no longer welcome. As the US and Great Britain adopt a policy of neither confirming nor denying that individual ships carry nuclear weapons, this effectively banned their navies from the country.

While *Rainbow Warrior* stretched her new wings in the Caribbean, and the mole in Auckland relayed intelligence of Greenpeace intentions back to Paris, New Zealand's anti-nuclear stand was causing a furore. The move threatened the long-standing defence agreement between Australia, New Zealand and the United States.

Called the ANZUS Pact, this 'mini NATO of the South Seas' – agreed at a time when a 'yellow peril' spilling down through Malaysia and Indonesia to the Antipodes was regarded as the main threat – was not in fact a military treaty. It afforded New Zealand no guarantee of security unless her defence happened to be in America's best interests. Nevertheless, it was widely perceived in the US as a kind of blood-brothers' pact. Americans felt betrayed. Howling for New Zealand's blood, they saw it as the sabotage of an important alliance. Half the US Senate supported retaliatory action. Important trade privileges were to be cancelled. New Zealand's status as a 'most favoured nation' trading partner, granted as a result of her support in the Vietnam War, must be withdrawn.

But Prime Minister David Lange would not be budged. 'We've decided we don't want to be part of anyone's tactical nuclear war,' he responded bluntly. 'We simply don't want to be defended by nuclear weapons because they cause more harm than anything that might threaten us . . .'

On American TV the prime minister added: 'There's only one thing worse than being incinerated by your enemy and that's being incinerated by your friends . . . The best hope is that slowly, undramatically, sanity will become part of the mosaic of world politics.'

David Lange (the surname from his distant German ancestry is pronounced Long-ee), aged 43, is an impressive, likeable, quick-thinking and eloquent figure. Weighing in at more than 18 stone (114 kg) he's also a burly one, and before his election had a risky stomach bypass operation to reduce his obesity from 24 stone (170 kg). As a barrister he made a name for himself as 'the poor man's friend'. His background was strongly Methodist. He had been in parliament only seven years, party leader for two, when he became prime minister, New Zealand's first to have a university degree.

Despite the widespread bankruptcy and hardship his party's radical financial policies were causing among farmers and manufacturers, Lange's direct and provocative thinking was keeping God's Own Country firmly in world headlines. New Zealanders were no longer ignored and unnoticed. But it was a difficult and challenging tightrope act for Lange to be pro-America and pro-Western alliance yet also anti-nuclear. He achieved both with sufficient effectiveness and grace to earn a nomination for the Nobel Prize for Peace, but his decision to ban the bomb offered President Reagan a challenge with global implications. If one Pacific ally simply opted out, saying to hell with Western solidarity, could the delicate arrangements giving the US Pacific fleets access to ports in Japan and the Philippines also be threatened? Would the persuasive Lange doctrine spread like an allergy through the Pacific? Could the blight unravel the entire security cocoon of South East Asia?

It was in this context that the French military authorities and nuclear experimentation chiefs in Paris were reviewing the projected voyage of the Greenpeace flagship *Rainbow Warrior* to Moruroa.

Three components of their vital modernisation were evidently being tested at Moruroa at the time *Rainbow Warrior* was making her Pacific Peace Voyage. One device was the M4, to be test fired before it was deployed in the new submarine *Inflexible*. The large explosion on May 8 was thought to have been the final test of its 150-ton kiloton warhead. Another was development of a 60-kiloton warhead for the new medium-range, ground-to-ground missile called Hades. The third was refinement of a new battlefield weapon that would be vital if Soviet tanks were to roll over the border into West Germany – the neutron bomb.

Alarmingly, there was word that *Rainbow Warrior* was being fitted with sophisticated gear to monitor those neutron tests. Could the ship get close enough to establish what kind of test it was?

Broadsides of clever propaganda from *Rainbow Warrior* would be bad enough. The prospect of the ship launching an 'nvasion of canoes to disrupt the whole season's testing programme could not be permitted. And these threats were only part of the problem France faced in the Pacific.

France had always disliked the sympathies loudly expressed in New Zealand and Australia for the separatist movement making trouble in New Caledonia. Her military planners were alarmed by the effectiveness with which muddle-headed protesters were undermining Western Europe's nuclear defence. Now the South Pacific Forum, on the verge of declaring its vast oceanic area a nuclear-free zone, was going soft. The virulently anti-nuclear but plausible policies of David Lange, albeit he was a socialist, were a dangerous cancer.

In France it was recognised that a sorry fate awaited any politician or military supremo who allowed the country's nuclear virility to be compromised. The armed services were in any case paranoid about protecting their nukes. And the authorities had long been obsessed with Greenpeace.

In his book about his first two protest voyages in *Vega*, David McTaggart describes how a young navy officer at a staff meeting put forward a plan to ram and sink the Greenpeace yacht. The plan was not accepted by the admiral in charge. Another operation to sink Greenpeace was reportedly ordered in 1978 when Valéry Giscard d'Estaing was president but countermanded at the last minute as not worth the risk. For years, according to French intelligence sources, anti-nuclear protesters have been repeatedly harried with minor food-poisoning, radio and mechanical sabotage and other types of harassment inflicted by French agents. In the changed climate of 1985, with French leaders irritated and alarmed by the growing anti-nuclear sentiment in neighbouring European countries, and political unrest in French Pacific territories, it was only a small step to envisage making a short, sharp example of Greenpeace.

That the environmental organisation was effective nobody could deny. It had already played a role in forcing French tests under-ground. Perhaps it could orchestrate such a world-wide chorus of opposition that the tests would be chased off Moruroa to some more distant island like Kerguelen, a bleak unpopulated 'territory' in the southern Indian Ocean. These were clearly matters a minister of defence should handle personally.

In private conversations with officials of other Western powers M. Charles Hernu, a long-standing friend and colleague whom President Mitterrand had appointed to the job, often reverted to the subject of Greenpeace, describing the group as dangerous nuisances. Greenpeace had it in for France, he thought, and was probably being manipulated through the peace movement by the Soviet Union. The French military believed Greenpeace was infiltrated by Soviet or communist spies. In some quarters, obsessed with oil-poor France's energy supplies, leaders even suspected Greenpeace of being at least partly financed by British Petroleum to stir up trouble for the French nuclear electricity generating programme.

At the highest level, Charles Hernu's team obviously concluded it was time for France to see Greenpeace off. But the complete story of how the defence minister and his security services took the decision to neutralise what they deemed to be a subversive and potentially dangerous bunch of troublemakers will probably never be known unless Hernu tells it himself. Later he would strenuously deny that he gave an order to sink *Rainbow Warrior*, or that he knew anything about such an order.

What is known is that on March 1 he received a note from Admiral Henri Fages, of the *Direction du Centre d'Expérimentations Nucléaires* (DIRCEN), the headquarters organisation of the French nuclear testing programme. Admiral Fages was chief of the test operations on Moruroa. Also in his charge was DIRCEN's own intelligence and security unit. The admiral was worried stiff about the activities Greenpeace was planning. His note urged the stepping up of intelligence gathering on the movements of the *Vega* and *Rainbow Warrior* 'to forecast and anticipate Greenpeace actions'. Three days later Admiral Fages of DIRCEN briefed Hernu personally, expressing angry fears that Greenpeace would be seriously disruptive.

Hernu then discussed the problem with Admiral Pierre Lacoste, head of the *Direction Générale de la Sécurité Extérieure* (DGSE). The DGSE is the foreign operations wing of the French secret service, the equivalent of America's CIA and Britain's MI6. When Admiral Lacoste read Admiral Fages' note he saw the word 'anticiper' had been underlined – not once, but twice.

In the French language 'anticiper' has more than one meaning. It's similar to the English word it resembles, most commonly meaning 'foresee'. It can also mean, in a vague way, 'to prevent', 'neutralise' or 'forestall'.

Was the word used in all innocence – 'Find out everything so we can be prepared'?

Or was it the kind of euphemism intelligence agencies concoct to lend respectability to their ends, a deliberately ambiguous instruction that set in train a disastrous chain of events – 'Greenpeace must be taken out'?

The defence minister ordered Admiral Lacoste to infiltrate Greenpeace and set up a surveillance operation in the South Pacific. The DGSE was already poised. Christine Cabon's cover was quickly consolidated. At the Paris Boat Show she had 'accidentally' encountered the ecologist, yachtsman and former Moruroa protester Jean-Marc Vidal. She had met him first in Corsica a few months before when she spoke enthusiastically of her admiration for Commander Cousteau, the diver. Now she told him she was bound for the South Pacific with a team of archaeologists and would like to help in ecology work. Vidal provided her with the letter of introduction that would be her ticket into Greenpeace. Meanwhile, other DGSE agents were being selected for the field team and a special unit was being set up within the service to handle the mission. It was called K Cell.

Costs of the 'surveillance' operation were estimated by Admiral Lacoste and his staff. One report would later put the figure at £300,000. The calculation was reputed to have been countersigned by General Jean-Michel Saulnier who, as head of President Mitterrand's military secretariat, carried the nuclear trigger codes in the briefcase that Americans call the football. Along with General Jeannou Lacaze, chief of the Army staff, Saulnier had evidently been sitting in on the meetings that planned and approved the intelligence operation against Greenpeace in March 1985. Lacaze had earlier commanded the analysis section of DGSE; Saulnier succeeded him in the top army job soon afterwards. It was never discovered by French media investigators whether the plan came to the attention of either President Mitterrand himself or Prime Minister Laurent Fabius. Normally, secret funds from the prime minister's office could be unblocked only with two signatures. Later, nobody would say who signed the paperwork and it is possible the system was bypassed.

Nothing ever came to light about the discreet orders that changed the mission of the DGSE's K Cell from surveillance and penetration of Greenpeace to that of hit squad.

It is plausible that since the DGSE was currently out of favour (see Chapter 11), control of K Cell and its field agents was taken out of Lacoste's hands and given to the man on the spot, Admiral Farges and DIRCEN. And that Charles Hernu, exasperated for so

94

long by Greenpeace actions, talked to Admiral Farges in a way that the latter might have interpreted as a green light to 'anticipate' the protest voyage in the most active sense of the word. Loathing Greenpeace, and having only a narrow perspective on the possible effects of their actions, DIRCEN might well have decided to employ K Cell to fulfil their dearest wishes – and blow Greenpeace out of the water.

Both Hernu and Lacoste vigorously deny giving such an order. Yet both might easily have known what DIRCEN intended; their official blessing would not have been required. If they knew, it's likely they supposed the ship would only be disabled. The mission would intimidate opponents and hearten French patriots. It would cause no loss of life. The bold signature of France was to be clearly evident, but leave no vestige of proof.

Wherever it originated, the order 'Sink the *Rainbow Warrior!*' had the effect of a rampaging torpedo.

It left a trail so Gallic, one DGSE officer sarcastically observed, that the only missing clues were a *baguette* bread loaf, a black beret and a bottle of Beaujolais.

It dismayed the French public. The display of incompetence prompted cartoonists and news commentators to depict the DGSE as Inspector Clouseau, the bumbling detective of the Pink Panther movies: one cartoon showed Clouseau dressed in scuba gear and standing to attention at President Mitterrand's desk.

It sank the ship. But it blew Greenpeace straight into the broad and loving lap of sympathetic public opinion around the world.

It threw an intense media spotlight on the French testing at Moruroa.

Then, in a style worthy of the best of Clouseau, the torpedo turned in its tracks, sank those who strenuously denied having pushed the firing button, and came within an inch of sinking the president and the French ship of state.

But Lieutenant Christine Cabon, as she infiltrated the office of Greenpeace New Zealand with her concept of the French rightness of things firmly entrenched behind her false identity and haughty manners, could hardly have imagined that a French torpedo was capable of such a spectacular and appalling malfunction.

7

SWIMMING POOL WARRIORS

The DGSE is skilled at muddying the waters in which it operates. It has never baulked from sinking a ship when required. Nor, for that matter, from bombing cars, kidnapping politicians and playing all the dirty tricks known in the intelligence game. Its commodious and antennae-capped headquarters building with nine floors has a screen of cement slabs protecting its many windows, giving the impression of rows of keyholes. It is situated in the Mortier barracks in northern Paris, in the shadow of the traffic-choked six-lane orbital motorway called *la périphérique*. The headquarters also happens to be adjacent to the popular Tourelles swimming pool which explains why the DGSE is known jocularly as *la piscine*.

The French secret services have had none of the intellectual traditions of the British services that concentrated mainly on Soviet targets, recruited university dons in wartime, and had some intellectual talent and social respectability at the top. In France secret operations were seen as thugs' work, hence the slang name for the DGSE's operatives – the *barbouzes* (bearded ones), implying cumbersome disguises and brutishness.

The DGSE, like much covert work in France even now, has its roots in the wartime resistance. Before the war France had only a handful of espionage agents who concentrated as much on Great Britain – France's bitter rival in the Middle East – as on Germany. From London, Charles de Gaulle masterminded a new organisation which, like the Resistance, drew on any talent it could find including plenty of gangsters looking for ways to redeem their pasts and guarantee their futures. The BCRA – *Bureau Central de Renseignement d'Action* (central bureau of intelligence and action) – sent agents on risky missions into occupied France but had an unsavoury reputation from the start. Flooded by opportunists, it grew into a huge, unwieldy and corrupt organisation with thousands of agents. Nine-tenths were dismissed in 1945 and the survivors moved in as leaders of a new organisation set up to take care of foreign intelligence.

The SDECE – *Service de Documentation Extérieure et de Contre Espionage* (department of foreign information and counter espionage) – quickly proved worthless in Europe, perhaps because of communist penetration, and turned its concentration on the French colonies.

Powerful in post-colonial Africa, SDECE made and un-made *coups d'état*. The staff of about 2,000 were mostly men of military background. It was not a service known for rapid promotion and there were racketeering scandals. One of those involved in the drugs case later filmed as *The French Connection* was not prosecuted in the US because he claimed to be an SDECE agent. The service operated in conjunction with French military units as well as mercenaries who hung out near to *la piscine* in a bistro called *Le Treillis*, a pun on camouflage suit. Retired officers of SDECE often moved into powerful jobs, becoming advisers to African rulers such as Omar Bongo of oil-rich Gabon. The service also drew heavily on volunteers among the large numbers of French expatriates who remained in the former colonies to operate airports, airlines, communications, local armies, and police as well as French diplomats, civil servants and businessmen. It was mainly patriotism – *la gloire* – that motivated these freelance and part-time intelligence agents, known as 'honourable correspondents'. France is thought to have had about 40,000 of them in 1970, but it's likely the number has diminished since the socialists came to power in 1981.

Though characterised by ruthless self-interest, SDECE operators chalked up some notable successes. They devised a scheme to remove fuel from Soviet aircraft to determine its secret anti-freeze ingredient. In the best traditions of James Bond they gassed and raided Soviet couriers travelling on the Orient Express as it steamed through a tunnel. In Tangier harbour they bombed at least three cargo ships carrying arms to Algeria, and as recently as 1982 planned a similar operation against a ship in Genoa, Italy, loaded with arms for Libya. It was SDECE agents who, in 1962, tipped off the Americans that the Soviets were deploying missiles in Cuba. In 1979 they learned of the imminent Soviet invasion of Afghanistan and also helped the Saudis plan the recapture of the Grand Mosque in Mecca after it had been taken over by Moslem extremists.

But SDECE was also responsible for some notable scandals. In 1956, during the Algerian War, with the connivance of the French air crew, SDECE agents arranged for the king of Morocco's Super Constellation aircraft, carrying the Algerian resistance leader Ben Bella to an Arab League Summit in Tunis, to be diverted. The air hostesses told passengers the window blinds had to be pulled down for secrecy. When the plane landed, not in Tunisia as scheduled but in Algiers, the French Army stormed aboard to snatch the wanted man. The affair further inflamed feelings not only in Algeria but also inside France.

In 1967 came the infamous Ben Barka affair when two SDECE agents picked up the Moroccan Socialist opposition leader in broad daylight in a Paris street. They handed him over to a Moroccan security chief who had come to Paris to torture and kill his victim personally in a villa in the suburbs. The agents, it turned out, were only doing favours for their Israeli friends who were then working closely with the Moroccans. De Gaulle loftily dismissed the episode as 'sordid and subaltern business' but it confirmed worst suspicions about the laxness of the secret service; de Gaulle's only action was to remove SDECE from the office of the prime minister and put it under the Ministry of Defence. Die-hard Gaullists in SDECE tried to block Georges Pompidou's path to the presidency in 1969 by smearing his wife, Claude. They circulated montage pictures purporting to depict her in orgies. Pompidou then put in his own man to run the service. President Giscard d'Estaing completed the discrediting of SDECE when he blatantly supported Bokassa, the tyrant president of the Central African Republic, then, deciding to overthrow him, first sent in the secret service to clear out of Bokassa's palace certain documents embarrassing to him personally.

At the same time SDECE was fighting a running battle with its sister service, the DST – *Direction de la Surveillance du Territoire* (counter espionage service) of the Interior Ministry – whose primary responsibility was to prevent terrorism, industrial espionage and Soviet subversion within France. A cop operation with tough, cunning leadership. DST thinks SDECE is a bunch of cowboys at best, traitors at worst. While SDECE works closely with arabs, the DST is close to Israel. When Abu Daoud, Palestinian leader of Black September, visited France in 1976 the DST picked him up and tried to hand him over to West Germany who wanted him in connection with the massacre of Israeli athletes at the Munich Olympic Games. But the terrorist had entered France on a safe conduct from SDECE and had to be released.

Despite an SDECE attempt to mastermind a palace coup against Qaddafi in Libya, which back-fired embarrassingly, the service improved its reputation through the late 1970s. Though the service verged on mutiny when socialists came to power in 1981, President Mitterrand decided to keep it. Subsequently its skills and morale were threatened by bungled leadership. On 4 April 1984, Admiral Pierre Lacoste was brought in to streamline the service and introduce a new anti-Soviet focus to its operations. He gave it a new name – DGSE; but his modernisation and re-organisation didn't get far. Though Lacoste had served in the office of Giscard's premier, Raymond Barre, and so looked bi-partisan, residual hatred of the socialists within the service blocked his efforts.

The professionalism of DGSE had already become a sore point. At the time of the Falklands War, in June 1982, President Mitterrand is reported to have ordered the agency to brief him on Argentina. The best it could do was provide an atlas map stamped 'secret'. Mitterrand was infuriated by such 'trite incompetence'. Another gaffe further enraged the president when, on the basis of DGSE reports, he announced that Libyan troops had withdrawn from Chad – only to be humiliatingly contradicted by the US whose satellite photographs showed they were still there.

For these and a host of other reasons, when the Greenpeace mission was launched relations between the government and the DGSE were already severely strained.

Under Lacoste's new organisation the service now had three divisions and 2,800 full-time employees of whom the 1,300 military held nearly all the key posts. One division gathered and processed information from agents in the field. One worked in counter-espionage, recruiting agents to act for France, penetrating other intelligence agencies and searching for defectors. The third, mostly autonomous, was *Division Action*.

The training centre of *Division Action* was at Cercottes, near Orléans, where the airfield (formerly a major NATO base until de Gaulle pulled out of the alliance) has a squadron of Transall transport planes used by French forces on foreign missions. On a headland at Aspretto, near Ajaccio in Corsica, was CINC (pronounced 'sank'), the combat swimmer training school for élite commandos; nominally run by the navy's air division, it was controlled by the DGSE's *Division Action*. Special mission training was also conducted at Noisy-le-Bcc, a fort near Paris.

Division Action's role was in the hands of a strongly military orientated staff. For operations, good men and women were often seconded from the 11th Airborne Division, a crack army unit. Also, field agents tasked for special missions were commonly 'honourable correspondents' or casual agents trained by DGSE but remaining as freelance to be dropped and disowned if an operation backfired.

From this 'James Bond' special operations wing of *la piscine* – noted for its extreme right-wing views and abiding hatred of socialists – was chosen the team and back-up crew to hit the *Rainbow Warrior*.

One of the controllers of Lieutenant Christine Cabon, the Greenpeace mole in Auckland, was Dominique Prieur, who was already working on her own cover for the operation. Nicknamed 'Doumie' and treated with special camaraderie, like a mascot, she was the first woman to be commissioned in *Division Action*. By the time she made captain in 1982 she had been on missions in Mauritius, Tunisia and Morocco.

An attractive slim blonde with an acid wit, Prieur was an experienced and professional agent. Now 36, she had come from a heroic background. Her father, Louis Maire, was captured four times by the Nazis and escaped four times, finishing the war in the Maquis operating in the mountains near Switzerland where the family lived. Her grandparents were both executed by firing squad ten days before the war ended and her parents later held their wedding service on the same spot. Maire took his family to New Caledonia where he managed the mining company's store then drifted to other jobs. Dominique was not brilliant at school but studious. At nine her parents divorced. Dominique returned to France with her mother and received posthumous medals for bravery on behalf of her grandparents. With an uncle who was an air force pilot, other relatives in a para-military unit of gendarmes and in the Foreign Legion, and her mother working at a military base near Besançon, not far from the Swiss border, it was no surprise that after working her way through college she joined the women's army corps. Commissioned in 1976, she joined the intelligence wing of the DGSE immediately.

In 1980 'Doumie' married Joel-Patrick Prieur, a lieutenant in the transport corps whom she had met a couple of years earlier at a military academy ball. They lived in the spacious commandant's flat of a barracks of the Paris regiment of the fire brigade (which in France is commanded by military officers) on the Left Bank, while her husband studied to get into War College. She had already been awarded a doctorate at the intellectually demanding Nanterre University in Paris, working under a professor well known for his anti-communist sympathies, and had written a thesis on the subject of Qaddafi's Green Book.

Her missions seem to have involved the infiltration of terrorist movements in North Africa with occasional forays among Europe's anti-nuclear groups. She would tell friends and relatives she was visiting her mother in Alsace, or taking a holiday, and drop from sight. No postcards, no telephone calls. Even her husband never knew specifically what she was doing. Later he explained: 'Sometimes she used to tell me simply that she was leaving on an assignment and I never asked questions – it was the best way to protect our marriage.'

Through spring 1985 the fire brigade flat on Rue du Vieux-Colombier saw a frequent visitor. He was a good-looking and physically fit military action man, Major Alain Mafart. Together, Prieur and Mafart pored over the photographs, maps and other intelligence about Greenpeace activities and New Zealand harbours relayed to them by Christine Cabon.

Mafart was clearly a top agent, different from James Bond only in his strong military background and affiliations. He was born the son of a military doctor in Indo-China who made General, spending his boyhood in Senegal and Marseilles. He learned to sail in Brittany and skied in Switzerland where the family had a chalet. Graduating young from a top Jesuit school he was sent to the US to take his mind off motorcycles. Too impatient to wait for France's compulsory military service, he enlisted as a paratrooper, served overseas and rose rapidly through the ranks. At a special staff school he graduated as top cadet then trained as a naval commando at Aspretto and joined what is now *Division Action*.

As an agent he operated in the Lebanon and parts of Africa, including Chad where France was embroiled in a series of small wars pitting Tuareg tribes against each other.

Brilliant, athletic, unruly, a detached personality but capable of turning on the charm, especially to women, Mafart was an accomplished adventurer. With a colleague in 1980 he paddled from St Tropez to Ajaccio, a 64-hour voyage in a tiny kayak. Then he used nine months of accumulated leave to make a long single-handed dog-sled expedition on the Greenland ice-cap; using traditional eskimo methods, he constructed the sled with his own hands. An expert and prolific photographer with several Hasselblad camera bodies and sets of lenses, he took frequent self portraits – a long-faced figure with blondish hair parted in the middle and a small fringed beard along the jaw, standing alone on the ice in his furs.

Subsequently Mafart devoted all his free time to following and photographing whales, first in California then at Tierra del Fuego. In 1983 he underwent plastic surgery after an operation for skin cancer on his face and was removed from active duty as a frogman. But he was then made second in command of the combat swimmer training school at Aspretto. Promoted to the rank of major in October 1984, now 35, he asked to be relieved of this command to study for the entrance exams to War College. In March 1985 he transferred to Paris. But first there was a little job to do in the South Pacific. With his interest in ecology and distant islands, the assignment was an offer he wouldn't refuse.

The cover plan Mafart and Prieur devised for their role in the operation required them to travel on Swiss passports as a honeymoon couple – Alain Jacques Turenge, a manager, and his bride Sophie Frédérique Claire Turenge, a sociology teacher. But they were only one section of the team.

Little is known about the leader of the *Rainbow Warrior* operation. Lieutenant Colonel Louis-Pierre Dillais, commander of the Aspretto combat school, was Mafart's former chief. He was an athletic man of 38, a couple of inches short of six feet tall, with short

101

brown hair. Unlike Mafart, who spoke excellent English, the leader spoke the language badly. But his competence as a secret agent and his ruthlessness could never be doubted.

The mission planners decided the only certain way of landing explosives and military scuba gear in New Zealand without arousing suspicion was to smuggle it in by yacht. In keeping with tried and proven DGSE procedure they also decided that while its own team of three could run the land-based side of the operation, they should look to the corps of freelances and honourable correspondents for the operatives who – so to speak – would be the ones to get their feet wet.

None of the evidence which subsequently came to light links Dr Xavier Maniguet with the DGSE. There is no certainty that he was approached by *Division Action*, provided with ample funds, and invited to embark on a modest sailing adventure in the South Pacific to help provide cover for a surveillance and/or sabotage operation. The doctor has strenuously denied being anything but an innocent caught up in a web of intrigue.

Maniguet was every inch a man of action and liked to look the part. Of smallish stature with bright blue eyes, his fair sun-bleached hair thinning and receding, he drove a Porsche, owned and piloted a bi-winged stunt plane, was parachutist, hunter and experienced scuba diver, and lived in an extraordinary house on the edge of an artificial lake in the countryside near Dieppe, Normandy. Constructed in two prefabricated cement balls half buried beneath turf and shrubs, with oval windows like portholes, the house was a stylish bachelor pad with furnishings heavy on shaggy rugs, maps and leopard-skin cushions.

A freelance doctor who specialised in tropical, aeronautic and diving medicine, Maniguet was also a reservist in the French Navy. He had worked in Asia and for several years had been working with French oil companies in the United Arab Emirates. Among his specialities was the treatment of oil-rig divers hit by the bends. His last job, highly paid, had been on an offshore oil facility run by Total near Abu Dhabi; he had returned from a long stint there only the previous December.

French oil companies abroad often provided cover for 'honourable correspondents'. Maniguet's qualifications and skills would have made him an eminently suitable candidate for that role. Or perhaps he was approached out of the blue, and was attracted by the excitement. He was evidently not a man to turn down the offer of a bit of excitement.

Maniguet's story is that he had made some money in the Gulf and wanted to learn to sail in the Pacific. He went to a travel agency called Odysée. A small family firm located in the most expensive section of Paris, it specialised in adventurous travel and had arranged previous yacht charters in the Pacific. Odysés told him a charter was already being organised from Nouméa, in New Caledonia, with an experienced skipper who had two other reputable crewmen available. Maniguet put his name on the contract and, in two cheques, is said to have paid over 110,000 francs (about £10,000) for the 50-day charter.

Later, when the story of Odysée's connection broke in the French papers, owner Claude Leroy and his wife immediately went on holiday. Before he dropped out of sight Leroy told *Le Monde*: 'It's the first time we had clients wanting to charter a yacht to go to New Zealand, especially in June when it's winter down there.'

The yacht waiting for the adventurous doctor in Nouméa was a strongly built fast cruising sloop called *Ouvéa*. It was owned by Nouméa Yacht Charters, run by Roger Chatelain. Reportedly, among Chatelain's business interests was a contract to dredge the lagoon at Moruroa atoll. The yacht had sailed to the northern part of New Zealand previously and in 1983 was reported stolen from Honiara, in the Solomon Islands, but later recovered.

The skipper whom Odysée had vouched for turned out to be Roland Verge, 35, a chief petty officer who had spent 15 years in the military including 11 years with DGSE. He had just returned from a quick trip to Nouméa to inspect the yacht. His crewmen, Jean-Michel Bartelot and Gerald Andries, were former petty officers and veterans of the Aspretto school.

For the voyage to New Zealand the *Ouvéa* crew adopted false identities with names remarkably similar to their own – Raymond Velche, professional skipper; Jean-Michel Berthelo, commercial agent; Eric Audrenc, photographer. Maniguet would later disclaim any knowledge of subterfuge. He did not himself adopt a false name.

The day after Maniguet finally agreed to the charter, when Christine Cabon was landing in Paris from Tahiti and Auckland, eyebrows were already being raised over a strange affair at a boat chandlery called Barnet Marine in the north of London, England. On May 29 a man claiming to represent a Belgian diving company selected a grey Zodiac inflatable dinghy (made in France) and a secondhand Yamaha outboard motor.

The customer showed little interest in the price, did not ask for a discount and took no trouble to get the forms to claim the tax refund he was entitled to because the goods were going abroad. He simply took a roll of new £50 notes from his pocket and paid over £1,400. A local minicab was called to take him back to his hotel. The porter of the Vanderbilt Hotel in Cromwell Road, Kensington, helped to carry the bulky, 180-pound (82 kg) packages to his room. Next day he checked out and took a taxi to Heathrow. The telephone calls he made from his room were to the Paris headquarters of DGSE.

The name given by the mysterious customer was Eric Andreine. Later, investigating police would be in no doubt that Eric Andreine, Eric Audrenc and Gerald Andries were one and the same.

Why had DGSE gone to such an elaborate lengths to buy a 10-foot (3 m) dinghy of a kind that is not only sold by the thousand in France but is manufactured there?

This was *la piscine* muddying the waters. It was laying a trail that it hoped would lead to British Intelligence. No love was lost between the secret services of the two countries. Although the British had at one stage relied on a French staging post in Senegal, it was widely believed in Britain that France had continued to make the Exocet missile available to Argentina throughout the Falklands fighting. The French had further compounded their froggish felony (as the British saw it) by planting explosives in the grounds of the French Embassy in London, during a visit by President Mitterrand, to 'test' British surveillance and security.

Nouméa is a blown-away French provincial town with the only casino and the only heavy industry in the South Seas islands. Its ambience is coconut Provençale – crowded beaches, chic boutiques selling sports gear and bikinis, white cement hotels and offices, and *pastis* under the sun umbrellas by the lagoon with coconut palms rattling in the tradewind.

For forty years up to 1886 the small island in the harbour was the prison of the Pacific, an islet of misery and despair where 40,000 convicts, many of them socialists deported after the 1870 Commune, were sentenced to terms far longer than the course of a natural life. From New Caledonia during the Second World War about one million Americans launched and re-supplied the forces that first halted the Japanese advance then chased them back through the Solomons and the Philippines. Then came a boom in nickel, chromite and manganese. The native Melanesians, called Kanaks, were enticed out of the bush to lift shovels. Colonials displaced from Algeria flooded in, along with new settlers like Dominique Prieur and her family. There was no urban infrastructure and people of all kinds lived in tents. The blue sky rained orange dust. And (as in Tahiti, from the bomb business) a monsoon of French francs.

When the world decided it had enough stainless steel for the time being, nickel crashed and the bubble burst. The French settlers could at least understand why the money tap had been turned off. But the Kanaks were left bemused, outnumbered and displaced. Only 20 percent of their country was designated for their use, mostly impoverished outlying islands. Now the Kanaks were struggling for independence and French interests were trying to prevent it. The legacy of bitterness and repression in New Caledonia ranks it nearer to the troubled countries of Africa and the Caribbean than to its carefree and peaceful neighbours in the South Seas.

While Mafart and Prieur made final preparations in Paris, no doubt being briefed personally by Cabon who had just returned from Tahiti, the sailors flew out to Nouméa to collect their yacht. They were accompanied by Lt Col Dillais who travelled separately to check they were not followed. He registered with the others at the Nouméa Beach Hotel but used the name Philippe Dubast, described in his passport as an analyst born in Rheims.

For a week the team prepared for the 1,000 mile (1,600 km) trip to New Zealand. Dillais rented a minibus for his team and settled all expenses in cash. Some diving gear was purchased but the main items to be used in the sabotage were either transported out from France or obtained from the large naval base in Nouméa. The *Ouvéa*'s lockers were stocked with provisions. Her water and fuel tanks were topped up.

The bulky rubber dinghy was stowed away, probably with the sails in the forepeak or at the bottom of one of the deep cockpit lockers. The skipper would have wanted to put the outboard motor, heavy air bottles and other diving equipment as near to the centre of the yacht as possible, and as low. They probably fitted under the cabin floor. Well wrapped in polythene, the explosives and other devices for making the bombs could have been chocked firmly into any dry spot.

Floating well down on her marks with supplies and secret equipment on board, on June 7 the 38-foot (11·6 m) yacht cast off her moorings and motored out of the marina. In the lagoon she hoisted sails, turned her bow towards the passage in the reef, and headed out into the Pacific, southward bound.

8

CRUISE OF THE *BARBOUZES*

The operation to sink *Rainbow Warrior* came close to disaster on day one.

On the 1,000-mile voyage south from New Caledonia the yacht *Ouvéa* stopped nearly halfway at Norfolk Island. But the *barbouzes* were such 'good' sailors that they carried no navigation chart of the island. After trouble finding a safe anchorage they gave up the idea of landing and pushed on.

The Pacific north of New Zealand is notorious for the fierce storms that give yachts a pasting. Many a globe-trotting yacht finds it the worst stretch of sailing water they ever encounter, and the *Ouvéa* was no luckier than the rest. Hammered by a heavy northerly blow (which ought, on the contrary, to have given them an exhilarating ride since the wind was astern) they decided it was imperative to put into harbour for a rest. So they said.

The most northerly port in New Zealand, tucked under the thumb of the fist of headlands at North Cape, is called Parengarenga. It is isolated, little populated, and is rarely visited by other yachts for the simple reason that its entrance is notorious for fiendish dangers. Again, the secret agents had no chart of the place. Nothing daunted, they sailed straight in.

From seaward they would have seen the narrow entrance between a steep scrub-covered hillside to the north and a spit of high sand dunes to the south. Dazzling even on a grey day, the bone-white sand is almost pure silica. Inside, they would see long inlets with shallow channels disappearing between mangroves in the folds of the hills. One headland jutting into the harbour had been 'broken in' for farming sheep, its rolling fields of grass making a vivid splash of green in the panorama of dark ti-tree scrub spotted with clumps of flax, opaquely turquoise water and snow-like dunes.

But what they could not have seen stretching clear across the harbour entrance was the bar, a ledge of hard sand, like a high doorstep on which the surf was seething.

From seaward, standing low in the cockpit of a yacht, only the backs of the breaking waves would be visible. But once the helm was put over and the yacht was running in, something about the shape of the waves and the white spray whipping ahead of them like smoke would have signalled danger. By then it would be too late to reverse course because the steep, racing waves would roll the yacht over. Survival would depend on keeping the yacht straight and sailing as fast as possible to stop her from broaching. You would start the engine, give her full throttle, hang on tight – and pray.

One moment the yacht would ride like a surf board on the curling wave. Next it would be lurching in the trough of fizzing foam, another cliff-face comber racing up astern. Several times her keel rammed the sand. The thump probably shook all four sailors to their back teeth. They were lucky to survive.

Having made it over the bar the yacht then had to thread the shallow channels up the harbour to the settlement of Te Hapua. There are no navigation marks and the channels are confusing even when you know the place.

Te Hapua lies at the end of a road of pale-coloured gravel that slashes through the rough scrub country. It ends at a small concrete wharf which is on the point of collapse. Under a macrocarpa tree near the wharf Jewel Susich runs the post office and store, its weatherboards painted brilliant yellow. In Te Hapua about 120 Maoris live in a strange assortment of decrepit shacks, caravans, and old buses, their windows patched up with corrugated iron and plastic. Every home no matter how humble has its TV aerial. Rusty hulks of dumped cars serve as breakwaters to prevent waves from eating into the grassy sward. Others are abandoned in the scrub. A few old fishing dinghies and punts used in oyster farming are pulled up on the shore. Horses push through the crude fences and roam the foreshore, grazing the short grass between clumps of rushes and tall white arum lilies.

The shop was quiet on the afternoon of Saturday, June 22. Most people were probably watching 'footy' on television. Jewel was catching up on the housework when her daughter Hope, aged seven, said some men wanted her in the shop.

Outside she found three men talking in a foreign language. All had dark hair. They looked strong, fit and sun-tanned. Their jeans and slickers were not the kind of outfits you saw in the small local farming towns like Kaitaia. They smiled and said hello. One was especially good-looking and spoke English. He explained that their yacht had been in a storm then asked a lot of questions. Where could they get a hot shower? How far was it to the nearest petrol station? Where could they get a map? The one question they did not ask was how to contact Customs.

Yachts were not completely unknown in this remote and difficult harbour. As many as four or five came in during the summer. But Jewel was a bit flustered by so many pressing questions. There was nobody to help out because her husband was away. First she sent

107

the Frenchmen up to the school where they might be able to get a shower. Then she telephoned Hec Créne (a French name, pronounced *crane*), the ranger of Te Paki Farm Park. He lived at Waitiki landing, half an hour's drive distant. 'There's a bunch of French blokes from a yacht asking questions and wanting a lot of things,' she told him.

Hec had put in a long day rescuing a mini-bus full of tourists that had bogged down in wet sand on the surf-swept Ninety Mile Beach on the other coast. It was already nearly dark. 'I'll come down in the morning,' he promised.

On Sunday morning Hec Créne, 64, a tall, craggy, white-haired man, drove to Te Hapua in his Land-Rover. Besides digging tourists out of the sand and organising facilities for visitors flocking to the lighthouse at Cape Reinga, one of his jobs as ranger was to keep an eye on visiting yachts on behalf of the Customs Department. But he was puzzled. As he drove over the ridge, looking down on Te Hapua with its red-roofed church, he saw the white shape of a yacht anchored off the decrepit wharf. But why would a yacht come to this out-of-the-way place in the middle of winter? In the far distance Hec saw the massive surf piled up on the bar by the easterly swell. How could a yacht come through that and live?

Only last Friday, the day before the yacht's arrival, Hec knew the big tugs hauling barges into the harbour to load silica sand for glass-making had been forced to turn back. Even for the tug masters with all their experience the bar was tricky enough on a calm day. Shallow channels through the sand were always changing. Any vessel that tried to go in on the leading lights would be a mile out of position. The chart had not been corrected since 1965. The tugmen would watch for the breaks and pick their way. If a killer wave piled up astern, putting the tug in danger of broaching, the engine was strong enough to reverse straight through the wave. The tough steel ship would come wet and spluttering but alive. It would be different in a yacht. Nobody with brains would go near the place in this kind of weather, though some had tried it. The French yacht *Drac II* had been wrecked during Christmas 1983 and the hulk was still visible on the beach. The sailing ship *Endeavour II* had grounded at the harbour entrance and was pounded to pieces. A fishing boat had recently been on the rocks. Even the Navy had grounded in the harbour and was towed off by a tug.

Besides, why risk coming into Parengarenga when there were so many safe places – harbours you could get the *Queen Mary* into – just a short sail down the coast? 'There's some dopey buggers come in here all right,' Hec thought as he walked out on the collapsing wharf.

The yacht was anchored fifty yards out in the channel. Hec waved at a couple of men on deck and gestured them in. They hauled up the anchor and started the engine. Hec took their lines as they tied up at the wharf. The yacht was a fast cruising sloop built of glassfibre, 38 feet (11·6 m) long. An orange rubber dinghy, fully inflated, was tied to the cabin top. A French flag flew from her backstay. The name *Ouvéa* was written in large black letters across her transom.

Hec was impressed with the look of the four men in their thirties. They were tidily dressed, courteous, obviously strong and in good physical trim. The sort I'd be keen to have on my fencing gang, he thought.

The English-speaker introduced himself as Xavier Maniguet and immediately asked where they could get maps and charts.

'What the hell made you come in here?' Hec asked.

'We had a storm off North Cape, it was very bad weather.'

'Didn't you see the remains of the French yacht out there?'

'Oh no, we were looking straight ahead.'

Hec took the doctor to Jewel's store and telephoned Customs officer Lew Sabin. The officer explained to Maniguet that Parenga-renga was not an official port of entry and they must clear Customs without delay. The nearest port was at Opua in the Bay of Islands, an easy sail of about 85 miles (136 km) further down the coast. They were not to bring food on shore, or throw food scraps over the side, and they were not to go ashore themselves more than they had to. Maniguet replied that he realised the importance of these rules. 'I am a physician so I understand well,' he said.

Afterwards Hec advised the Frenchmen to anchor out in a sheltered part of the channel and wait. When they saw the tugs come in they would know it was safe to leave. He was on the point of getting into his Land-Rover to drive away when they called him back. 'Come on board and have a can of beer!'

For half an hour Hec chatted with the French yachtsmen. They said they were coming on a diving holiday. They showed Hec through the boat, opening lockers to explain where things were stowed. The neatness of the little galley, with its lift-up lids over the sink and cool-box, intrigued him. He saw the sails bunched up in bags in the fo'c'sle. All was neat, clean and dry, hardly what you would expect of a yacht that had taken a severe beating in a storm. But Hec had no reason to be suspicious. New Zealand wasn't Israel or Northern Ireland. A ranger's business was litter and vandalised lavatories and buses stuck in the sand. Not foreign commandos. Just before noon he bade them all good luck and drove home. A decent bunch, he thought.

But when Hec Créne was ostentatiously shown over the boat it is possible the yacht's illicit cargo of explosives and military scuba gear had already been secretly unloaded. Perhaps during the night, the *Ouvéa* crew had quietly loaded the stuff into a rubber dinghy and paddled up some mangrove creek where they cached it in a place easy to identify and reach later by road. Or was the stuff sealed in plastic and simply dropped over the side, to be recovered from a dinghy with a grappling hook?

The easterly swell died during the night. Next morning, Monday, the *Ouvéa* sailed out of Parengarenga just as the tugs and barges were coming in. She negotiated the bar safely then turned her bow to the south-east, heading down the coast. At this time *Rainbow Warrior* was still at Port Vila in Vanuatu, about to set sail for Auckland.

Even in winter, when the weather is not so different from the English Channel in summer, the north of New Zealand is a paradise for sailing (less so for diving, because the water is clouded by run-off from rivers). If New Zealand were projected through the centre of the world it would lie roughly between Land's End and Madeira. The South Island would make a 500-mile (800 km) chain of snow-covered alps, rising to more than 10,000 feet (3,000 m) straight out of the sea, stretched across the Bay of Biscay. The North Island, with its long Northland peninsula jutting like a finger towards the tropics, would be a rolling, fertile country dotted with lakes and volcanos just off Portugal. Long and narrow, the country is a little larger than the British Isles yet it has only 3·2 million people. A quarter live in Auckland, a sprawling, comely, business-oriented city at the north end of the country. Wellington, the political capital, and the South Island cities of Christchurch and Dunedin, are less than half Auckland's size. The rest of the population is thinly scattered over a lush green country with 63 million sheep, seven million beef and dairy cattle, and vast areas of untouched forest country called 'the bush'.

Unlike Australia, the country has no snakes, no transparent deadly jellyfish, no poisonous octopus and no man-eating sharks. Apart from a small spider living in rotting logs on the beach, and the stingray that can lash your foot if you stand on one in the shallows, there's nothing to give you so much as a nasty nibble. The police don't carry guns. The biggest menace is other drivers. The empty roads are a delight but New Zealanders drive on the theory that there is never anything coming – so go for your life, no worries.

The peninsula jutting northwards more than 260 miles (418 km) from Auckland is only four miles (6·4 km) wide at its narrowest but the two coasts could hardly be more different. On the western side the stormy Tasman Sea pounds long straight beaches of hard sand, much of it so black it scorches the soles of your feet. The three big harbours opening into the Tasman, their splayed fingers stretching nearly to the opposite coast, are shallow, muddy, treacherous and little used. With their weatherboard buildings and wide verandahs shading the pavements, the rural villages still have the air of the pioneer days of the 1930s when there were few roads in Northland and bullock teams dragged massive kauri logs out of the bush for shipment to Auckland by sailing scow. But the eastern coast, where the *Ouvéa* was sailing, is a different world.

Washed by the Pacific and generally calm because the prevailing westerlies blow off the land, the coast is a succession of islands, promontories, rivers, beaches of soft white sand and lovely harbours. The coves, inlets and creeks are just made to hear the splash of a cruising yacht's anchor after it has ghosted in on the tide. You could sail here for a year and swing in a different and lovely anchorage every night. The country is high and rugged. Headlands thrust out into the ocean like bare-knuckled fists. The beaches between them are backed by farmland and bush-covered ranges. The water is clean and clear, interesting for diving and refreshingly warm for swimming. Navigational hazards are few but reliable winds and sparkling seas make delightful sailing.

The harbours, sheltered and beautiful with small waterside communities, lie a comfortable day's sailing apart. Half-way to Auckland, on a river tucked behind a massive headland with a spectacular volcanic spire, is the town of Whangarei, an agriculture and light-industry centre. Auckland itself lies in a sheltered gulf sprinkled with small islands. At the Bay of Islands and at Auckland many of the islands are designated as national parks.

The only blight on the endless procession of little beaches and coves along this spectacular coastline is the profusion of seedy motor camps, shabby beach homes and tourist developments designed as if aesthetics and planning principles were eternally delayed in one of New Zealand's notorious dock strikes. But even in high summer a French visitor would find them remarkably uncrowded; in winter they are deserted. North of Whangarei, thin and twisting gravel roads lead to beaches, coves and creeks with hardly a house to be seen, though there might be a fisherman or two and a bunch of tents during summer weekends and at Christmas. There is no road access to many inlets where a yacht can anchor but you can hike in along bush tracks.

Along this coast it's unusual when you do not see a white sail on the horizon, when a secluded anchorage does not have a yacht or two swinging an anchor, when yachtsmen are not rowing ashore in

111

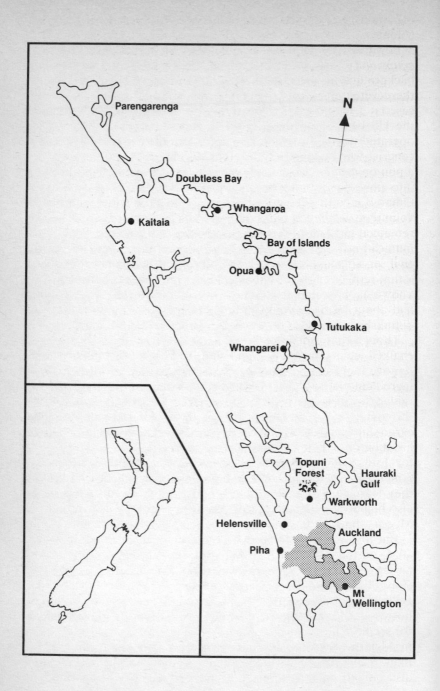

dinghies for a barbecue of cockles in the shade of a gnarled pohutu-kawa tree.

The DGSE would undoubtedly have known of the area's reputation as a 'smugglers' coast'. In 1976 at least one yacht in the celebrated 'Mr Asia' drugs racket landed 450,000 sticks of marijuana worth NZ$2·8 million at Doubtless Bay, an extensive bight that the *Ouvéa*, after leaving Parengarenga in mid-morning, should have passed around late afternoon.

The French yacht ought to have sailed into the Bay of Islands to clear Customs at the port of Opua bright and early on Tuesday. In fact she did not arrive until Wednesday afternoon. The 'lost' day and a half has never been accounted for. If the explosives had not been landed at Parengarenga under the noses of Hec Créne and the Maori community there, where had the yacht put in? She might even have made a rendezvous with other members of the team.

Posing as the newly-wed Turenge couple from Switzerland, Alain Mafart and Dominique Prieur had flown into Auckland on the same day that the yacht scraped into Parengarenga. They had rented a small campervan and were staying at a hotel before starting a tour. Next day another traveller signed into an Auckland hotel as Jean-Louis Dormond and rented the first of a series of cars and campervans. (Later, French newspapers linked 'Dormond' with Lt Col Dillais, chief of the combat frogman school at Aspretto, who, using the name Dubast, had been superintending the yacht's departure from Nouméa.)

Either 'Dormond' or the 'Turenge' couple could have driven to a rendezvous pre-arranged with the aid of information and photographs provided by Christine Cabon. If no campers or fishermen were around to observe what they were doing it would take only a couple of flashes of headlights to signal the yacht that the coast was clear. The explosives and other equipment would be quickly run ashore in the dinghy and stashed in the campervan. The whole job could have been done in five minutes.

In the Bay of Islands the *Ouvéa* crew sailed between the twin towns of Russell and Paihia, which are joined by a little red ferry, and continued up the inlet to Opua. Here there is a commercial wharf, a supermarket and gas station built on the foreshore with special landing places for yachts, and a post office.

Ocean-cruising yachts generally visit New Zealand during the warm summer months to avoid the hurricane season in the tropics. When the rains and wind of winter come most are only too keen to head north, following the sunshine. It was unusual but not exceptional to find a French yacht asking for the Customs in the middle of winter. But the Customs officer was completely satisfied. He saw

113

only a typical cruising yacht with a nice bunch of guys on board. They had diving equipment, an outboard motor, a few cameras . . . everything you would expect. After being cleared late in the afternoon they strolled along the wharf to the friendly store to stock up on fresh food and supplies.

Next day the yacht anchored off the town of Paihia. According to some reports, the Turenge couple received a telephone call from Paihia that day at their Auckland hotel. Then the yacht headed out through the islands to try a dive but found the water too cold and cloudy. Instead they pushed on, rounding Cape Brett then heading down the coast to the small harbour of Tutukaka where they topped up the fuel tanks at the fishermen's wharf. Another day's sailing took them to Whangarei.

On Friday, June 28, the *Ouvéa* motored up the river into the town basin. As usual it was crowded with yachts, many of them from overseas, and it was hard to find space. A small navy pontoon used by Sea Cadets was empty so the yacht was tied up with her bow to a piling and her stern positioned so her crew could jump on to the pontoon. John Mackenzie, living on board his home-built steel yacht *Albatross* moored on the other side of the piling, saw them come in. 'They were pretty fair sailors, very bronzed,' he recalled later. 'And they pissed over the side, even in daylight, pointing at the cars going along the road, no worries.'

Frenchman Paul Farge, 61, who had lived on his trimaran in the harbour for years, noticed the French flag immediately and hailed the crew to come over for a drink. 'I'm afraid I've only got some New Zealand plonk,' he told them.

'Don't worry, we've got a good bottle,' they said, and brought over a Châteauneuf-du-Pape.

Paul said he had sailed from France to Tahiti in 1950–1 with Jacques-Yves le Toumelin in his yacht *Kurun*. Both the skipper and his yacht were well known, not only in France but among ocean-cruising yachtsmen everywhere. But Paul got only blank looks. The *Ouvéa* skipper boasted to Paul that he was a professional sailor and that he helped to run a sailing school in Marseilles. Paul thought it strange that he had never heard of the famous French voyager. He told them they were crazy to come in winter but they just shrugged. They had already found out the diving was bad, they said, but it was the only time of year they could make the trip because Dr Maniguet had business commitments.

Paul was puzzled again when they admitted they had stopped at Norfolk Island on the way down from New Caledonia but couldn't find a good anchorage because they had no chart. He promised to photostat a chart for them so they could call at Norfolk on the way home. But when he heard how the yacht had come so close to being totally lost on Parengarenga bar, as they took her into an unknown harbour again with no chart, Paul found himself wondering what kind of sailors they were. Not professionals, for sure.

Rural towns in New Zealand do not have much reputation for night life, even on a Friday when shops stay open late. But the place would seem lively enough when you had been bouncing around the South Pacific for three or four weeks. The four Frenchmen strolled up James Street to Reva's Pizza Parlour, a small and cosy establishment decorated with paper lampshades. It was owned and run by Reva Meredith, a blonde Californian who had made her break for a fresher, cleaner life in New Zealand 15 years before.

Reva's place is something of a Pacific crossroads. It's famous among globe-trotting yachties for providing the last pizza before Australia. On a Friday night in Reva's you're likely to find the crew of a yacht you last encountered in the Greek Islands or Panama or some atoll anchorage in the Tuamotu archipelago. Reva recognised the four Frenchmen as yachtsmen right away but it was busy and she had no time to chat. They ordered red wine and pizzas and got talking with others at adjacent tables. When they had eaten, Reva put the visitors' book on the table for them to sign.

A large and dog-eared blue lecture book, its lined pages were filled with entries from yachts registered all over the world – *Nanook of the North* of Canada, *Sea Venture* of San Francisco, *Lady Oz* of Adelaide, *Dazzler* of Alaska, *Toucan* of Hong Kong, and scores of others.

With wine and pizza inside them the *Ouvéa* crew must have felt in rip-roaring form. The worst part of the voyage was over. The main part of their mission had been accomplished. It had been a narrow escape but they had avoided being wrecked at Parengarenga. Now they had two weeks in port to look forward to. A couple of girls at the next table were chatting and laughing with them. One, it turned out, was a hairdresser called Carol. Her husband was a police officer in the town. How cocky they must have felt scrawling their entries in the book (see overleaf).

Beneath the enigmatic last remark (meaning: Perhaps there is something else in New Zealand) somebody had drawn a stick figure in a sun hat lying with its chin in its hands and looking at a crudely sketched and mysterious object. It could have been a keyhole, a submarine or a cypher. It might have been two Mexicans fishing on a raft. It could also have represented a large hole in the side of a ship with water pouring in.

For the three tough and well-trained though beardless young *barbouzes* of the DGSE, and the sporty playboy doctor, New Zea-

For a sailing initiation, Tasman Sea was
a good one (. . .) "Para Renba Renba" also
with a 185 cm boat and 100 cm water deep (. . .)
The main interesting lesson is that a 40 horse
power Engine on a sail ship is very very
useful, very convenient, very efficient and
in fact why to get a mast??

> Xavier Maniguet (not the skipper
> of course)

(Of course) Xavier n'est pas un pur yacht man

Voilà France (Carol)

> the skipper
> Raymond

Peut-être y a t'il autre chose en N.Z.

land must have seemed a walkover, like Rambo operating in the garden of an old folks' home. The place was completely open, unsophisticated, trusting. New Zealanders were friendly but feeble, so easy to fool. The covert military hit-men, men of muscle and charisma, probably felt they were being charmed to death by smiling zombies. For a European technocrat, New Zealand has the air of a place living in a permanent weekend. Its people are invariably busy building and painting their boats, repairing their houses, drinking beer, having barbecues, talking sport and yacht-racing. The country's outstanding contribution in the two world wars that had ensured the freedom of modern France was entirely forgotten there. Because of its nuclear-free policy, in fact, New Zealand was seen by the French as a spineless sort of place. What sort of national leader was it who could say to the rest of the world, as this country's burly prime minister had done when explaining that he was opting out of the Third World War – 'What happens if we get hit by a nuclear warhead? I'll tell you what happens. We fry.'

The country used to be called by the Maori people *Aoteoroa*, land of the long white cloud. The commandos could be excused for thinking the cloud was still around and the nice New Zealanders had their heads in it.

For ten days the *Ouvéa* waited in Whangarei. Dr Maniguet flew to Queenstown where he rented a car, visited Fox Glacier and went skiing in the Southern Alps. On his way through Auckland he tried unsuccessfully to obtain permission as a qualified pilot to land a small plane on the glacier. Obviously he was a ladies' man; one investigator later reckoned Maniguet had slept with eight women in seven days.

The others killed time and made preparations. The chore of guard-duty in the yacht was rotated. Every night one slept on board and the other two shared a hotel room. After one night at the Grand Establishment Hotel they moved to Motel Six, on Bank Street, the main road north, just out of the town centre. The hexagonal room with two single beds, a good-sized kitchen and a bathroom must have suited them because they remained there all through the week of July 2–7. Every morning before eight the one who had slept in the yacht drove up in their rented red Ford Telstar saloon, parked outside unit 1a, and came in for breakfast.

Barry and Joan George, who own the motel, remember them as friendly, respectable and, perhaps because of their military training, remarkably tidy. Their standing order for breakfast was juice, coffee and mountains of toast with jam which Barry carried into the room on a tray and put on the table. Sometimes there were girls in the room. 'But you know how it is,' Barry said later. 'In situations like that you keep your head down and try not to notice things.'

On Sunday, July 7, Dr Maniguet drove up from Auckland in a rental car and took over the motel unit that the *Ouvéa* crew vacated. 'He seemed well off, rather suave,' said Barry.

'Sexy and rich,' his wife added.

The *Ouvéa* was moored between two pilings a boat's length away from the riverbank. Inside her lay the steel ketch *Iron Butterfly* in which Ian and Dereth Hancock were living with their two young sons. 'They were super-fit, very powerful, dressed in that smartly casual French way,' Dereth remembers. 'They always waved and smiled and said hello. I usually make a point of talking with overseas people and I'd like to have tried my French but they were always busy, coming and going with various bags and boxes.'

All week while Maniguet was away the three military men were busy on board. On four afternoons the trio played squash at the new Kensington fitness centre. In the evenings they ate at different restaurants in town and sometimes went to Pips Nightclub. They saw a lot of their new friend Carol from the hair-dressing salon. She had met the Frenchmen by chance, talking to them because she did a lot of travelling herself and enjoyed meeting tourists in her own town.

Roland Verge and another spent NZ$400 on sportswear, including New Balance jogging shoes. 'They had lots of cash, lots of fifty-dollar bills,' reported Kevin Johnson, owner of the sports shop. Once they had a small accident, bumping a Honda Accord, and apologised profusely in French though there was no damage. Mostly, they spent time combing the chandlers in town for a bizarre range of gear.

At one boating shop they bought a small grapnel intended for anchoring a dinghy in rocks and weed. They insisted it would be just right to anchor their rubber dinghy when they went fishing in the harbour. In fact, too light and the wrong shape to grip on a bottom of sand or mud, it could hardly have been less suitable. It would have been ideal, however, to use in 'dredging' for a bulky object lying on the seabed. With the grapnel they bought 40 feet of light rope and a splicing tool.

At Carter Marine the French crew bought charts of the coast and a blue foul-weather jacket, and asked shop assistant Simon Langer what lights a small boat like a Zodiac was required to carry after dark in New Zealand. When he told them they needed only one all-round white light, and that a torch did the job mighty fine, they bought a cheap one.

On five successive days they returned to the same shop and pored over bits of navigation and electronic equipment. Manager John

Blomfield was asked to supply a repair kit for a Zodiac. Then they bought a small sea anchor – a drogue made of sail-fabric – which they said they wanted to use on a lifebuoy.

From another chandler they bought an outboard motor that they left in the back of their rented car, parked next to the Hancocks' car. Overnight the Hancocks' car was stolen. The Frenchmen's vehicle was broken into and the outboard motor, with other equipment, disappeared. One of them went to the Police Station and in a casual way told the constable on duty at the front desk: 'We've lost an outboard motor – if one is handed in it could be ours.'

'Don't you want to make an official report?'

'Oh no, we just wanted to let you know in case it turns up.'

Next day they were back at the chandler with another strange request. Their satellite navigator, a delicate electronic instrument that uses signals from satellites to pinpoint a vessel's position on the ocean to within a few hundred yards, had to be connected to the power supply in the *Ouvéa*. But the wire, they told John Blomfield, had been stolen from their car.

An expert sailor, John was puzzled rather than suspicious. There was no shortage of good gear on their boat so it was odd that the sat-nav should have been in their car. Why would a thief take a wire but leave the instrument itself, worth about £1,000? It was obviously a secondhand one and John wondered if they'd pinched it. He supplied the wire and the sat-nav was apparently fitted satisfactorily. The yacht was now capable of making a spot-on rendezvous anywhere in the open ocean.

The agents also did a lot of driving. Explaining that they needed carrying capacity to transport supplies to the yacht, they exchanged their rented medium-size Ford saloon for a blue Australian-made Holden Commodore station wagon. The Ford was turned in with 838 miles (1349 km) on the clock, enough to cover the whole length of the Northland peninsula nearly four times. In the station wagon they drove another 192 miles (308 km).

Although the agents left a trail a mile wide in Whangarei they covered their tracks perfectly when driving. Most likely they had two important missions to carry out. One was to recover the explosives and sabotage equipment landed earlier from the yacht. The other was to make a thorough reconnaissance of the whole coast north of Whangarei to find and check out a secluded bay or inlet where one or two members of the team could be dropped off to assist in the sabotage operation (see Chapter 9).

A number of facts suggest the theory that the explosives, along with the outboard motor and deflated Zodiac rubber dinghy intended for use in the sabotage mission, were dumped in shallow water on a secluded part of the coast, perhaps in Parengarenga. Using the yacht's own small orange inflatable, with the yellow drogue to steady it, they could have paddled out to the site under cover of darkness. Then, using the grapnel and perhaps diving with flippers and snorkels, it would have been an easy matter to recover the smuggled equipment, carrying it aboard the *Ouvéa* again, in Whangarei, in broad daylight. What could be more ordinary than an outboard motor being taken to a yacht?

If this were the case it seems the outboard's packaging must have leaked while it was submerged, letting water into the engine. Unwilling to pin the success of the entire mission on a cranky and damp motor the team decided to buy a replacement. But this was stolen. By now their bank-roll could have been getting depleted and paying cash for a second outboard motor might have cleaned them out. The agents then decided they had to make do. The wet outboard was stripped down and dried out in the yacht's cabin, then reassembled. Next door in *Iron Butterfly* Dereth Hancock noticed the Frenchmen always used the outboard motor to power them ashore, though the distance was only fifty feet (15 m) and it was just as easy to haul yourself along the mooring lines. Often the motor was left running for hours at a time, once through an entire day. Were the agents checking its reliability and giving it as much use as possible?

On Saturday, July 6, Barry George as usual took breakfast for three on a tray into Unit 1a and found a different atmosphere. Instead of tousled heads still in bed the Frenchmen were up and dressed. They had visitors. Barry doesn't remember exactly how many: at least two and a woman, he thinks. Some were smoking. They were talking intently. He put the tray down and went out, thinking no more about it. Around this time a small pop-top campervan, with the dark and light blue stripes of the Newmans company, was seen on the forecourt. It was not owned by guests in any of the other units. Moreover, it was identical with the motor caravan rented from Newmans by Alain Mafart and Dominique Prieur who were roaming the country as the newly married Turenges from Switzerland.

For the last two nights the Turenges had been staying at the Beachcomber Motel on the outskirts of Paihia, one hour's drive further north. It was one of the few motels with a view of the Bay of Islands and was handy to scores of small beaches and headlands in isolated spots. Mafart had registered, signing 'Turenge, 105 Avenue du General Dizot, Paris.' This was a non-existent address. They stayed in unit 12, a double room, but slept in single beds. Roslyn Tanner, the manager, doesn't remember them having luggage. As the couple prepared to leave that Saturday morning a little dog jumped inside before Mafart could close the door. When staff tried to get the dog out the agent became somewhat flustered and insisted on doing it himself. Perhaps there was more than a honeymoon couple's nighties and pyjamas among the luggage on the floor of the van. One police theory that later emerged was that in unit 12 the couple might have been assembling the bombs.

On Saturday the 'Turenges' were driving on a road to the coast from the country town of Warkworth when a chip of road stone thrown up by a truck smashed the windscreen. It was only an hour's drive to Auckland, perhaps longer with the shattered windscreen punched out and wind whistling round their ears. At Newmans' headquarters in Mount Wellington, close to Auckland Airport, they changed the vehicle and set off again. Yes thanks, they told the friendly reception staff in excellent English, they were having a lovely holiday.

As *Rainbow Warrior* sailed in to a hero's welcome at Auckland, on the afternoon of Sunday, July 7, all four of the *Ouvéa* crew were at the Golden Palace Sauna and Massage Parlour opposite the carpark of Whangarei's busiest pub. 'They were regular blokes, super-friendly to women, who used the facilities of the place,' reported manager Graham MacDonald. It was their last day of rest and play for some time.

Early Monday afternoon two forestry workers were trimming felled pines in the State forest at Topuni, on State Highway 1 a few miles north of Wellsford. Nearby was a level roadside area, where the County Council stockpiled heaps of road metal, often used by drivers as a lay-by. It was well off the road, a good spot to let the kids – or dogs – out for a run. Just across the road was a pretty little stream. When a Newmans pop-top camper stopped for a few minutes then drove away the workers took little notice. But a few minutes later a blue Commodore station wagon pulled in and stopped. Then it sped away and returned again. The two men – one resembling Roland Verge – peered anxiously at their watches and seemed to be looking for something. Foresters often had trouble with people dumping garbage, or sneaking into lonely clearings to grow marijuana. The men became suspicious (their identities are not disclosed because both are members of Plymouth Brethren, a reclusive religious sect that permits no radio, no television, and very little contact with non-believers). They decided to investigate.

In the back of the station wagon, as they strolled over, they saw an outboard motor and large bundles wrapped in blue canvas.

'What's your trouble?'

'We were meeting our friends here. They've got a campervan. Have you seen it?'

'We saw one a few minutes ago but it took off, heading north.'

The station wagon zoomed out into the highway, nearly causing an accident as it turned into the traffic. The forestry men wrote its registration number in the dust on the tailgate of the gang truck. Before clocking off for the night they reported the incident to the office and the number was noted.

That night the *Ouvéa* crew celebrated with a slap-up meal at a modern restaurant called The Forum. Local businessman Murray Broadbelt was dining with his company's senior managers and their boss, who was up from Wellington. The French agents, with a couple of girls, were squashed around a circular table next to them. Murray noticed the party because one had a dictionary and they were talking about the menu. Some dishes had French names. Instead of just telling the waiter in typically laid-back New Zealand style, 'I'll take the chicken' they were ordering *poulet sauté aux fruits* in French and the waiter was looking nonplussed. They were tanned, weather-beaten, hardy-looking types. Murray thought they might be a crowd of businessmen from Tahiti or New Caledonia. It came as a shock to realise how limited his schoolboy French was.

It was their last night in Whangarei and the *barbouzes* were celebrating. Their skipper's 38th birthday was on Wednesday when they would be busy on more important affairs. A woman who was with them paid the bill by cheque but after a few minutes one of the Frenchmen ran back, told the waiter to tear up the cheque, and settled in cash.

It was just before noon next day – Tuesday, July 9 – when the four Frenchmen cleared Customs, let go the mooring lines that secured them to the piles fore and aft, and headed down the muddy river between the widening avenue of mangroves. The west-south-west wind was blowing straight into the bight behind Whangarei Heads at 20 knots, and there was a cold front coming up from the south. The yacht had a rough time beating out to clear the heads. A sail ripped out. Once round the headland the wind would have come abaft the beam, giving them a fast downhill ride.

It was a perfect wind for a northward-bound voyage to Nouméa. If that was where they were intending to go so soon.

Early the same morning, in the far-north town of Kaitaia, Erna Rogers had just opened the doors of her seven-day dairy when a Newmans campervan parked under the pohutukawa tree outside. Looking out through the window of the shop she could see the upper part of the vehicle. The bow of a grey inflated rubber dinghy was tied to its back window. The couple who came in spoke with French accents. They bought some instant coffee and pots of yoghurt, telling her they were 'just travelling around'.

Why were Mafart and Prieur so far north? It seems they had collected the dinghy and outboard from the *Ouvéa* crew the previous day, after the forest rendezvous that went awry. One explanation is that all the equipment required for the operation had been recovered earlier but the explosives were kept hidden until the last possible moment. Erna's Highway Dairy is situated on the outskirts of town, on the road leading north to Parengarenga. When Erna saw the agents that morning their camper was heading south.

While the *Ouvéa* was thrashing out of Whangarei against the gale it appears certain that the Turenges' campervan now had on board all the equipment required for the support of the sabotage mission next day. Their destination that evening was Parakai, near Helensville. Parakai is a small resort built around one of New Zealand's many hot mineral springs. The main pool is a typical outdoor municipal swimming pool with slides, diving boards and twisting tubes to ride down on mats, but the water comes out of the ground at 145 degrees F (63 degrees C). There are also special spa pools where you can soak up the benefit of the minerals in the water. Around the 'thermal resort' is a tree-shaded motor camp, three motels, a few shops and a large pub. Conveniently, Auckland is only 40 miles (64 km) distant.

The couple checked in at the Hinemoa Motel on Springs Road. The twelve modern units stand in a line but all are slightly offset, like angled-parked cars. Miniature town houses built of white cement with tiled roofs, the two-storey units have car-ports and courtyard gardens. The bathrooms have spa pools fed directly from the hot spring. The windows look out on shrubs of Australian red-hot poker and the tall trees of the motor camp.

Twice before, once for two nights, the Turenges had stayed at the Hinemoa. Ironically, the unit they were given this time had been purchased the year before as an investment – reportedly for just under NZ$46,000 – by the prime minister, David Lange, and his wife Naomi.

The stage was now set for the sabotage of *Rainbow Warrior*.

The yacht *Ouvéa*, with the three military frogman-saboteurs and enigmatic doctor on board, had cleared the country and was sailing north, the rugged coast of secluded harbours just off her port beam.

The cargo of explosives, diving equipment, rubber boat and outboard motor, to be used in the operation, had been landed safely and presumably were packed in the lockers of the 'honeymooners'' campervan parked outside the prime minister's motel unit one hour's drive from Auckland.

Jean-Louis Dormond, later claimed by journalists (though not formally by New Zealand Police) to be Lt Col Dillais, had checked

123

into a room on the seventh floor of the Hyatt Kingsgate Hotel. His window looked directly down on the Greenpeace ship berthed at Marsden Wharf. That night the *Rainbow Warrior* crew had invited a party of Auckland supporters, including a Member of Parliament, on board for drinks. The ship's dimly lit maindeck was thronged with people. The darkness around the vessel was split by the flash of Fernando Pereira's camera as he photographed the visitors.

The warriors of the rainbow slept peacefully enough in their bunks. It was likely to have been a less restful night's sleep for the *barbouzes*, warriors of the swimming pool.

9

OPERATION RAINBOW

Auckland (pop. 800,000) is a city of beaches and volcanos. It sprawls over an isthmus between two harbours that reach towards each other like hands with splayed fingers. The city fronts the Waitemata Harbour which opens off a broad island-studded gulf on the Pacific coast. Its back door is the Manukau Harbour that runs in from the Tasman Sea on the west coast. In two places the mangrove-lined tidal creeks of their upper reaches come within a mile or so of meeting. Wherever you are in Auckland you are dazzled by views of one harbour or the other but they are markedly different. The Manukau is shallow and muddy, fringed on the south side by farm land and on the other by dark bush-covered hills; beyond them, black-sand beaches and black-rock cliffs are hammered by the Tasman surf. The Waitemata, clean and deep, is fringed by calm beaches of soft white sand and gnarled pohutukawa trees which, at Christmas, burst into masses of spiky red flowers like fireworks.

On the neck of gently rolling country between the two harbours more than fifty volcanic vents are sprinkled through the city. Dormant but not extinct, most were formed about 60,000 years ago; one is only 700 years old. Some are perfectly round craters now filled with water and forming lakes or harbour coves, created by explosive bursts from beneath the surface. Others are high cones where lava welled up in slow fountains of fire to form what are now green molehill mountains. Grazed by sheep and landscaped with large trees, they are dotted through the suburbs that sprawl along the bays and up into the bush-covered ranges. Nearly every house is a wooden bungalow, each with its trim lawn and flower-filled garden on a quarter-acre section. Some areas of Auckland do have a disproportionate share of social problems: it is the biggest Polynesian city in the world, with a large population of indigenous Maori people and their close cousins from Western Samoa, the Cook Islands, and other South Pacific neighbours. But nowhere in this sea-and-garden city with its fresh ocean breezes and excellent roads is any neighbourhood that in European or American terms might conceivably be distinguished as 'slum'.

A couple of miles outside the entrance to the Waitemata Harbour, perfectly round and symmetrical with a flattish triple cone at its summit, is Rangitoto. Auckland's newest volcano, the island is the centrepiece of the city. Three miles (5 km) across, its scrub-covered flanks sloping languidly to a height of 850 feet (260 m), it forms the backdrop to every beach, every harbour view.

When 'Jean-Louis Dormond' checked into the Hyatt Kingsgate Hotel on Saturday, July 6, he would have walked into his luxurious seventh-floor room (NZ$121 a night), opened the curtains, and looked straight down on the dazzling harbour with Rangitoto in the background. Even a sardonic secret agent must have been struck by two amazing features of this harbour – the brilliant light-turquoise colour of its water and, even for a mid-winter weekend, the great number of yachts and motorboats afloat on it.

Auckland calls itself 'City of Sails'. Every third household owns or uses a boat. The city's anniversary regatta, in January, stages simultaneous races for more than fifty different classes of yacht ranging from expensive ocean-racers to tiny pram-type dinghies helmed by seven-year-old boys and girls. Its creeks and inlets are stuffed with boats swinging at moorings. The beach carparks are cluttered with boat trailers left by 'yachties' who launch their boats from the sands. In gardens and back-yards through the suburbs you find all kinds of boats under construction, from motor launches for local fishing trips to large ketches being built with their own hands by husband-and-wife teams with blue-water dreams in their eyes. For the frogmen-commandos making preparations for a sabotage operation, the city's love of water and sail proved both a blessing and, as it turned out, a curse.

From his seventh-floor window, the commando chief had the city of sails at his feet. The commercial wharves lay directly below him with Marsden Wharf seemingly within spitting range. Looking left he would see the bigger wharves for cruise liners and freighters, and the city centre tower blocks. Beyond lay the small dock for fishing trawlers, the oil berth with storage tanks, the huge and crowded boat marina at Westhaven, and the spindly steel arch of the eight-lane road bridge crossing to the north shore of the harbour. To his right the harbour foreshore was a succession of bays linked by a waterfront drive, each one a different suburb looking out over the harbour and gulf islands.

Immediately opposite the city wharves, barely half a mile (800 m) across the harbour at its narrowest, the Frenchman looked at the naval base in the suburb of Devonport and the North Shore peninsula with its string of beaches and suburbs. On the map this peninsula resembles a miniature Italy. The 'toe' is a flat-topped headland, covered with houses and a single prominent high-rise, called Stanley Point. Its 'heel', called North Head, is a round green hill, originally a volcano, that juts out into the harbour.

It's likely the chief of the swimming pool warriors sat at his window, even sipping a beer, as his target steamed into the harbour that wintry, sunny Sunday afternoon. He would have had one of the best views in Auckland of the Greenpeace ship's arrival. With binoculars he would have seen the pilot launch going out to meet her at the port limits, off Rangitoto Island, and the harbour pilot scrambling aboard by rope ladder. Then the flotilla of yachts and launches converging on *Rainbow Warrior*, only to be left behind as the pilot gave orders for Full Speed.

Staying in the deep water of the buoyed shipping channel, *Rainbow Warrior* cut through the yachts out for a mid-winter sail, made the ninety-degree turn round North Head, then headed into Marsden Wharf. From his window the Frenchman would have been able to look right down on deck for the ship was only about 600 yards (550 m) distant. Perhaps he strolled down the hill from the hotel, crossed Quay Street, and joined the well-wishers thronging the wharf as the doughty, salt-caked little ship touched her dark green hull with its vivid rainbow against the timber pilings.

Through the early part of the week 'Dormond' surely observed the constant stream of visitors to the ship. He could have gone on board himself without much trouble, just smiling and – if challenged – saying he would like to look around. There was no guard on the gangway, no security of any kind. Did bombs ever go off in New Zealand?

On Tuesday night, after the *Ouvéa* had set sail from Whangarei and Alain Mafart and Dominique Prieur were keeping up the pretence of honeymooners at the prime minister's motel unit at the hot springs, Greenpeace held a reception on *Rainbow Warrior* for friends and supporters. It was a low-key affair with a few bottles of New Zealand wine. A crowd of guests took their drinks out on the maindeck. The night was fresh but not cold, and stayed fine. A spot of rain in the night dried up the next morning.

Now it was Wednesday, July 10.

In Papeete, Burt Reynolds was playing at the 'Drive-in Gauguin'. Ruth Manea, Miss Tahiti '85, made a glorious return to her home island of Tahaa where her papa informed the papers: 'Next year she will pass her Baccalauréat, that is what's important.' And on Moruroa the jack-up drilling rig was grinding down through the coral under the lagoon, making a shaft for the next nuclear test.

The 'affaire' which all France was following with rapt attention just then was the case of Christine Villemin, a provincial housewife suspected of drowning her four-year-old son 'Little Gregory', a drama (complete with poison pen letters) of the pent-up frustrations in rural village life. President Mitterrand was in the foothills of the

Alps, paying homage to the 3,500 Resistance fighters killed by the Nazis in summer 1944. Top French restaurants were imposing quotas on American customers to preserve their unique character. And the papers, interestingly enough in light of the storm about to break over the French government's head, ran extensive coverage of the 'Argentine Nuremberg' trial in which junta officers were accused of state-sponsored terrorism and crimes against humanity. French commentators fiercely rejected – as did the Nuremberg prosecutors – defence arguments that the accused were 'only following orders'.

Auckland, too, was having its dramas. There was grim news about cracks in the cross-harbour bridge that formed a vital link between the two halves of the city. The motor show was opening. And Bob Jones, charismatic leader of the defeated New Zealand Party, was alleged in banner headlines to have punched a newspaper reporter on the chin.

At the end of the day taxi-driver Jim Titchener headed home over the cracking bridge, followed the highway that skirts the marshes on the north side of the harbour, and turned his Holden taxi south towards Devonport.

A tall and powerfully built figure with a mane of thinnish grey hair, the fierceness of shaggy brow belied by a quick smile and a twinkling eye, Jim was long-serving mayor of the borough. He was looking forward to getting home for tea so he could get on with his planning committee papers. Near the naval base he turned towards the 'toe' of the peninsula, following the concrete road to the cul-de-sac at the tip of Stanley Point.

On his left, as he reached the end of the road, the houses looked across the main harbour to the city wharves, only seven-tenths of a mile (just over 1 km) distant. But Jim swung into his driveway on the right. The windows of his modest, L-shaped bungalow looked over the muddy shallows of Ngataringa Bay, tucked behind the peninsula.

Next to Jim's house is a quarter-acre patch of grass called Blair Park. It slopes down from the end of the road to a copse of trees. A narrow concrete path leads down one side of the park, makes a couple of zig-zags through the trees, and comes out on a patch of grass where dinghies are racked in wooden lockers. A long wooden ramp or slipway, decked with boards and horizontal slats to give feet a grip, slopes steeply down into the water. The slipway is overlooked by no houses and is visible only from the Bayswater area more than half a mile (900 m) distant across the mudflats. It is, as Jim says, one of the most secret places in Auckland. And it was here that the operation to sink *Rainbow Warrior* was launched.

Jim and his wife Barbara were having 'tea' – in New Zealand it's

128

Her campaigning days over, the Greenpeace flagship *Rainbow Warrior* lies in the harbour mud at Marsden Wharf in Auckland, New Zealand, where she was sunk by two bomb explosions at 11.38pm on Wednesday, July 10, 1985. One man was killed but twelve other crew members and visitors scrambled to safety. *(Picture: Rob Tucker)*

Detectives inspect the hole made in the hull of *Rainbow Warrior* by the first explosion. **Upper:** The bomb could have been attached with cord to the bilge keel that protrudes from the side of the hull at the same level as the policeman's feet. *(Picture: Gil Hanly)* **Lower:** In the engineroom, shrapnel sprayed through the deckhead and penetrated the upper cabins, the passageway and the funnel casing; water flooded in at the rate of six tons per second. *(Picture: Terry Salmon, RNZN)*

How the bomb equipment was smuggled into New Zealand. **Upper:** Off the end of this wharf in the isolated harbour of Parengarenga the French yacht *Ouvéa* dropped anchor after a hazardous crossing of the bar at the harbour entrance; later, military diving gear and explosives were secretly landed. **Lower:** The roadside pull-off where forestry workers believe they saw the yacht's crew rendezvous with the 'Turenge' couple to hand over the sabotage equipment.

Agents of the French secret service involved in Operation Rainbow:

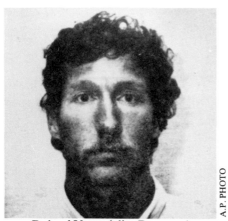

Roland Verge (alias Raymond Velche), skipper of *Ouvéa*, escaped

A.P. PHOTO

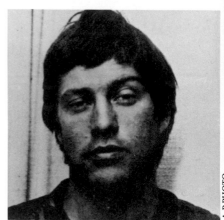

Gerald Andries (alias Eric Audrenc), combat swimmer, escaped

A.P. PHOTO

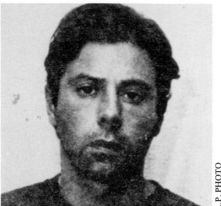

Jean-Michel Bartelot (alias J-M Berthelo), combat swimmer, escaped

A.P. PHOTO

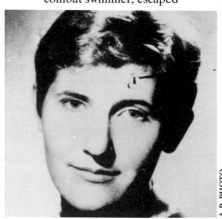

Christine Cabon, infiltrated Greenpeace offices, escaped

A.P. PHOTO

Major Alain Mafart (alias Alain Turenge), sentenced to 10 years

AUCKLAND STAR

Dominique Prieur (alias Sophie Turenge), sentenced to 10 years

AUCKLAND STAR

Dead: Fernando Pereira, 33, Greenpeace photographer, drowned when the ship was sunk by bombs. *(Picture: John Miller)*

On a white-water rafting trip after the bombing, the man known to NZ Police as Jean-Louis Dormond **(above right)**, alleged by the French press to be Lt Col Louis-Pierre Dillais, chief of the underwater combat school. From a room like this **(below)** on the seventh floor of the Hyatt Kingsgate Hotel, overlooking Auckland Harbour and Marsden Wharf, 'Dormond' is thought to have orchestrated the secret operation.

STANLEY POINT

DIVER ESCAPE

From his north-facing hotel window, the officer thought to have
co-ordinated the operation looked straight down at *Rainbow Warrior*
berthed at Marsden Wharf. Immediately opposite, on the far side of the
harbour, is Stanley Point where the saboteurs were observed carrying their
laden Zodiac down a steep path to a dinghy slipway. In darkness the
inflatable would then have motored across the harbour and drifted with its
motor cut beneath Marsden Wharf itself or a nearby wharf.

ZODIAC ESCAPE

AINBOW WARRIOR

After the bombs had been fixed to the hull of the Greenpeace flagship, timed to explode at 11.38pm, the saboteurs made their escape. It's known that the inflatable with one man turned right and went down the harbour where the outboard motor and an air cylinder were ditched. As a second air bottle was found in the upper reaches of the harbour, it's likely the diver (perhaps two) swam to the left, drifting with the flood tide to a landing point among the yachts or commercial craft.

Upper: Operation Rainbow was launched from here. Jim Titchener, mayor of Devonport, showing where his wife Barbara saw the saboteurs drop their Zodiac inflatable on the path (left). They launched it from a wooden slipway (right), one of the most 'secret' places on the Auckland harbour waterfront. **Lower:** It ended here. From Marsden Wharf (arrowed, right), one saboteur motored in the Zodiac across Mechanics Bay to the bridge (foreground) where he ditched an air bottle and the outboard motor. Vigilantes near the Outboard Boating Club (arrowed, left) watched him unload equipment into a campervan at the roadside.

the main meal of the day – around seven o'clock. Barbara was talking about her visit to the hair-dresser that day when she looked out through the French windows and saw two people carrying an inflated rubber dinghy between them down the path. They were not walking but trotting, with quick short steps as if the load were heavy.

In the hastening twilight it was hard to pick out the strangers' features. The one carrying the front of the dinghy, just reaching the first bend in the path, was half hidden below the grassy bank. Barbara noticed rather dark hair, possibly curly.

Carrying the stern of the dinghy Barbara saw a tall man with fairish hair, perhaps a little thin on top. He wore a light-coloured wet-suit but his arms were bare. He was a lean, fit-looking type.

What made Barbara look twice was the colour of the inflated rubber dinghy. It was a light colour, probably grey, unusual in this city of boats. 'Look at that, I've never seen one of those,' Barbara remarked to her husband. Then she added, 'It doesn't look like a navy one . . .'

At that moment the rear man reached the turn in the path and lost his grip. 'Oh look,' Barbara exclaimed, 'they've dropped it!'

Sitting with his back to the windows and concentrating on his tea, Jim turned to look over his shoulder. But the dim figures had gone. The couple thought no more about it. They saw nobody else. The incident stuck in Barbara's mind because she couldn't imagine why divers would be going out in the dark. And why were they carrying their dinghy down this steep path instead of simply pushing out from Stanley Bay near the dockyard, where it was only a step from the road to the sandy beach? Though Barbara kept half an ear open she heard nobody coming back up the hill, though it's possible the divers had made an earlier trip down and up again while she was in the kitchen dishing out the tea. One or two people carrying other equipment such as an outboard motor might have passed by without being noticed.

With only four or five driveways off that part of the cul-de-sac, the two men and Dominique Prieur stood little chance of being noticed when they drove there, probably in the campervan, just before seven o'clock. Prieur had injured her back in a parachuting accident a few years before and is unlikely to have done much lifting or any diving. She probably stayed at the wheel as the men quickly unhitched the Zodiac inflatable and loaded the outboard, air bottles and sabotage charges inside it. The wheels on which the dinghy was trailed, manufactured as an accessory by Zodiac, would be unclipped and tossed in the camper. The dinghy was no doubt loaded with all the gear inside it. Taking short, shuffling steps the men set off down the path, past the Titcheners' windows, while Prieur drove away.

The saboteurs had chosen their launching point well. Once down the path they were completely out of sight. The chances of meeting anybody on the slipway at this hour, a week-day evening in winter when all good New Zealanders were having tea, were negligible. And even if they had met somebody it's certain they would have had a cover story ready if necessary.

On the wooden ramp they arranged the gear carefully in the dinghy and clamped the four-horsepower motor to the transom. You can imagine the divers swirling their masks in the water, snapping the rubber straps over their heads but wearing the masks high on their foreheads, stowing the black swimming flippers close to hand, checking that the flashlight was accessible in case they saw another boat . . .

The Zodiac slopped into the water. One man would keep a hold on the edge of the ramp while the other yanked the starter rope. The small Yamaha turned over quietly. With a gentle push the loaded dinghy cleared the ramp and motored into the darkness.

Beneath the houses on Stanley Point the vertical cliff drops about 40 feet (12 m) to a reef of rocks covered by the sea at high tide. The tide would not be high until 1.04 am. It was now nearly dead low so the reef was clearly visible in the glow of city lights reflected from the cloudy night sky. Well out of range of any lights from the houses along the clifftop, the small inflatable with its wet-suited figures riding low on the dark water gave the reef a wide berth. No doubt speed was kept down to reduce any chance of detection from the whiteness of the wake. There was lots of time. As the dinghy rounded the point and headed for the beacons marking the wharves on the other side of the harbour, the saboteurs had only 1,200 yards (1,100 m) to cover and they were alongside *Rainbow Warrior*.

Although the starting place of Operation Rainbow is known, and the precise spot where it ended would also be discovered, the identity of the saboteurs remains a mystery even now. Also baffling is the type of bomb they planted, the timing devices used and even the number of men involved in the sabotage operation.

Afterwards, many theories would be aired. Some would suggest as many as twenty undercover agents were involved. Others pointed to the *Ouvéa*. It would be standard military practice, surely, to have two divers planting the bombs with one man in the dinghy. If this were the case, who was the third man? It would have been only too easy for the yacht to have sneaked into an isolated bay during her first night at sea to off-load one or two of her crew. The drop could have been accomplished in seconds. 'Dormond' or the 'Turenges' could have been waiting at the pre-arranged rendezvous in the rental car. A flash of the headlights confirms that all is well as the yacht

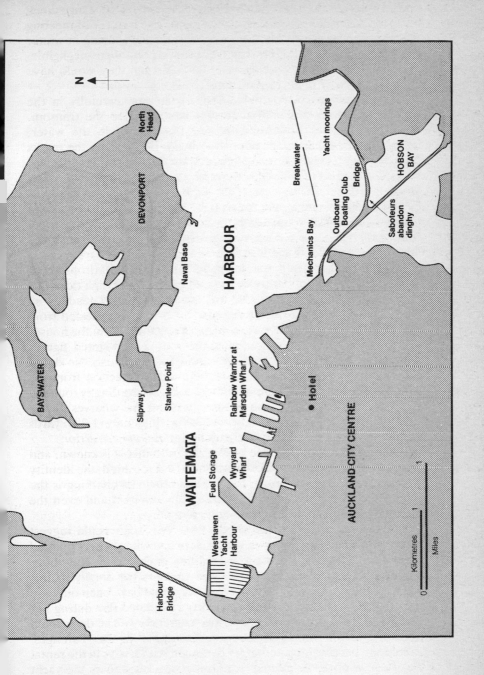

N

North Head

DEVONPORT

Naval Base

Stanley Point

Slipway

BAYSWATER

HARBOUR

Breakwater

Yacht moorings

Mechanics Bay

Outboard Boating Club

Bridge

HOBSON BAY

Saboteurs abandon dinghy

WAITEMATA

Fuel Storage

Wynyard Wharf

Rainbow Warrior at Marsden Wharf

● Hotel

AUCKLAND CITY CENTRE

Westhaven Yacht Harbour

Harbour Bridge

Kilometres
0   1
Miles
0   1

131

sails in. One or two men swim ashore, or paddle in by dinghy. Then the yacht disappears into the darkness, either 'hiding' at sea a few miles off the coast or sailing on to a different and more northerly rendezvous where the men would be transferred to the yacht again the following night.

But for reasons that emerged much later it seems the two men in the dinghy could well have been Lt Col Dillais, commander of the combat-frogman school, and his former deputy, Major Alain Mafart. Dillais was known to have been in charge of the Greenpeace 'surveillance' mission, as described later by Admiral Lacoste, and had been in Nouméa to supervise the yacht's departure. Police had strong reasons to suspect that he had entered New Zealand under the name Dormond; the French press later reported a strong resemblance between Dillais and a photograph of the 'Dormond' sought by police. Mafart later admitted he was one of the support team but could easily have had an active role. Both officers would certainly have had the competence to undertake this relatively simple operation: more men would not have been essential to the mission. Though Dillais was evidently commanding, he would not have been the kind of man to hang back from the centre of any action. He was a fit, active soldier who would later spend part of his time in New Zealand on a white-water rafting trip in the South Island.

Everything was on the commandos' side. The sky was mostly overcast with a bit of a lop on the water for perfect concealment. The moon wouldn't rise until four minutes after midnight then would be hidden by cloud. The tides were near neaps, when the movement of water was least, so currents were minimal. Even if they were spotted little attention would be paid in this city of sails to a couple of men motoring up the harbour in a rubber dinghy.

As it turned out they were seen at different points by several witnesses whose names police later kept a well-guarded secret. Like Barbara Titchener, however, none thought them suspicious enough to warrant raising the alarm. If Central Operations had been called with a report that 'a rubber dinghy was moving in the harbour' would the police really have responded with sirens and flashing lights? It is unlikely they would have shown much interest.

As the inflatable cruised towards the city the saboteurs saw coloured lights winking on the foreshore, each one indicating the seaward end of a different wharf. Marsden Wharf itself, shorter than the other piers, had no navigation beacon. Captain Cook Wharf, on its right as the commandos saw it, was marked by two red lights and a yellow, all mounted vertically and flashing in unison. Bledisloe Container Terminal to the left of Marsden Wharf, brightly floodlit, was a useful point of reference.

But the stubby length of Marsden Wharf confronted the saboteurs with a problem. It meant the approach to the wharf from seaward was illuminated by pools of light from the wharves on either side. It was still early in the evening and *Rainbow Warrior* had a lot of visitors on board. People were often to be seen standing at the end of the wharf looking out. There was usually a fisherman or two about. If the frogmen were simply to cruise in out of the darkness, crossing the pools of light then disappearing into the vaults between the open pilings of Marsden Wharf, near their target, they ran a grave and probably unacceptable risk of arousing suspicion.

The commandos therefore had two options. One was to head boldly and confidently into the pool of dim illumination cast by the wharf lights as if making for one of the yachts or launches tied up further along. They would have a minute or so to scan the wharf, checking for observers. If it was clear, they could then swiftly alter course and disappear into the shadows beneath the wharf. Once among the heavy wooden pilings and cross-braces supporting the wharf any small boat would be completely hidden and undetectable.

Another option was to hide the inflatable under a less frequented wharf nearby and swim the rest of the distance underwater, following a wrist compass. If the sabotage team comprised three or more men it is likely the two frogmen slid into the water while the inflatable was well out of range of the wharf lights. Trained and hardened combat swimmers would have had no difficulty swimming the last couple of hundred yards or so to Marsden Wharf. Any tools and explosives they had to carry would have been made neutrally buoyant once they were under the surface so there was bulk to transport but no weight.

Though hardly textbook practice it is equally likely the mission was carried out by only one frogman with the dinghy man, trained in the business, able to provide support if necessary.

In either case the inflatable might have slid into a concealed position at an adjacent wharf, standing by with spare equipment in case support – or rescue – were needed. The motor must have been shut down because the eerie and cavern-like space beneath the wharf would have acted like an echo chamber. Captain Cook Wharf, jutting further out into the harbour and more deserted because the guard on the gate discouraged casual strollers, was little more than 600 feet (185 m) from the Greenpeace ship's berth. A frogman could have swum back and forth several times, fetching the bombs and other equipment from the dinghy.

After eight days of rain the water was thick with suspended silt washed out of the hills. The Royal New Zealand Navy divers who were on the scene a few hours later reported that a powerful torch turned towards the face from arm's length was reduced to the faintest glimmer. In daylight, a diver could not see his hand more than a couple of inches from his face-mask. The sabotage swimmers were working completely blind.

If the inflatable were concealed among the slimy and mussel-encrusted pilings supporting Marsden Wharf the man sitting in it all alone – would it have been Dillais? – must have heard above the swash of the waves the cheery welcomes of the Greenpeace crowd going on board *Rainbow Warrior* for the meeting of skippers in the peace flotilla sailing to Mororua. He might have permitted himself a sardonic smile when he caught the strains of 'Happy Birthday' floating out of the four messroom portholes opening on the ship's starboard side, towards the wharf. Though the pilings would be in total darkness the dim illumination over the ship would have revealed to a commando's sharp gaze the band of colours where the rainbow sprang from the waterline and arched towards the ship's stem. He would see the white blob of the dove of peace and be able to read the name Greenpeace written in man-high letters along her bulwarks. Perhaps these features gave him a grim satisfaction as he waited while the frogman – was it Mafart? – did his work.

Feeling his way beneath the surface, the frogman would first locate a point of reference on the ship's hull so he knew exactly where he was, probably the screw. Two bombs were to be fixed. The first was to blow a hole in the side of the vessel so she filled with water and sank. But the mission planners knew the ship would be refloated: harbour authorities would not leave a wreck blocking access to a wharf for ever. Once she was raised a hole in her side would be easy to repair. Therefore the second bomb was intended to damage her in such a way that repairs would be uneconomic. They intended that *Rainbow Warrior* would never sail again. For this purpose one bomb was laid on top of the propeller shaft and firmly lashed down. But finding the most effective spot to attach the other charge was more difficult.

To sink the ship quickly the saboteur would aim to blow a hole that instantly flooded the engine room, the ship's largest single compartment. To make the biggest possible hole in the steel hull-plates he needed to position the charge midway between the bulk-heads at either end. But how would he find the ship's tenderest spot when he was on the outside of the hull swimming in the dark and in water so silty that he couldn't see more than two inches?

The saboteurs appear to have hit on an ingenious solution.

Apart from additional accommodation and laboratories for scientists, *Rainbow Warrior* had been a North Sea trawler of a standard type. The mission planners would have had no difficulty finding plans of her layout and construction. Working from the plan, they would measure off the distances to help the diver find the critical spot. The sabotage team would have prepared two thin nylon ropes, knotted at certain points to represent those distances. These ropes the frogman now took from the inflatable, or unclipped from his belt.

Tying one rope to the screw, he swam forward along the bottom of the ship until he came to the first knot in the rope. At this point he fixed a heavy steel construction tool – known from its shape as an 'F' clamp – to the bottom of the keel. He made a turn of the rope on this datum point and continued swimming until he came to the end of the rope. He then let himself drift upwards, running his fingers over the weedy and barnacled bottom-plates of the ship until they touched the bilge keel. Angled outwards and downwards like a longitudinal fin about eight inches (20 cm) broad, the bilge keel runs most of the length of the hull and is intended to dampen the ship's rolling in heavy seas. It is not solid throughout its length but has gaps every few inches. Like an underwater handrail, it might have been made for the job of attaching bombs. When the diver pulled the rope taut and touched the end of it on the bilge keel, he knew he had found the exact spot where the blast of his bomb would cause maximum damage.

Nothing is known about the type of bombs used. The obvious military solution would be limpet mines. Not much larger than a cake tin, a limpet mine uses magnets to glue itself to the steel hull-plates. The diver only has to steer it to the right spot and – *clunk!* – it's on. Careful searches of the sea-bed by naval divers later on, however, and thorough sifting of mud and sand dredged from under the wreck, revealed no trace of magnets.

From the size of the hole blasted in the side of the ship, some engineers later reckoned the charges must have been as big as 50 pounds (23 kg) of explosive. But Royal New Zealand Navy diving and underwater demolition experts had a different theory. Water is a medium that cannot be compressed. The effect of an explosion beneath the surface is therefore greatly magnified by the weight of water around it. The blast from the bomb attached to *Rainbow Warrior*'s hull-plates took the path of least resistance, through the steel to the air space in the engine room beyond. To achieve this with spectacular effect the charge might have been as small as ten pounds (4·5 kg).

With bombs this small, both could have been carried a considerable distance by only one swimmer. He would want them to have nearly neutral buoyancy otherwise, if they were heavy, he would pop up to the surface as soon as he let go of them. It is possible their weight could have been compensated with a flotation device as simple as a small cube of polystyrene foam, or a plumber's float of the kind used for ballcocks in water tanks. The method of attaching the bomb to the smooth side of the ship could have been equally simple.

The ten-pound charge of dynamite or plastic explosive, sealed with its timing device in heavy polythene and attached to the float, could have been tied to the ship's bilge keel with a length of string. A slight positive buoyancy, to ensure the bomb drifted up towards the surface until restrained by the string, would have held it gently nudging the curving steel plates which the blast would penetrate. The saboteur might alternatively have used a strong underwater epoxy that sets in a flash. Or a device as simple as a rubber suction cup. There is also a possibility the bomb was lashed to the concrete cross-member, called a whaling, that runs horizontally between the piles. The whaling was later found shattered by the explosion.

Now the frogman was working only five or six feet (2 m) beneath the surface, jammed in the narrow space between the rough steel plates of the ship's hull at one shoulder and the rough concrete whaling at the other. Above, he would have seen the deck and wharf lights glimmering on the surface. And he would draw confidence from the certainty that nobody was looking for him. The commandos were planting their bombs on a ship that flew the British flag and she was in the harbour of a friendly nation. They were not operating behind the lines in enemy territory. There were no sentries patrolling with jackboots ringing on the deck, as in films. But even if one of *Rainbow Warrior*'s crew or visitors had peered down into the scummy water between ship and wharf the frogman would have remained undetected. He was using special French military diving equipment that cleaned the air as the diver exhaled, and recirculated it so he left no tell-tale bubbles.

While one or more frogmen fitted the explosive charges to the hull, some of the Greenpeace crew were talking with a young French businessman who came on board unannounced to look over the ship and wish them well. Only later, when the ship was lying on the bottom of the harbour, was any suspicion aroused.

Rien Achterberg, who had been working in the Greenpeace office by day as the ship's shore manager, and was sleeping on board at night, was sitting in the galley at about 7.30 pm when he saw the man peering curiously into the porthole. Rien stuck his head out and asked if he wanted to come on board. The visitor, aged about 23, snappily dressed in a khaki safari suit, introduced himself as François Verlan. He claimed he had always been interested in Greenpeace and was on his way that evening to Tahiti. Rien talked

136

with him in his cabin and they exchanged addresses. Rien started to show him around but was sidetracked. Later Rien saw him with a piece of Steve's birthday cake and a glass of wine, looking as if he was settling in for the evening. With important matters being discussed it wasn't the best time for outsiders to be lurking around, no matter how pure their motives, so Rien told him they didn't usually have visitors at night and it would be best to leave. Rien escorted him to the deck but was sidetracked again and the Frenchman wandered up to the ship's bridge. Rien ran after him, shouting, 'No, no, this is the way . . .!' The visitor apologised courteously and left with a wave of thanks, crossing the gangway to the wharf just a few feet from his compatriot then finishing his secret work beneath the surface.

The timing of the operation suggests the bombs were fired by a time-delay device set at three hours. The diver might have first triggered the time-fuse on the engine room bomb. Then he went deeper and swam aft along the bottom of the ship, two minutes later setting the time-fuse on the prop-shaft bomb. At that moment the Greenpeace leaders and peace flotilla skippers were going down the steps into *Rainbow Warrior*'s fish-hold to begin their meeting. While they were discussing the tactics and communications problems of their protest voyage to Mururoa, the time-fuses were already operating just a few feet away, on the outside of the hull-plates.

Later there was speculation that François Verlan had been a DGSE mole spying out *Rainbow Warrior* to ensure minimal casualties and that the devices might have been triggered by remote control from on shore. If this were the case it seems unlikely that the bombs would have been fired with as many as 13 men and women still on board, some of them asleep in the lowest part of the ship.

Out in the harbour the saboteurs now had only escape in mind.

The trail of clues investigators were to discover later suggests the team split up. The intention was to confuse subsequent investigation. The DGSE was muddying the waters.

The swimmer (or swimmers) flippered away from the wharf and headed out into the harbour. The flood tide was running at just over one knot. If he merely trod water, without swimming, the gentle current would have swept him westwards, up the harbour towards the bridge. Bobbing up at intervals he would see in his face-mask the end of Captain Cook Wharf go by, then Queen's Wharf and Prince's Wharf. A drift of only 1,800 feet (550 m) – nothing to a trained combat swimmer with fins and air bottle – would take him past the wharves to a large basin opening on his left. He could have angled inwards, paddling another 1,300 feet (400 m) to the Western Viaduct where fishing trawlers, small freighters and an assortment of small ships were berthed. In the jungle of mooring ropes, fenders, pilings, floating debris and ladders a frogman would find plenty of camouflage. Picking his spot and his moment, he could ditch his flippers and breathing gear, scramble up a ladder in the shadows, and duck into a vehicle awaiting him on the edge of the wharf.

Alternatively, he might have drifted another 1,600 feet (490 m) heading for the three flashing lights – one yellow, two greens – marking the outer extremity of the oil-tanker berth at Wynyard Wharf. Here was another of Auckland harbour's secret places, a reclaimed finger of land, longer and wider than a wharf, for the storage tanks of Shell, BP, Mobil, Europa, Caltex and other oil companies. There are netting fences around the installations, with 'No Smoking' signs, but otherwise the area is open to the public. The reclamation in 1,800 feet (500 m) long and more than 600 feet (180 m) wide. At the seaward end the road finishes at a pavement and a yellow-painted wooden railing much scarred by weekend fishermen using it as a cutting board for slicing bait. Beyond the railing is a slope of big volcanic boulders, spotted white with bird droppings and oyster shells, leading a few steps down to the sea.

No film director could invent a better setting for a rendezvous of secret agents. There are no streetlights. The road and the rocks are black. Even at weekends the place is deserted but for three or four fishermen and perhaps an elderly couple sitting in their car watching the yachts go by. It's the sort of spot where you wouldn't be surprised to find a campervan with the curtains drawn: a couple of tourists getting a free night's sleep in a peaceful place by the sea yet near to the heart of the city.

After leaving the frogmen at Stanley Point, Captain Dominique Prieur might have crossed the harbour bridge and driven here, waiting until the dark figure of a frogman slipped out of the water, shrugged off his empty air tanks which he ditched, then climbed up over the rocks and ducked under the railing to reach the pavement. Had there been a fisherman or courting couple in evidence she would have operated some simple pre-arranged signal such as switching on the sidelights.

If he saw the camper with sidelights switched on the frogman only had to drift on a few more yards and come ashore on the grassy walking track between a wall enclosing the tank farm and the rocks. Just past this point the frogman would have come into Westhaven, the yacht marina crammed with boats of every description. The floating pontoons, pilings and boats would provide more than ample cover for a trained man to get unobtrusively ashore.

But this is mostly conjecture based on the fact that a French military re-breather bottle was later found in the *inner* reaches of the harbour where it had been carried by the tide. It is positively known that the inflatable dinghy, driven by one man, turned right after leaving *Rainbow Warrior* at Marsden Wharf. It passed outside the four wharves of the giant container terminal then headed across the seaplane base at Mechanics Bay.

Here the road called Tamaki Drive, following the foreshore through beach-side suburbs like Okahu Bay, Mission Bay, and Kohimaramara, crosses the wide mouth of a shallow inlet called Hobson Bay. Lined with Pohutukawa trees, the causeway is exactly a mile (1·6 km) long. Halfway along, on its landward side, are the launching ramps and clubhouse of the Outboard Boating Club (OBC). Just before it regains the land the road crosses the Ngapipi Bridge, spanning the channel connecting the tidal flats of Hobson Bay with the sea.

Overlooked by the houses of Remuera, Auckland's richest suburb, the bay inside the bridge is filled with moorings for motor launches. Yachts and high-masted vessels cannot pass under the bridge. For many months the owners of the boats in Hobson Bay had been plagued by pilfering and vandalism. Because of the high import taxes, boating equipment in New Zealand is expensive and valuable. There is a flourishing secondhand market for such things as dinghies, outboard motors, electronics and even smaller items like boat-hooks and ropes. The owners became so fed up with damage and losses that only a few weeks before, in collaboration with the OBC, they had started nightly vigilante patrols. Some watchers kept guard from their boats anchored in the bay. Others sat in their cars on the roadside, or paddled through the moorings in dinghies.

It was around 9.30 pm when the lone saboteur drove his Zodiac under the arches of the Ngapipi Bridge. As the current of the flood tide swept him through he unscrewed the Yamaha outboard motor from the transom and dropped it into the sea. He also ditched an air bottle and possibly other equipment. Then he paddled to the right, following the embankment of black boulders towards the clubhouse.

In the light thrown over the water by the streetlamps the two vigilantes, patrolling near the OBC launching ramps and looking out over the reflection-sprinkled water, noticed the dark shape of the inflatable creeping along the foreshore. (Their names were protected because they were key witnesses. One man was reported to have been so frightened of retaliatory action against his family or himself by the French military that he sold his home and moved to a new address.)

Some fifty or sixty yards from the clubhouse the inflatable reached a small wooden ramp leading up, over the boulders, to a gap in the

139

roadside railings. On the pavement at that point there is a bus stop and a red telephone kiosk. The man was seen to look left and right, searching for something, and the watchers realised he was wearing a wet-suit. Mysteriously, he jogged away along the pavement and returned before long with a small pop-top campervan in the Newmans colours that had been waiting further up the road. The driver parked near the bus stop and opened the camper's side-door.

The vigilantes' curiosity turned to suspicion, then alarm, as they saw the wet-suited figure scramble up the slope from the inflatable to the pavement. He was carrying bulky objects and made several trips. They thought the stuff had been raided from the many yachts swinging at mooring buoys on the seaward side of the road. Like all neighbourhood watch schemes, the vigilantes had been warned by police advisers not to intervene but to call for help. They telephoned Police Central and reported their suspicions. Before the police turned up the suspected raider was seen chaining the inflatable to the broken railings. Then he climbed into the front passenger seat of the Toyota camper. As its engine started and the lights came on the vigilantes realised the raiders would escape. One of them stepped out of the shadows, ran a few steps into the light to get a closer look, and was in time to read the Toyota's registration plate as it drove away.

Eighteen minutes after the telephone call a police patrol car arrived. The officers took note of what had happened but it was too late to take any action. It was always intended that the Zodiac should be found because it laid a false trail, pointing to British involvement.

Two hours after the inflatable was abandoned and the campervan vanished into the darkness, the two time-fused charges exploded and sank *Rainbow Warrior*.

The first bomb, as intended, blasted a hole in the side of the ship big enough to drive a car through. Water poured in at about six tons a second, flooding the engine room instantly. The explosion blew the generator to bits, ripped through wires and conduits and sprayed shrapnel around with such force that it cut like jagged armour-piercing shells through the deckhead and funnel structure.

The second bomb also did its work well. From the damage it caused, its force was later calculated to be the equivalent of about 360 tons. It bent the top blade of the propeller and sheared the six bolts, each two inches (5 cm) in diameter, fixing the propeller to the stern-shaft. The shaft, nine inches (22·8 cm) of solid steel, was bent. The sternpost was fractured top and bottom so the rudder was left hanging. It cracked the stern frame in two places, and blew in the aft-peak ballast tank which was full of water and formed the deck of the accommodation flat where Fernando Pereira was standing.

Every weakness in the old ship was highlighted by the jolt, with seams and rivet holes strained so water poured in. *Rainbow Warrior* was not insured. Both the ship and Fernando Pereira's life were lost.

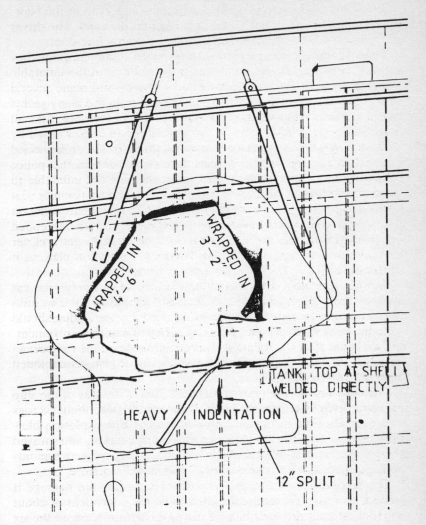

Engineers' diagram of the hole that sank *Rainbow Warrior*

10

THE FRENCH CONNECTION

ATTN GREENPEACE
URGENT URGENT URGENT
IO JULY 1985
FROM LEWES
USA, CANADA, AUSTRALIA, PLS DISTRIBUTE TO REGIONAL OFFICES

RAINBOW WARRIOR WAS SUNK SUPPOSEDLY BY TWO EXPLOSIONS IN
THE AUCKLAND HARBOUR APPROXIMATELY 2¾ HOURS AGO. PLS
DO NOT, REPEAT NOT, BOTHER THE AUCKLAND OFFICE AS
TELEPHONES ARE JAMMED. WILL HAVE MORE INFO IN AN HOUR
OR SO . . .

Her campaigning days over, *Rainbow Warrior* lay on the bottom of
the harbour. The rise and fall of the tide washed silt through
her shattered cabins. Some electronics were salvaged from the
wheelhouse, just above the reach of the water, but most were ruined
by salt water. Divers rescued the crews' belongings so they had
clothes to wear, though everything was soaked. Hordes of spectators
lined the nearby wharves to gaze at the wreck of the peace ship, the
Red Ensign still fluttering amid the baggywrinkle in the shrouds of
her mizzen mast. Peace workers raised NZ$20,000 for Greenpeace
in the first two days. Post Offices provided special collection facilities
throughout the country.

Mostly because of its mysterious circumstances the sinking made
front-page headlines around the world except in France. Only when
the news from New Zealand mentioned sabotage did the Paris papers
give the story three paragraphs on an inside page. There was no
shortage of candidates with a grudge against Greenpeace, a group
that made a profession of interference and provocation.

The attack might have been made by private interests, such as a
powerful industrial corporation fearing embarrassing exposure by
Greenpeace campaigns, or an embittered sealer or whaling captain
put out of work. It might have been a political act: right-wing
extremists trying to end Greenpeace meddling, leftists in some
tortuous plot to subvert. Press reports suggested at different times
that the bombs had been planted by white settlers in New Caledonia
who hoped a commando operation against Greenpeace would intimi-

date anti-French groups in the Pacific; by BOSS, the South African secret service operating with the help of British or American agents; by Greenpeace itself, to attract sympathy and harm France's reputation. Seven international directors of Greenpeace had been planning to sleep on board and decided only at the last minute to get some peace and quiet at the Piha Surf Club: the sabotage might have been an attempt to assassinate the leadership.

Equally, the bombs could have been the work of dangerous cranks. Greenpeace in Auckland received a letter bearing a death's head and the slogan 'Better Dead Than Red'. The message concluded: 'We are Veterans of Vietnam, Africa, professionals, well trained to strike where it hurts . . . and we'll crude you all like the *Rainbow Warrior*.'

Interestingly, there was no statement from a terrorist organisation claiming responsibility, no blackmail message. The prime minister, David Lange, called an urgent meeting of the government's committee on terrorism to evaluate the situation and ensure precautions had been taken against further actions. Even the French embassy, in Wellington, stepped up its security.

Though the publicity gave an immeasurable boost to their cause, Greenpeace workers around the world were chilled to realise they had become a target of terrorism. The organisation was proud of how much it had achieved without resorting to violence. Nonviolence was the essence of its philosophy. It was embarrassing, uncomfortable and rather frightening to be associated with what Prime Minister Lange was labelling 'a sordid act of terrorism'. In London the Greenpeace office door was kept locked and callers had to use the intercom. Mail was checked for letter bombs. In Paris other tenants tried to evict Greenpeace from its offices in case the building was bombed. American Greenpeace director Peter Bahouth flew into Auckland on the morning after the bombing and was met at the arrivals gate looking shell-shocked after a Customs officer had told him brightly: 'I hear your trawler's at the bottom of our harbour . . .'

Other members of *Rainbow Warrior*'s crew who had slept ashore, like Henk and Bunny, were telephoned with the news at 7 am. Numbed, they joined their friends who had been awake all night and helped to cope. Reporters jammed the lines with calls from all over the globe. Visitors crowded the tiny sixth-floor office suite. There were tears for Pereira, and for the ship on which they had lavished so much work and affection. Among the sacks of sympathetic letters that poured into the office during the following hectic days was a postcard from Israel expressing outrage and horror at what had happened. It was signed 'Frédérique'.

At Auckland's Central Police Station, an ugly grey nine-floor fortress with mean windows, it was clear from the outset that the investigation would be a big one and a long one. But there were problems. The CIB (Criminal Investigation Branch) was seriously below strength. Men had been lost to an early retirement scheme. A spate of homicides had spread the remaining manpower thinly; the year would turn out to be the country's worst ever for murders. Within hours of being put in charge of the investigation Detective Superintendent Allan Galbraith, head of Central CIB, demanded manpower. A total of 66 detectives were posted immediately to the *Rainbow Warrior* case from all over the country. With divers, searchers and other experts called in as required, the team involved as many as 130 investigators. Half the Fraud Squad section on the fifth floor was cleared to make space for a Rainbow case HQ.

On the dour side with a pale, narrow face under a mop of dark hair, Allan Galbraith, 45, was a deliberate, careful, and tenacious policeman. Not shy but slow to speak, he gave an impression of unhurried deliberation. He started on the beat after emigrating from Glasgow in 1957. Later he specialised in narcotics, served in Bangkok, and worked with the London bomb squad for several weeks before compiling the NZ police instructions on how to deal with explosive devices. Now his priority was basic procedure. Establish the facts. Correlate reports of survivors and eye-witnesses. Protect the wreck from activities that could disturb any evidence. Watch airports and investigate passenger lists for names suggesting links with known terrorist organisations . . .

Police questioning of survivors had begun in the early hours of the morning in the small waterfront police station. Sipping tea with a blanket over her shoulders, Margaret Mills was upset by the abrasive tone. She overheard a policewoman tell a colleague with doubting sarcasm: 'Mills *says* she was asleep at the time . . .' But the police attitude changed dramatically when the navy divers confirmed beyond doubt that the ship had been victim of an attack. The case was murder and sabotage.

It was late in the day before the police team, following up other incidents reported during the night of the bomb, visited the Outboard Boating Club and heard that a man in a wet-suit had sneaked ashore and left an inflatable dinghy chained to the railing. Moreover, the vigilantes had noted the plate number of the campervan in which he was driven away. The number was immediately traced to Newmans' rental fleet.

When detectives contacted the Newmans office at Mt Wellington, near Auckland's airport, at about 9 pm, two girls were still working late but the computer was shut down and instant answers were not available. Worse, the vehicle's documentation had been sent to Wellington where the renters were scheduled to end their tour of the North Island in a week's time. The girls searched through records of all the foreign passports to have crossed the counter in the past weeks and identified the hirers as a couple called Turenge, from Switzerland. 'Will you put a hold on them when they come in?' the police officer asked. 'It's very important.'

The girls telexed the request to Wellington office and also telephoned the 'meet and greet' staff coming on duty in the Auckland office in the morning.

As counter clerk Becky Hayter arrived for work, knowing nothing about the police request, she found a couple waiting outside to return a hired camper. They explained their plans had changed. Instead of going to Wellington they wanted to return the vehicle at once. As the NZ$42-a-day charge had been paid in advance, they were entitled to a refund of the seven unused days. Becky explained that a cheque for as much as NZ$294 required two signatures. It was still only 8.30 and none of the managers had arrived at work yet. The Turenges told her they would wait.

Meanwhile, two other girls were talking nearby (fearing reprisals, none wanted to be named). One said, 'Look, there's the Turenges who came in with a smashed windscreen last weekend.'

The other, who had heard about the police message, was startled. 'The Turenges?' she exclaimed.

One girl phoned the police from another office while her colleagues offered the couple coffee and made conversation. The man said their holiday had gone well. The woman turned down her mouth. No, it hadn't been much fun.

Operations manager John Hammond, late because he had been collecting customers from a motel, arrived just before nine o'clock. The girls behind the counter were apprehensive and 'in a bit of a twist'. When the situation was explained he made a pretence of preparing the paperwork for a refund. Confident of their cover though they must have felt they were burning holes in the carpet, the DGSE agents waited patiently at the counter.

After abandoning the Zodiac, Mafart and Prieur had headed south, first to Thames then to Hamilton. Learning from the newspapers that a man had been killed in the sabotage, they telephoned their contact in Paris then altered their plane reservations to get out of the country as soon as possible. But they were also careful civil servants. One thing government employees did not do was abandon a rental car without collecting a refund. Otherwise their expenses claims would not add up.

Instead of a cheque the agents were confronted by a police officer in plain clothes who showed his Warrant then introduced himself in a quiet voice. The agents quickly glanced around the office. Other police officers were strategically positioned. 'Would you mind coming with us?'

The arrest was made so smoothly that other clients at the counter noticed nothing unusual.

While the two campervans they had used were taken in for finger-printing and forensic investigation, the Turenges were questioned in custody. Permitted to make a telephone call they dialled Paris. The number was quickly traced to the headquarters of DGSE. Soon afterwards a police officer let slip a telling phrase while talking to reporters. They were working, he said, on 'the French connection'.

There had been a 'gut' feeling from the beginning that France was involved in the sinking of *Rainbow Warrior*. The ship's mission explained it all: the motive was self-evident. Feelings were running so high that an armed police officer shadowed the French consul in Auckland; his home and office were put under 24-hour precautionary surveillance.

Though the French Embassy in Wellington publicly dissociated the French government from any sabotage attempt – 'In no way was France involved . . . we do not deal with opponents in such ways' – every development in the police investigations fuelled the notion that the sabotage was linked with France.

The arrested 'Swiss' couple, identified as Alain Jacques Turenge, 34, a manager, and Sophie Claire Frederika Turenge, 36, a sociology teacher, were known to be French speakers. In court they pleaded 'not guilty' to five charges, including refusal to produce identification, making false or misleading statements about their married state and entering the country on passports with false or misleading particulars. As always throughout the whole affair Det. Supt Galbraith and his team guarded their tongues, giving little or nothing away.

But it was clear the Turenges were agents of some kind, and obviously French. Even the prime minister, David Lange, alluded to it. At a press conference not long afterwards, Lange said the bombing operation was well-funded, meticulously planned, external in the sense that New Zealand was only the venue, and it clearly had political overtones. But there was no evidence to link any government or intelligence agency with the crime. When asked what countries might be involved in the attack Lange reportedly commented: 'You will be able to surmise from all the publicity and reports so far that there is a very strong French connection.'

Every development reinforced suspicion of French involvement.

In this 'City of Sails' the name Zodiac was well-known as a French trademark. Among those who came forward when police appealed for witnesses was Barbara Titchener, who had seen an unusual grey inflatable being carried down to the water at Stanley Point on the evening of the bomb blasts. The Zodiac was also seen moving across Mechanics Bay towards the Ngapipi road bridge. Next day police divers found a nearly new 4hp Yamaha outboard motor on the seabed near the dinghy sheds, just inside Hobson Bay. The engine had been used for fewer than ten hours. With its petrol-oil ratio of 100-to-one, it was a type of motor more common abroad – and in France, naturally – than in New Zealand.

Besides, detectives had flown to Lyttelton, in the South Island, to interview the master and crew of the French cargo ship *Helene Delmas* which had been berthed in the container port at the time of the explosion; another freighter, the *Bounty III* of Tahiti, had sailed from Auckland on the night before the explosions and was also being sought. Through Interpol, police had tracked down the young Frenchman seen on board *Rainbow Warrior* a couple of hours before the sinking. He was being interviewed by *gendarmes* in Tahiti and was later questioned again by an Auckland detective but released.

At the same time, Det. Supt Galbraith's appeals for information on the movements of the arrested couple's Toyota Hiace pop-top camper produced a flood of sightings. Among them was a call from forestry workers at Topuni. They hadn't seen the news broadcasts themselves because, as Plymouth Brethren, their religion forbade them to watch TV or listen to radio. But their mates had told them all about it. They had seen the Toyota meeting a Holden station wagon in the roadside pull-off north of Wellsford, and had written the station wagon's number in the dust on the back of their gang truck.

Tracking the number to a Whangarei car-hire firm, detectives rapidly established the link between the mysterious Turenges and a French yacht called *Ouvéa*. Inquiries about town quickly convinced police that the crew of young Frenchmen had a lot of questions to answer. On Sunday, July 14, police learned the yacht had arrived at Norfolk Island at 5 pm the previous evening and was lying there at anchor making ready to head for New Caledonia. At dawn on Monday a Royal New Zealand Air Force Andover carrying no less than nine detectives, forensic technicians and police photographers took off from its base at Whenuapai, outside Auckland. Its mission: to dash 660 miles (1065 km) to Norfolk Island and catch the yacht before it sailed into international waters.

Once a British penal colony where descendants of the *Bounty* mutineers settled after Pitcairn Island became overcrowded, Norfolk is Australian territory. It's a small, picturesque holiday island of rugged cliffs, tall dark pine trees and rolling green hills. For visiting yachts the lack of a good harbour providing shelter in all weathers is a drawback. The police team landed in the middle of the morning and found Dr Xavier Maniguet had already left the yacht. He had flown to Sydney on the daily flight the previous day.

Accompanied by local police officers, the New Zealanders boarded and went over every inch of the *Ouvéa*. Grudgingly co-operative – not that they had much choice – the French agents allowed themselves to be grilled and photographed. Bureaucrats to the last, they had kept every receipt to justify the expenses of their mission. The detectives took away an armful of maps, photographs and addresses with which they later reconstructed every minute of the yacht's stay in Whangarei.

But they could find no legal justification there and then formally to request the Australian authorities to prevent the yacht from sailing. To have asked the Australian police to bend the rules and detain the yacht for a few days, Galbraith explained later, would have been unfair – 'If it backfired it might have cost their jobs and caused an international incident.' Though 'relatively amiable' the three remaining crew were impatient to depart for Nouméa and protested at the delay. Disappointed, the police had to let them go.

Dr Xavier Maniguet later told reporters in France it was never his intention to sail back in the yacht himself. He had agreed to do so only because the crew insisted. On arriving at Norfolk Island he saw a headline in a local newspaper saying that President Reagan had a tumour. Thinking it must be cancer Maniguet's professional curiosity was aroused and he bought a copy to learn more about it. Only then did he see a news report about the sinking of *Rainbow Warrior*. When he telephoned Paris he discovered an aunt was dying. For this reason he took an immediate flight to Sydney.

In the airport, as he waited to be called for his connecting flight to Singapore, his baggage already checked through, police arrived and prevented him from boarding. That night in his hotel room he saw a TV news report of the hunt for the *Ouvéa*. For the first time, he said, he realised he was himself a prime suspect. In the morning he went to a film where he was picked up by two Australian and two New Zealand detectives who questioned him all night. Then he, too, was allowed to leave.

Tracked down in a Singapore hotel a few days later by Auckland reporter Tim Murphy, of *The New Zealand Herald*, Maniguet denied any knowledge of the bombing. He said he had decided to sail in mid-winter because June and July were the holiday months in France and he had no other choice. Adamantly he insisted he was 'just a tourist' and couldn't imagine any link with the sabotage of the Greenpeace ship. He had left the yacht in Norfolk because he was sick of sailing and had professional commitments in Singapore and France. He admired the Greenpeace stand against killing of whales and seals, and was amused when he heard Greenpeace was planning a direct action at Moruroa. 'I thought it was unusual but I wasn't upset about that,' he told Murphy. 'Everyone has their rights.'

Detailed inquiries by the detectives who saturated Whangarei revealed many strange aspects of the *Ouvéa*'s stay, such as the Frenchmen's purchases of sea anchor, grapnel, and sat-nav fittings. Their movements were back-tracked to the yacht's mysterious arrival at Parengarenga. On holiday in Brisbane, Australia, ranger Hec Créne was quizzed by telephone about what he had seen on the yacht and the behaviour of her crew.

Detectives interviewed hundreds of wharfies, harbour board employees and others working near the waterfront. A laser at Auckland University was adapted to try a revolutionary New Scotland Yard technique of revealing fingerprints.

On the foreshore of Hobson Bay, close to where the Zodiac and outboard motor had been dumped, a resident walking a dog discovered an air bottle washed up on the beach. It had French words and military markings. A second one, identical, was found on the muddy shore of Pollen Island, near Te Atatu, in the inner part of the harbour. This type of air bottle was not available in New Zealand. Detectives in gumboots, assisted by a helicopter, trudged miles of mudflats at low tide in a fruitless search for additional clues.

The Turenge couple, whose applications for bail had been repeatedly refused, were finally given their freedom late in the afternoon of Wednesday, July 17. It was exactly a week since *Rainbow Warrior* had been bombed. So late in the day, the pair were not able to raise the required sureties of NZ$4500. They were returned for the night to Mt Eden Prison. Next day, with heads covered by jackets and jerseys, they were driven to their lawyer's office in the city centre where police waited to re-arrest them on further passport charges. They were bundled back to jail.

Then the forensic experts, soon after returning from Norfolk Island, furnished the proof that clinched the French connection.

Painstaking laboratory analysis of the minute scrapings removed from the inside of the *Ouvéa*'s lockers and bilge compartments revealed traces of explosives. Had this been known earlier the yacht and her crew would certainly have been detained on Australian territory. But the vital evidence came just too late. Dr Maniguet had flown from Singapore to Paris where he dropped from sight. The *Ouvéa* had sailed immediately from Norfolk Island and was heading for New Caledonia, a short voyage of only 460 miles (740 km).

Two days after leaving Norfolk the yacht crew reported their position by radio as 100 miles (160 km) north-west of the island and on course for New Caledonia. A reporter was told by radio that the Frenchmen were in heavy weather and didn't expect to reach Nouméa for at least six more days. Five days later, at 6.20 am on Sunday July 21, they gave their position to Australian journalists radioing from Norfolk as 30 miles (48 km) north-west of the Iles des Pins, off the southern tip of New Caledonia's main island. They should have been only about four hours' sailing from Nouméa.

Det. Supt Galbraith thought he now had a strong case. In a packed courtroom the 'swimming pool' agents Dominique Prieur and Alain Mafart, still clinging to their cover names, were charged with the murder of Greenpeace photographer Fernando Pereira; they were further charged with conspiring to commit arson, and wilfully damaging the *Rainbow Warrior* with explosives. Auckland police then obtained warrants for the arrest of the three *Ouvéa* crew on charges of murder, arson and conspiracy to commit arson involving *Rainbow Warrior*. The authorities in New Caledonia were immediately notified.

But the *Ouvéa* was never seen or heard from again. The yacht disappeared from the face of the ocean and the affair took a dramatic new turn.

An RNZAF Orion maritime reconnaissance aircraft on a routine surveillance flight between Auckland and Fiji made a discreet foray into French air space in an attempt to find the yacht but saw nothing. Her last radio message appears to have been deliberately misleading. The *New Zealand Herald* discovered that the reported position corresponded with Goro Reef where a yacht called *Phoenix* had grounded in heavy weather and was the centre of intense rescue activities. The rescuers would surely have sighted the *Ouvéa* had she been in those waters. French authorities issued an all-points bulletin to police posts and military units in New Caledonia, but the matter was not treated seriously until July 28 when the *Ouvéa*'s charter period came to an end. Then aircraft and a French navy vessel were reported to have started a search but the effort was half-hearted.

At the highest levels of command the French authorities knew exactly where the *Ouvéa* was. She had been scuttled at sea. The DGSE had launched a back-up plan to remove their agents from any possibility of capture. Later, reporters discovered that the French Navy's nuclear submarine *Rubis* had sailed from Nouméa on July 5 and arrived at Tahiti three weeks later. The importance of the yacht's satellite-navigator, and why it had to be fitted in Whangarei, was now apparent. As trained naval frogmen the three agents could have scuttled the yacht and swum down into the submarine while it remained submerged, showing nothing more than a periscope. If Dr Maniguet were indeed a member of the team, perhaps it was the fact that he was the only one not trained in this procedure that had compelled him to leave the yacht in Norfolk Island. But would the French really have resorted to such an elaborate plan when it would have been so easy, among New Caledonia's many small islands, to scuttle the yacht in deep water off a reef then paddle ashore to be picked up by patrol boat, helicopter – or simply a truck?

At the same time yet another of the 'swimming pool warriors' was slipping the net.

Among the papers and other items taken from the *Ouvéa* at Norfolk and brought back to Auckland was evidence of links between the Turenges and the crew. The blue storm jacket which the *Ouvéa* crew had purchased from John Blomfield's chandlery was found in the Turenges' camper with its labels removed. On the back of a street map detectives also found the address of an art studio in Ponsonby, an Auckland suburb. The studio owner, recognising her own handwriting on the map, remembered talking with a French woman archaeologist who said she was working in Auckland for a few weeks. The trail led straight to the offices of Greenpeace where police compiled a comprehensive dossier on the so-called Frédérique Bonlieu. It was thought some of the photographs and maps she had collected while working there, and sent to her 'friends' in Paris, were among those found in the *Ouvéa*. Interpol was sent a description of the woman and asked to help trace her.

But word of the intensive police inquiries was leaked, most likely through inadvertent loose talk. Though *New Zealand Herald* reporter Karen Mangnall and some of her Greenpeace friends had shared their flat with the mole, it was the opposition newspaper *Auckland Star* that broke the story. Police 'pleaded' with the editor not to run it. On July 26 the story was front page news with banner headlines: 'French may have infiltrated Greenpeace'.

At that time Det. Supt Galbraith had identified the mole as a French agent taking part in an archaeological dig in Israel. He had formally asked Israeli Intelligence if the woman was under surveillance and was awaiting a reply. A senior detective stood by to dash to Israel and apprehend her. Within 12 hours of the story being published in Auckland and flashed abroad on news agency wires Cabon had fled.

The dig, sponsored by the University of California, was at Dor,

12 miles (20 km) south of Haifa. Later her colleagues reported she left suddenly after getting a telegram from Paris saying her father was seriously ill. In fact Cabon's father had been dead for some years. It was suggested in press reports that the two messages from the DGSE in Paris and police in Auckland had arrived in Tel Aviv at the same time and the Israeli authorities, knowing of Cabon's previous undercover missions to infiltrate Palestinian terrorist cells, had delivered the French one first. On Saturday, July 27, she took the TWA flight from Tel Aviv to Paris. As a precaution against terrorist reprisals she was later reported to be secretly undergoing plastic surgery to change her appearance.

It was the trail of telephone calls made by the Turenge couple, the *Ouvéa* crew and Dr Maniguet that led detectives to the seventh-floor room of the Hyatt Kingsgate Hotel occupied at the time of the bombing by 'Jean-Louis Dormond'. Unlike the 'Turenges' he stuck to his original cover plan. He checked out of the hotel on the day after the bombing, crossed Cook Strait to the South Island by ferry, and, until things cooled down, took to the tourist trail, skiing and white-water rafting. Inquiries throughout New Zealand tracked his route between Paihia in the north and Queenstown in the south; both places had also been visited by Dr Maniguet. The three rental vehicles he used, including a Toyota campervan, were traced. On July 22, twelve days after the bombing, Dormond turned in his hired campervan early, saying he was having difficulty driving on the left side of the road, and flew out of the country from Christchurch.

Meanwhile tons of mud were being sucked from beneath *Rainbow Warrior*'s hull and washed through special sieves mounted on a barge alongside. Working blind, police and navy divers sorted inch by inch through the foul and rotting debris accumulated in the ship's cabins and compartments, picking it clean of anything that might give a clue to the origin of the explosion. Among more than 800 itemised exhibits the divers also recovered Margaret Mills' spectacles. But there were no magnets suggesting a military limpet mine and no clues to the type of charge. 'We'll never know what kind of charge it was unless somebody tells us,' said Lt Hugh Aitken, staff diving officer.

A set of technical drawings of the ship, wet, stained and oily, were also recovered by the divers. They were sent to the naval dockyard at Devonport where engineers began planning salvage of the stricken ship as soon as the six-week search for evidence was completed.

For the quiet Scotsman heading the hunt for the saboteurs – Allan Galbraith worked 50 hours of overtime in the first two weeks – failure to get his hands on the key agents was a disappointing blow. His team had started promisingly with the vigilantes noting the

Turenges' campervan number but then their lucky streak had withered. Of the seven people then suspected to have had a hand in the operation, not counting the enigmatic Dr Maniguet, only two had been apprehended. In the eloquently understated way typical of New Zealanders, Det. Sgt Trevor Tozer, press officer of Auckland Central, admitted, 'Yes – there's a number of people with whom the Super would like to have a yarn.'

In the 5th-floor *Rainbow Warrior* room – stuffy when the windows were shut, hellishly noisy when they were opened – Galbraith's massive inquiry ran at full spate for weeks. In the middle of it he had to move with his wife and two children to another house in Hillcrest on the North Shore. A bunch of CIB colleagues rallied round and moved all his belongings. On news bulletins he cut a somewhat grim, determinedly guarded figure. But this was no ordinary police investigation. Soon his 66 detectives were scattered through half a dozen countries, travelling almost the equivalent of five times round the world unravelling the mystery newspapers headlined as *L'Affaire Greenpeace*. The wage bill alone, for 65,000 hours of detective work, was thought to exceed NZ$1·5 million.

Besides Norfolk Island and Australia, Galbraith sent a squad of three to Nouméa, to find out what they could about the *Ouvéa* crew and to stand by in case the yacht turned up. Another detective hitch-hiked on a RNZAF flight to Tonga to check out seven Frenchmen – five of whom had no passports – in a yacht called *Shanti*; the skipper of the yacht was reported to be a Frenchman who had earlier been charged in Brisbane (but was later released) with gun-running to New Caledonia. A New Zealand detective had flown to Tahiti to follow up on the gendarmes' quizzing of the *Rainbow Warrior*'s mysterious French visitor, François Verlan, just before she sank; now Galbraith wanted to speak to the man again but he had dropped from sight. Other detectives were investigating the Turenges' background in Switzerland. The Swiss authorities found no trace of them and would later deliver a sharp diplomatic protest note to the French, demanding an explanation for the use of forged Swiss passports.

Now Galbraith ordered his team on to Paris but it was much on his mind that not only did New Zealand have no extradition agreement with France (the complex legal issue was rooted in an agreement made between France and 'Great Britain and her colonies' as long ago as 1868), but no French national was *ever* known to have been surrendered by France to another government.

At the end of July, three weeks after the blast, Galbraith's investigations had reached a frustrating stalemate. It was obvious that old-fashioned police procedure, no matter how thorough, patient,

153

persistent and worthy, could be no match for secret-service intrigue and superpower politics.

Police knew the setting and the timetable of the drama enacted to a tragic climax on the Waitemata Harbour. They had arrested two key members of the cast and identified at least three others but didn't know their real names. The operation had clearly been produced and directed from France: official involvement was suspected but a long way from being proven. There were a lot of gaps in Galbraith's reconstruction of the operation but at least he knew what those gaps were.

Though he hadn't discovered exactly where the *Ouvéa* had landed the explosives and sabotage gear, he knew the crew had control of it until the hand-over meeting which they had nearly missed in Topuni Forest. He knew the job had been professional and he knew who was behind it. Though the principal saboteurs – those who planted the bombs – had covered their tracks, Galbraith had two key members of the team locked up. The man he still knew as Alain Turenge might well have been one of the frogmen but he had no evidence to prove it.

The back-up team, too, would have had a clear run had they not been spotted by vigilantes at the OBC. Even then the Turenges might have escaped had they left the country immediately instead of remaining to pick up a refund of a few dollars to square their expenses claims.

The agents had evidently suffered from bad forward planning. Cabon had failed to brief them properly on what to expect. First they had nearly been wrecked at Parengarenga. Then the French made the serious error of underestimating the curiosity of New Zealanders. Far from being simple-minded and docile like their sheep and cows, as the secret agents obviously believed, the people in rural districts of New Zealand were so intensely interested in foreigners that weeks later they still remembered small incidents and were able to report in detail on strange or odd things a bunch of them had done.

For some time Galbraith and his men worked on the theory that it was members of the *Ouvéa* crew who had planted the bombs. People at Marsden Wharf soon after *Rainbow Warrior* was bombed reported seeing a yacht sailing nearby, but this was the yawl *Django* shifting her berth. Other reports that the *Ouvéa* had been seen in Auckland were also discounted at an early stage.

There was some circumstantial support for the theory that one or two of the *Ouvéa*'s trained military frogmen were put ashore soon after the yacht sailed north from Whangarei and were picked up again after placing the bombs the following night. A print resembling the New Balance jogging shoes that a couple of the Frenchmen had bought in Whangarei was found in the Zodiac. Some of the witnesses who had seen the Zodiac in Mechanics Bay and Hobson Bay reported that the man in it was wearing a red knitted hat and resembled the *Ouvéa* crew member 'Jean-Michel Berthelo'; photographs found on the yacht showed 'Berthelo' wearing a similar red wool hat. Galbraith and his men had also decided that an experienced military diver could have handled the operation single-handed. As two spent oxygen bottles had been recovered it seemed more likely there were two divers.

But police were puzzled by a fundamental contradiction. If 'Dormond' or the 'Turenges' had driven the saboteurs north after they had planted the bombs, taking them to a point north of the Bay of Islands where they could have re-boarded the *Ouvéa* around three or four o'clock in the morning, how did the yacht sail about 480 miles (775 km) in only 62 hours in order to arrive at Norfolk by 5 pm two days later?

The *Ouvéa* was a fast cruising yacht and had a powerful diesel engine. Driven by a strong crew with spinnaker hoisted in a following wind she would have made exhilarating bursts of ten knots or more. Over the whole journey she could easily have averaged the eight knots required to fit the time-frame.

But there was no following wind. On the contrary, the yacht had the weather on her nose. For the first few hours conditions were good for fast sailing, with a 25- to 30-knot breeze on the beam. Then a cold front came across the Tasman and the yacht was headed by winds out of the north-west at 15 to 20 knots with rain and drizzle. Pinching into the wind with sails a-flutter and engine running the yacht might have averaged six knots, though the going would have been hideously uncomfortable. Advised by ocean-racing yachtsmen and navigation experts, detectives concluded it was just possible – but on balance unlikely – that the *Ouvéa* had any role beyond the delivery of the sabotage equipment. The highly visible and merry-making behaviour of the yacht's crew while they were in New Zealand seems to reinforce this conclusion. On the other hand, if 'Turenge' were the saboteur and he knew the yacht would be well out of the country at the time, he might easily have laid a smokescreen by wearing a red hat like 'Berthelo's'.

At the same time, painstaking combing of airline passenger lists had produced the names of several French 'tourists' yet to be eliminated from police inquiries. Though Galbraith later dismissed as 'nonsense' press reports that as many as twenty French mercenaries were in Auckland, other DGSE agents could well have been standing by in deep cover. They could have taken part in the operation. Or – alarmingly – they could be mounting a para-military rescue mission to spring the 'Turenges' from jail.

The security precautions put in hand were on a scale never before seen in New Zealand. Four detainees at a military prison on the outskirts of Auckland were summarily bundled out to other quarters. Like a miniature Colditz the compound was surrounded by coils of barbed wire and floodlit, and guarded day and night to provide secure and unassailable quarters for one prisoner, 'Sophie Turenge'. Her 'husband' was given a private cell in Auckland's top-security prison at Paremoremo on the other side of the city.

Galbraith was hedging his bets, keeping an open mind, and counting the days until his prosecutors had the arrested couple in the witness box and he could start getting some answers out of them. So far, they had told police nothing.

The police team needed a lucky break. It came suddenly and from a completely unexpected quarter, confirming what all had suspected about the French connection.

On the day after the first New Zealand detective arrived in Paris, President Mitterrand dropped a political bombshell of his own. And the spotlight shifted abruptly from Auckland to the other side of the world.

11

MITTERRAND ON THE BURNING DECK

Despite its brave front the government of France had been wriggling desperately for nearly a month, since the day after the bombs sank *Rainbow Warrior*.

When arrested in Auckland on passport charges, the 'Turenge' couple had been permitted a telephone call. They dialled 846.87.90 in Paris, a number secretly assigned to 'Ministry of Defence, DGSE'. The phone itself was in a flat in a tower block with handsome concrete balconies, located a few hundred yards from DGSE headquarters on the Boulevard Mortier. The call alerted *la piscine* to its agents' fate. It was traced by New Zealand detectives. And the call from the South Pacific was also intercepted by French security services and reported to the GIC, an inter-ministerial committee supervising the wire-tapping of long distance calls to and from France.

The DGSE started an immediate damage-control operation. It was moving to 'exfiltrate' the *Ouvéa* crew from the South Pacific. The Mortier flat was vacated and the French PTT, which handles post and telephones, had assigned the phone number, back dated, to a fictitious subscriber. But the DST – the DGSE's rival agency which handled security within France and was controlled by the Interior Ministry – was smelling a rat. Always ready to suspect the DGSE of being clumsily accident prone, it had a direct line to the Auckland investigation through the police liaison officers provided by the Ministry to 'help' Galbraith with inquiries in Nouméa, Papeete, and metropolitan France.

Within a week President Mitterrand had been informed of the agents' plight and was aware of the risk that the fiasco in Auckland could engulf France in an international scandal. On July 17, while the *Ouvéa* was being tossed around in a storm north of Norfolk Island, Interior Minister Pierre Joxe crossed the Rue du Faubourg St Honoré from his ministry to the president's office in the Elysée, carrying a summary of reports from his counter-espionage service, the DST, identifying the Turenges as DGSE agents on mission in New Zealand.

A generation younger than Mitterrand's closest confidants, Pierre Joxe, 50, had been the president's political ally since 1971 when Mitterrand cast France's socialist party in its current form by merging disparate small parties. Joxe was one of four younger socialists who had regular working breakfasts with Mitterrand. As the son of a prominent left-wing Gaullist who had been a cabinet minister and a diplomat, Joxe himself had a more élite background than most of his socialist colleagues, many of whom are former schoolteachers. This background seemed to make him more militant and certainly more effective. He had never relinquished his membership of the CGT, France's communist-controlled labour union, and Mitterrand had finally put him in charge of France's security services. Joxe brought an almost Leninist passion for professionalism to every task. Faced with a bungled intelligence mission, Joxe's reflex was to protect the president. And his first question was bound to be: have we got the option of 'plausible denial'?

President Mitterrand could have summoned his intelligence chiefs for a meeting, but did not. Delaying tactics suited his temperament. He was known in France as 'the Florentine', a euphemism in many people's minds for Machiavelli, mainly because of his habit of letting his defenders and opponents, and even his rival lieutenants, fight out an issue in public while he waited for the opportune moment to make his own move.

For the time being, the only evidence firmly linking France to the sabotage in Auckland was the 'Turenge' couple whose identity was yet to be established by the local detectives. When operating under foreign cover identities most French agents preferred to be Swiss rather than Belgian. Switzerland had recently modified its passport design to make it harder to counterfeit, an indication of how unhappy it made the Swiss authorities to co-operate, even involuntarily, with the undercover activities of other governments. Also, French and Swiss security forces waged a permanent undeclared civil war over the illegal flight of French capital to Switzerland.

In this inauspicious diplomatic climate, on July 25, Mitterrand drove across the Swiss border for an impromptu visit. With him was the Foreign Minister, Roland Dumas. With the Swiss ministers for foreign and economic affairs they made a three-hour boat trip on Lake Neuchatel. Neither the purpose nor the tenor of their discussions were disclosed. If Mitterrand was hoping to persuade the Swiss to corroborate the Turenges' claims to Swiss citizenship he did not succeed.

French defence experts claimed that an operation of such magnitude as the Greenpeace attack could not have been launched without high-level clearance. 'It's indisputable that Charles Hernu must have been informed,' declared Jean Rochet, former director of the internal intelligence agency, DST. For weeks, as the scandal deepened, Hernu maintained his innocence. Even when *Libération* described the operation as 'state terrorism' and called for Hernu's resignation, his only reaction was to cancel a long-scheduled trip to Japan, going instead to see Mitterrand at his country home in the pine-forested Landes, near Bordeaux. As he emerged he poured scorn on reporters' pointed questions about his political health. 'I've never considered resigning,' he said, adding jocularly: 'I don't know how I'd draft the letter.'

It remains an open question how much Charles Hernu, the Minister of Defence, knew at this stage. Probably a great deal, if not everything. Nor is it clear whether Hernu told the president what he knew or deliberately chose to isolate Mitterrand from the situation, perhaps with assurances along the lines of, 'There are loose ends but my shop has it under control'. The full story may never be known because their friendship runs too deep to be divided by politics.

Even before he became the pivotal French character in the Greenpeace affair, Charles Hernu, 62, was an unusual figure in the socialist government.

Starting single-handedly he had turned the socialists around on the nuclear issue, in the late 1970s swinging the party behind the *force de frappe*. The change sharply enhanced the socialists' political credibility. Their anti-nuclear posture, in a country priding itself on its Gaullist heritage of national independence guaranteed by the deterrent, had virtually foreclosed the socialists' chances of being elected. Hernu's instinctive feel for the French consensus continued after he became defence minister in 1981. He consistently topped the polls as the cabinet minister with the broadest national appeal and was the only cabinet minister likely to keep his job if the socialists lost the parliamentary elections coming up in March 1986 and the conservatives formed a coalition government under President Mitterrand.

For Mitterrand, Hernu was especially precious because security policy – and specifically nuclear control – was a key presidential responsibility. Hernu's popularity suggested Mitterrand could co-exist with a new conservative government, helping defuse calls that Mitterrand should resign if the socialists lost control. More subtly, Hernu symbolised the reconciliation of the socialists with the French military.

The bearded, jovial Hernu – mayor of Villeurbranne, a suburb of Lyons – was closer to the affable politician of pre-war days than to the modern technocrat. After a good war in the Resistance and a spell in the army he entered socialist politics, became the youngest member of parliament in 1956, and rallied to Mitterrand's flag. As bluff as Mitterrand is byzantine, Hernu was unfailingly loyal. He was the only outsider always invited to accompany Mitterrand on his annual family pilgrimage to the rock of Solutré, a hilltop in

Burgundy where Mitterrand hid when he was on the run as an escaped PoW. Hernu's fidelity to Mitterrand was perhaps the only thing that transcended his passion for the military.

Son of a gendarme, grandson of a cavalry officer, Hernu adored being accepted by the military. Landing on aircraft carriers, clambering down missile silos, photographed in flight gear, catching a whiff of the cordite on exercises, Hernu was in his element. Above all, he shared the military's protective ferocity towards the nuclear deterrent.

He also shared the animosity of French nuclear commanders towards Greenpeace. An official from another Western nuclear power, who met Hernu frequently on professional and social engagements, was struck by it: 'Hernu was obsessed with Greenpeace. He always seemed to get around to mentioning it. We even commented on this fixation among ourselves. Hernu was always saying they were going to get Greenpeace . . .'

For the United States and Great Britain, more accustomed to dealing with anti-nuclear demonstrations, Greenpeace was business as usual – just another nuisance. The sharply more hostile French attitude is explained by the absence in France (alone among Western nations) of any significant peace movement. Even the communists in France supported the nuclear deterrent for the reason that it helped to keep France out of the NATO military alliance. To French élite opinion, Greenpeace was linked to the peace movement, therefore probably manipulated by Soviets. To the French public at large, Greenpeace was a movement of Anglo-Saxons with its secretariat in London, therefore part of an ancestral campaign by the jealous British to drive the French out of the Pacific. Nor was France fertile territory for ecological protection, least of all for a movement that many people felt – rightly or wrongly – was targeting French interests with unwarranted tenacity and pugnacity.

French officials therefore had few qualms about sinking *Rainbow Warrior*. If the operation dramatised France's determination not to tolerate interference with her national interests in the Pacific, so much the better. Their crime was to be caught. The agents, with their botched attempt to flee the country then the telephone call made after their arrest, had provided the government's political opponents – not to mention New Zealand and world opinion – with a guillotine poised above the presidential neck. The priority now was to ensure nobody pulled the handle, and in case they did, to blunt the blade.

With this aim a quiet luncheon took place on July 30 between the Elysée chief of staff and an intelligence adviser to opposition leader Jacques Chirac, mayor of Paris and leader of the neo-Gaullists. In

Le Train Bleu, an old-fashioned roomy restaurant in the Gare du Lyon, discreet by virtue of being so public, the two men agreed that if France were forced to defend herself publicly against allegations from New Zealand, an ideal investigator acceptable to both sides would be Bernard Tricot, 65, a respected senior civil servant who had handled sensitive inquiries as de Gaulle's chief of staff in his presidential office. Politically opposed to the socialist government, Tricot was therefore acceptably 'above suspicion'.

At this stage a plausible – but unproven – foreign charge that France's socialist government had destroyed a Greenpeace ship to protect the nuclear test programme might even be helpful to Mitterrand in consolidating his over-riding design to burnish his credentials as the guarantor of nuclear independence. It could also improve the outlook for 'co-habitation' between a socialist president, defending France, and a conservative parliament, running the country's business, after the imminent elections. Thus the government, having prepared a fallback position, temporised.

Though he had the ability to rebound with unexpected audacity, Mitterrand's tendency throughout his career to play a waiting game had more than once proved nearly politically fatal. The pattern had prevailed in every crisis of his presidency. In 1984, for example, the president looked on while his party marched towards political suicide in an unpopular crusade to nationalise church-run private schools. Long after what most observers thought was the point of no return, Mitterrand dumped Prime Minister Pierre Mauroy, a traditional socialist, replacing him with technocrat Laurent Fabius, at 37 the youngest prime minister in the country's history, who directed socialist policy back towards the centre. It was a more popular course but precious time and political assets had been wasted while Mitterrand – who refuses to wear a watch – trusted his own sense of timing.

Now his time was running out. After the short reports of *Rainbow Warrior*'s sinking little had been published in French newspapers. On Wednesday evening, August 7, advance copies of two news weeklies to hit the stands next day – *VSD* (the title is an abbreviation of the French words for Friday, Saturday, Sunday) and *L'Evénement* (Events) – reached the presidential office. In the summer 'silly' season when news was scarce, sensational allegations were being made. The first New Zealand police officer had arrived in Paris the previous day and his presence might have been played down. But now the lid was blown off.

Long articles in both Paris magazines accused French intelligence agents of sinking *Rainbow Warrior*. Their stories had the essentials: the French government had mounted a complicated, costly operation to sink the Greenpeace flagship. There was the unmistakable whiff

161

of historic scandal. Suddenly France had a new 'affair'. The attack on the Greenpeace flagship seemed likely to claim fresh unintended victims, this time political casualties in Paris.

The few hours of advance warning had given the government time to act. At 1.10 am next morning Agence France Presse, the state-financed news agency, issued a bulletin: 'The prime minister has ordered an investigation into the sabotage of *Rainbow Warrior*.' Two minutes later came a second flash: 'The president insists on a rigorous inquiry.' A few hours later Fabius named the investigator as Bernard Tricot. 'If any criminal acts under French law are uncovered,' Fabius briefed Tricot in a letter of appointment, 'you will immediately inform the courts.'

The surprise move by the government, its first public reaction to the sinking, was timed to dominate the early morning radio news shows that were the main sources of information, especially during August when the nation was on holiday. The intention was to overshadow the allegations of the two news magazines. That very night Captain Joel-Patrick Prieur abruptly decamped from the spacious official headquarters in the Vieux-Colombier barracks in Paris where he had lived with his wife until her departure and dropped out of sight.

The initial magazine reports contained factual errors and garbled details. Their versions of events underwent many speculative reworkings through subsequent weeks. But the two scoops established the pattern of future revelations. Repeatedly the press published new evidence, usually on the basis of tips. The new allegations sparked new government investigations that broadly confirmed press reports – and provoked new questions, fresh leaks.

Reporters in France functioned with a very Gallic blend of technical expertise, good contacts and highly developed hunches. Writing in *L'Evénement*, Pascal Krop, 36, acknowledged basing his story largely on press reports from New Zealand. His alertness stemmed partly from his professional passion for the subject: he had just co-authored a book on '*la piscine*'. In the rival *VSD*, a more sensational tabloid magazine that relished espionage stories, Jacques-Marie Bourget (his story won a top French award as the scoop of the year) hinted that the saboteurs were frogmen from the Aspretto base. He focused on the fatal weakness in any French government defence: the Turenges held in New Zealand. 'Sophie T. is neither Swiss nor a schoolteacher,' he wrote, 'but a captain in French intelligence.'

Clumsy spies and government incompetence offered juicy targets to French reporters, many of whom cheerfully confess to a 'Watergate complex', a fear that they appear to knuckle under to authority and lack the virility of aggressive US reporters whose investigative scoops climaxed in the overthrow of President Nixon. French reporters had been kept out of Chad earlier in the year when the French army was battling Libyan troops. French reporters, in 1973, had ignored President Pompidou's cancer (and France's political paralysis) for months. French reporters had never got to the bottom of President Giscard d'Estaing's rumoured capers in Africa. But subtle changes were occurring. In fact the French press, while earning scant recognition for its improvement, had for years been steadily growing more professional and more independent. Reporters were waiting for a spectacular chance to prove they were no longer 'pussy cats'.

The leading Paris publications quickly revamped *VSD*'s scoop and got on the story, though motives were somewhat mixed. The weekly news magazine *L'Express*, with veteran investigative reporters who kept the story running, and the leading morning paper *Le Figaro*, both conservative, were openly campaigning against the government. France's most distinguished investigative publication, *Le Canard Enchaîné*, which single-handedly broke the story of Giscard's diamonds, needed to squelch the idea that it investigated only the political right; the *barbouze* tragi-comedy was irresistible to the satirical bent of its writers. *Libération*, a leftist paper tracing its origins to the May 1968 student revolt, kept everybody on their toes with punchy headlines, racy prose and its readiness to despatch educated and streetwise reporters halfway round the world on an editor's intuition. Most important of all *Le Monde*, the 'establishment' paper, desperately needed to restore credibility. The paper was struggling with an old-fashioned image, plunging circulation and a reputation for being soft on the left. It had barely emerged from a bruising internecine power struggle. The Greenpeace affair enabled the new editorial team to redeem the reputation (and some of the readership) of *Le Monde* by repeated news breaks (often shared with *Le Canard Enchaîné*). Above all, *Le Monde* treated the story as a major event from the outset.

Within a week French reporters had ferreted out the other essential details from their intelligence sources. The *barbouze* community in Paris pored over the pictures of the Turenge couple photographed on their way to court in Auckland. Despite 'Sophie's' wig and large round spectacles, and 'Alain's' hand upraised in a gentle attempt to ward off the cameras, they were identified positively as the DGSE agents, Mafart and Prieur. Only France's state-controlled television played down the story. Other media, sceptical of government statements, despatched reporting teams to the South Pacific to track the French agents' movements and squeezed their sources for more and deeper insight. Starting with the identification of the Turenges, it was disclosures in the French press that kept up a remorseless pressure on the government.

Reporters reconstructed the voyage of the *Ouvéa* and the antics of its crew in Whangarei. Leaks continued to implicate intelligence commanders. Three French detectives were despatched to Nouméa to investigate the disappearance of the yacht. Some developments bemused readers. Just before the agents' real identities were published, *Libération* reported that a young woman had paid cash for six-month subscriptions for daily copies to be airmailed to 'Monsieur Turenge' and 'Mme Turenge'. Similar subscriptions had been arranged at three other papers. The total cost was about £1,000. Was this a normal reaction for a Swiss honeymoon couple? When the papers arrived in Auckland police checked them for microdots and other secret messages.

Only a week after the Tricot investigation was launched *Le Monde* claimed the government was pressing for fast delivery so it could stem the tide of disclosures and speculation. Ministers were meanwhile scattering for the August 15 holiday, the only week in the year when there was no meeting of the cabinet. That day *Le Monde* would headline the news that DGSE was behind the sabotage of *Rainbow Warrior*.

But when the first newsbreaks came the government's reflex had been to counter-attack with its own private leaks and a public cover-up. French leaders still hoped they could stonewall New Zealand's investigators who, on the same day, issued international warrants of arrest for the military crewmen of the *Ouvéa*. Perhaps they hoped the unpleasant situation there would be remote enough to escape notice in France during the long summer holiday. On the day of the first news breaks, Mitterrand had written personally to David Lange extending the full co-operation of French judicial and police services to the New Zealand detectives arriving in Paris to press their investigations in light of the new information. 'I wish you to know right now how deeply I, together with the Government of the Republic, disapprove of the criminal deed committed on your territory and for which there is no excuse on any count,' the president wrote. He added: 'I am determined that this case be handled with the utmost strictness and that your country be able to rely on France's total co-operation.'

But the French hardly had to resort to subterfuge to put obstacles in the way of New Zealand detectives. Galbraith's men were not allowed to knock on doors and demand answers, as they could at home. Instead they had to go through the bureaucratic hoops of a cumbersome and antiquated procedure called a Rogatory Commission. First they were required to list all the avenues of inquiry to be conducted, and at a special hearing convince a magistrate of the Judiciary that the questioning was germane to their inquiry. This meant, in effect, setting out the whole of their case (to Galbraith's fury, key elements were leaked to the press within hours). The questioning was then conducted on New Zealand's behalf by an examining magistrate who documented and delivered the answers. To follow up on the questions the detectives then had to begin all over again, making their case for a new Rogatory Commission before a different magistrate.

Mitterrand must have been tempted to repeat de Gaulle's haughty dismissal of the Ben Barka scandal as 'a subaltern affair' or even, in the words of Talleyrand, 'worse than a crime, a mistake'. Perhaps he was inhibited by his old suspicions that he was being trapped by intelligence agents: as a young cabinet minister he had been framed by allegations that he was leaking secrets to the communists. Mitterrand was also hampered by the manifest lack of eagerness on the part of Fabius, a prime minister with no experience of cloak-and-dagger diplomacy, to enter the fray. Fabius is alleged to have told advisers, in a 'hypothetical' discussion on France's options: 'It is something we could never admit.' A confession of guilt, Fabius thought, would further damage his government's credibility with militant socialist party members and shatter its claims to moral superiority over conservative predecessors.

Both Mitterrand and Fabius consistently maintained they had no knowledge of a plot to blow up Rainbow Warrior, either before the explosions or for weeks afterwards. But with Mitterrand playing cat and mouse and Fabius trying to ignore the unsavoury distraction from the country's economic problems, the government could gain time by pitching red herrings to the press.

First came the Nouméa connection. The Ouvéa had come from New Caledonia where right-wing French settlers hated the socialists whom they blamed for deliberately stirring up separatist sentiment among the indigenous Melanesians. With its frontier atmosphere and political agitation, the island teemed with active and retired French mercenaries and intelligence officers. This brand of Frenchman despised ecologist and pacifist alike, and suspected New Zealand of agitating for New Caledonia's independence. With shootings and violence going on, an act of terrorism could easily be credited to frustrated settlers. The destruction of Rainbow Warrior might strain relations between France and New Zealand but it would force the Paris government to stiffen its public defence of France's right to keep her Pacific territories and continue her nuclear tests there. A few hours after the sabotage became an 'affair' with magazine allegations and the subsequent appointment of Tricot, *Le Monde* appeared early in the afternoon with its first major story: 'French military and police sources believe the operation was the work of right-wing fanatics or possibly even extremists in New Caledonia.'

To most of the French press, caught napping over the New Zealand inquiries and suddenly confronted with a huge accumulation of evidence pointing to a French connection, the explanation seemed plausible enough. It was hard to believe France's own secret agents could have been so clumsy. 'All that's missing from this "made in France" picture is a French loaf of baguette bread, a beret and a bottle of Beaujolais,' snorted a DGSE source quoted in *France-Soir*.

A refinement of this version of events blamed the attack on right-wingers who had managed to infiltrate and hijack a routine surveillance operation by French intelligence, itself known to harbour many ideological opponents of socialism. This 'sabotage of the sabotage' version had a persistent half-life, particularly in the pro-government paper *Le Matin*.

The second red herring was more subtle because it pitted French intelligence against the redoubtable and wily MI6 of Great Britain. It emerged full-blown over the weekend of August 10 when a report on *France-Inter*, the most popular government-run radio station, asserted that British intelligence had sunk *Rainbow Warrior* and framed France.

As there were no ready-made fanatics to hand, and MI6 had no obvious motives for sinking Greenpeace, one had to be fabricated. Evoking ancestral animosities, a reporter said Britain's intelligence services bore a grudge because of the success of French-made Exocet missiles against British ships in the Falklands War. It alleged French agents were carrying out a surveillance operation on Greenpeace which was discovered then 'turned' by the British. One reporter said he had been shown copies of the Turenges' orders for a pure surveillance-only mission.

A rash of newspaper stories elucidated other possible British motives. Britain was jealous of France's residual role in the Pacific. Britain wanted to tarnish the reputation of France to reduce her influence in Europe. Evidence was provided. *France-Inter* 'uncovered' a message claiming responsibility for the sabotage. It was a message in English signed 'Veterans of Vietnam' which Auckland police had already dismissed as irrelevant. Other evidence could be deduced. The arrest of the Turenges, for example, was easily explained: British intelligence had spotted the couple passing through London Airport en route for New Zealand and tipped off Auckland. Why French secret agents should travel through London at all, and buy equipment there, unless the DGSE already envisaged the gambit of blaming perfidious Albion, was a question left to other investigative reporters to ask. Furious British newspapers hailed these allegations as typical of the French 'dirty tricks department'. (Only a few weeks later it transpired that *France-Inter* had written a formal apology to the British government for its 'unfounded' allegations).

The DGSE laid some defensive groundwork by claiming its interest in Greenpeace was legitimate because the organisation was 'manipulated' by Soviets. In the international arena, support came from an unexpected quarter when the *Wall Street Journal*, the American financial daily, stated bluntly that the French Government had its priorities straight if it was involved in sinking the Greenpeace ship. Headlined 'Mitterrand's Finest Hour' an editorial in its Asian edition endorsed the sabotage. 'No one is suggesting France was smart to blow up the Greenpeace vessel in another country's harbour or allow someone to get killed,' the paper said. 'But it is an absurdity that Greenpeace should be allowed to arrogate for itself the right to interfere in [nuclear] tests that are part of Western defence against a growing nuclear threat . . .'

At Marsden Wharf in Auckland, six weeks to the day after she was sunk, the patched and sludge-filled hulk of *Rainbow Warrior*, stripped of her masts and all the fittings that divers could remove, was refloated. With her anchor carried forward to ensure she did not slip back into deep water, the old ship was gently lifted out of the mud as air was pumped into thirteen five-ton airbags fixed around her hull. Tugs towed her tenderly into the dock at the Devonport naval base where, high and dry, the full extent of her damage was revealed.

Greenpeace, riding high on a tidal wave of public sympathy and support, pressed on with its delayed protest at Moruroa. Four yachts, including the faithful *Vega* making her fifth protest voyage, backed financially by Auckland peace groups, set sail from New Zealand. 'The French have rammed our boats before and now they are both nervous and angry,' said David McTaggart. 'The yachts in the peace protest are vulnerable and must be protected.'

Fortunately a new mother-ship was right to hand. When *Rainbow Warrior* was sunk an 880-ton ocean-going tug, donated to Greenpeace by the Maryland Pilots' Association (a finder's fee of US$500,000 had to be paid), was in the process of fitting out in Amsterdam for a new campaign in the Antarctic. Greenpeace planned to land two men and supplies on the southern continent. They would remain for the winter and be picked up again a year later. This, the organisation claimed, with tongue more than slightly in cheek, earned it the right to sit at the conference table of world powers controlling the future exploitation and protection of the continent.

After the bombing the 218-foot (66-metre) tug, renamed *Greenpeace* and seen off with a champagne party thrown by well-wishers in London, was despatched to Moruroa. *Paris Match* published a colour spread of the landing barge that the ship carried as deck cargo for later use in Antarctica, claiming it was convincing proof that the ecologists planned to invade the atoll.

The Elysée, for its part, publicised orders from the president instructing French forces to repel any breach of French sovereignty – by force if necessary – around the test site. And Mitterrand himself played the card of patriotism another way. In a television interview he solemnly reaffirmed the independence and nuclear strength of France with a phrase reminiscent of Louis XIV: 'La dissuasion, c'est moi.'

And, like a party watching the waiter open the first bottle of champagne, all France waited for publication of Bernard Tricot's rushed report.

12

UNDERWATERGATE

The surprises in the Tricot Report started with its speedy completion. Delivered on Sunday, August 25, just seventeen days after it was commissioned, the twenty double-spaced typewritten pages plus three sketch maps (a plan of Auckland Harbour conspicuous by its absence) were quickly mimeographed. At Matignon, the prime minister's office, reporters elbowed into the scrum beleaguering the press officer next day to grab a copy before supplies were exhausted.

The report was good news for the government. That afternoon the establishment paper *Le Monde* published it under the headline: 'Report Clears French Intelligence Services of Blame'. Next day the Paris-based *International Herald Tribune* said the investigation had exonerated the government and its main intelligence agency without being able to say who did it. Tricot's findings, it added, seemed to lessen the threat of a major scandal. By rushing the report into print the government showed it shared this judgement.

Bernard Tricot, imbued with the primacy of French national interests, had done exactly the job for which he had been picked. He had protected the state. In fact, he confided later, his original draft had denied French guilt even more emphatically but he had toned down his conclusions after being passed some 'disturbing' clues by New Zealand's ambassador in Paris. All in all, Paris insiders concluded, Tricot had come up with a version of the facts that gave the government enough cards to bluff it out.

Acknowledging the French Government, at a high level, had plotted against Greenpeace, Tricot explained the presence of agents in New Zealand by saying their mission was only to spy on the protest group, not attack its ship. But he confirmed that the Turenges, the mole and the *Ouvéa* crew were all part of the same design. Much of this information had already been uncovered by the press. But some items, including the real identities of the yacht's crew, were new.

And there were numerous surprises, especially in the unexpected amount of detail in Tricot's version.

The report traced the growing French concern about Greenpeace's Moruroa campaigns to the end of 1984 when Admiral Henri Fages, commandant of DIRCEN, the nuclear test centre in the Pacific, had become convinced that DGSE was not taking Greenpeace seriously enough. Fages quickly went over the head of the organisation's chief, Admiral Lacoste, to Charles Hernu himself. The defence minister responded sympathetically and quickly.

France promulgated new regulations to ban the passage of foreign ships through parts of her territorial waters during arms tests and declared an exclusion zone around Mororua Atoll for the duration of the test programme in spring and summer. While this ban was being announced in Tahiti on May 23, Fages was back in Paris reviewing with Hernu their anti-Greenpeace campaign, now in high gear. Tricot reported that the French planned to intercept *Rainbow Warrior*'s communications and jam transmissions to black out news coverage of the showdown in the Pacific. Navy commandos had been specially trained to intercept small, high-powered speedboats before they could reach the reef. Anyone who did manage to get ashore was to be arrested. Video cameras and other equipment would be confiscated. A cautionary note was included: tact was to be exercised to avoid offending British susceptibilities if, as expected, *Rainbow Warrior* flew the Red Ensign.

All these plans were listed in a memo left by Fages for Air Force General Mermet, scheduled to succeed him as commander of DIRCEN in June. Fages, who never commented publicly on allegations about his role in the affair, admitted to Tricot his 'distress' that Lacoste was not taking things seriously enough. Tricot noted in his report that Farges left his job in June but did not say that the admiral in fact stayed on for a month to ensure a smooth transition of command, well beyond the July 10 night of the sabotage in Auckland.

Probing Hernu's orders to DGSE, Tricot reported that in the best traditions of intelligence operations, to safeguard politicians' need for 'plausible denial', the orders had been mainly oral. Both Hernu and Lacoste maintained they had ordered an operation only to gather intelligence, albeit one big and expensive enough to require approval from Mitterrand's top military aid, General Jean Saulnier.

A former commander of France's strategic nuclear bombers and missiles, Saulnier would have readily seen the need to guard against a spectacular Greenpeace protest that ridiculed France's ability to protect her nuclear programme. When questioned by Tricot both Saulnier, who was now chief of staff, and General Lacaze, his predecessor, said they recalled plans and funds for an operation in New Zealand but only for spying.

A slightly different recollection came from Admiral Lacoste who said they had decided to infiltrate Greenpeace to see how its plans could be foiled. In giving Lacoste his orders in March, Hernu had used a Fages memo recommending steps to 'predict and anticipate Greenpeace's actions'. Hernu had shown Lacoste the memo but did not give him a copy to keep. Tricot saw the document, however, and noticed that Hernu (or an aide) had twice underlined the word 'anticipate'.

Semantically, Tricot had a smoking gun. The word could not mean 'predict' in its most common and more passive sense because that would have been tautological, a grammatical error unworthy of a French admiral's correspondence. It had been used in the active voice. It meant pre-empt, prevent, perhaps – in the jargon of spycraft – even 'neutralise'.

When questioned again, Hernu agreed it meant infiltration. Lacoste interpreted it more strongly, but certainly not to include dirty tricks or even non-violent 'soft' methods of harassment, he said.

Working his day down the chain of DGSE commanders, noting that the leadership changes since 1981 had harmed morale and discipline, Tricot remained convinced that no orders were given, in writing or verbally, to sink *Rainbow Warrior*.

Spies had to be sent to New Zealand, he was told, because France had no permanent DGSE network there (in fact DGSE had agents in deep cover but would not have wanted to jeopardise them in an operation liable to involve crime and subsequent police investigation). The five agents listed by Tricot were Mafart, Prieur and the *Ouvéa* crew; he did not include Dillais. All five were exculpated. Mafart had been out of the frogman unit for more than a year. Prieur was not trained for underwater missions and suffered from a bad back. The *Ouvéa* had overlapped with *Rainbow Warrior* in New Zealand for only two nights, too short a period for the Frenchmen to have planted the bombs.

Implicitly Tricot rejected the simplest explanation of the *Ouvéa* crew's behaviour – that they were a bomb delivery squad who took advantage of their mission in the tropics to live it up – and described them instead as disciplined soldiers. Their performance was consistent with orders to familiarise themselves with sailing conditions in the South Pacific and make themselves conspicuous enough to wangle an invitation to join a future Greenpeace expedition, perhaps as skipper and crew of a protest vessel. Their credentials as seafarers had been established by their 'exploit' of seamanship in sailing into Parengarenga in bad weather. Fraternisation had also gone well, noted the strait-laced Tricot. 'I ascertained that our fellow Frenchmen acquitted themselves gallantly with the distaff part of the local population although this applies, of course, only to the bachelor crew members.'

Though he hadn't been able to interview Mafart, Prieur or Cabon, Tricot said he could not believe any of these officers would disobey

171

orders and lend themselves to a separate bomb plot. The commander and his deputy of DGSE's Action Division had both assured Tricot that in their judgement a sabotage operation on the territory of a friendly nation would have damaged French interests.

Tricot's report therefore arrived at 'the certainty that the French government did not order damage to the ship.' It added: 'There is no reason to believe (and many reasons to doubt) that the DGSE instructed its agents to exceed the government's plan.'

Of course there were caveats. Tricot said he could not rule out the possibility that these officers 'conspired to hide part of the facts from me'. He believed the five French officers were innocent 'in the present state of my information'. In a television interview he admitted: 'I could have been fooled'. His report concluded with a one sentence recommendation for a fuller inquiry.

What Tricot did not do in his report was offer any plausible alternative culprit. If France didn't do it, who did? But this obvious question went unanswered. He did not address the role of Admiral Farges and DIRCEN which, DGSE sources were privately complaining, had gone overboard. Tricot hypothesised that foreign powers might have spotted the French agents and mounted an operation for which France would be blamed (the British gambit again). Or it might have been French political fanatics with good intelligence contacts trying to discredit the socialist government (the New Caledonia angle). This time the Paris media quickly turned up its collective nose at such threadbare theories. The Tricot Report, said one opposition politician, was 'taking the French people for imbeciles'.

The scorn poured on the report was almost universal. 'Tricot Washes Whiter' headlined *Libération* and this irreverent verdict stuck in peoples' minds. The paper compared the report to a fairy story by Lewis Carroll and said its conclusions were too good to be true. In London the *Daily Mail* said the report reeked of complacency and Bonapartist arrogance, adding that, as whitewashes go, it was a pretty thorough job. The *Daily Telegraph* gave more than a third of its front page to the report, also describing it as a whitewash, but a predictable one. In New Zealand the *Auckland Star* said in an editorial that Tricot's report, riddled with deceit and insincerity, was such a blatant whitewash it insulted the intelligence. 'It is time to stop mincing words,' the paper said. 'The sooner France gets out of the Pacific the better.' Putting its finger on an ironical twist, *The Times* in London pointed out that the kindest thing said so far about the report had been the comment by David Lange, prime minister of New Zealand. He had said the report couldn't possibly be the whitewash job it was made out to be – 'It was too transparent for that.'

For David Lange's quick tongue the report was a gift. The DGSE, he said, seemed to have viewed his country as a Club Med for its agents. Demanding an immediate official apology for 'outrageous violation of sovereignty' by the five French spies now admitted to have operated in New Zealand, the prime minister bluntly suggested that the French ambassador be recalled. In a three-page statement he described the report as inconclusive, contradictory and certainly incredible. Tricot had made an international fool of himself, Lange told reporters. When implying a British connection he had not clung to his report but had leapt from the iceberg to the *Titanic*. Filmed for French television, Lange said New Zealand had always looked on France as an honourable country but this was no longer the case – 'France has killed our friendship.'

Greenpeace, predictably, condemned the report as insulting. International director Steve Sawyer, still in Auckland coping with the aftermath of the sabotage, said it showed France was not only willing to use murder and arson but also deceit to protect her nuclear weapons and testing programme.

Ignoring the newspaper jibes and Lange's anger, the Paris government held its ground. In a television appearance next day Prime Minister Fabius publicly adopted the Tricot Report. He called on New Zealand to come forward with its evidence, pledging that any French people guilty of crimes would be punished. He instructed Charles Hernu to pursue the investigation to clear up the unanswered questions in Tricot's report and said the government would support calls for a parliamentary commission to inquire into the affair. 'The French Government is determined that no relevant facts shall be kept dark,' he said in a statement. And he added: 'Our condemnation of this act of sabotage is not, as has sometimes been said, directed at the inefficient execution of a questionable scheme: it is an absolute condemnation of a criminal act.'

Meanwhile, almost unnoticed in the uproar, the three DGSE men last seen leaving Norfolk Island on board the yacht *Ouvéa* had turned up. Tricot, it appeared, had been driven into the countryside near Paris to meet them at a secret rendezvous. Now, acting on his advice, one hour before the report was published the three men calmly 'surrendered' themselves at the headquarters of the French criminal police on the Quai des Orfèvres in Paris. An examining magistrate promptly interviewed Verge, Andries and Bartelot and decided the international arrest warrants from New Zealand were too incomplete to hold them. Released immediately, they dropped completely from sight and were afterwards alleged to be hiding in Africa.

It was a smack in the face for the New Zealand detectives who,

173

unaware that their wanted men were in an office only a few doors away, were at the police headquarters trying to get permission to interview them. It was the first of many occasions on which the French government backed away from its pledges to bring to justice 'anyone suspected of a criminal act'.

This news, coinciding with new revelations in New Zealand papers that traces of explosives had been found in the *Ouvéa*, moved David Lange to new heights of scathing fury. 'Three people do not scuttle a very expensive yacht and suddenly pop up in Paris,' he said. 'They were smuggled out of the South Pacific and into France. At every step of the way their journey was funded by the French government. They got there because the French government saw to it.' The use of a French navy submarine, Lange added, was 'clearly an intelligent surmise'.

In London, Tricot's insinuation that the bombing of *Rainbow Warrior* had been a British frame-up raised a storm. To some politicians, in light of the close co-operation that existed between intelligence organisations in Western Europe, the idea had 'a regrettable ring of truth'. Others pushed for an official inquiry on the grounds that a British ship had been sunk by espionage, an act of war. But investigative journalists soon tracked the purchase of the abandoned Zodiac to a Frenchman whom they linked with *Ouvéa* crewman Gerald Andries. *The Observer* headlined its detailed story: 'Dinghy clue may sink French.'

L'Affaire Greenpeace now seemed to have all the makings of a scandal that could topple a government. Dubbing it 'Watergate-sur-Seine' and 'Underwatergate', foreign papers drew obvious parallels with the Watergate crisis that pitched US President Nixon out of the most powerful seat in the Western world. In fact, for reasons peculiar to the French political character, this affair was never likely to climax with the direct downfall of a French president. In Paris, and even more so in the provinces, French opinion remains perplexed by Nixon's downfall, by the spectacle of the American nation hounding out of office an apparently competent president because he spied on his political opposition. A country with vivid memories of political turbulence, France clings to the presidency instituted by General de Gaulle as a symbol of political legitimacy and stability. Politicians feared that unleashing a cycle of impeachment could degenerate into political paralysis. And French people are too cynical about the frailties of politicians to be morally outraged over a little political skulduggery. The president was psychologically untouchable. The prime minister seemed made of Teflon.

But crucial parliamentary elections were in prospect. The electorate would have a lot to say about a party that dragged France's name through the mud and bungled so appallingly on matters to do with future security of that symbol of French nationalism, the nuclear deterrent. In Paris there was all-round heartfelt support for a quick termination of the affair which, *Le Monde* said, had made France look ridiculous. In the corner of its daily page of Greenpeace coverage this staidest of newspapers started running a cartoon figure of a frogman with an angelic halo. *Libération* neatly summed up the government's predicament: 'either the government is lying and should be sacked or the government is incompetent and should be sacked'. Even the pro-socialist *Le Matin*, in an editorial by its editor Max Sallo, who had been a government spokesman until recently, commented: 'Better a noisy ending than unending noise.'

Despite the press clamour France's opposition leaders were conspicuously muted. Mitterrand decided to capitalise on the military card. In another of the surprise moves typical of him, the Elysée announced the president would leave next day (Friday, September 13) for the South Pacific. Flying by Concorde, he would pause en route to witness a test-firing of the European space rocket Ariane. At Mururoa Atoll he would witness an underground nuclear test and attend a meeting of the South Pacific Co-ordination Committee. This committee of France's high commissioners, ambassadors and civil and military representatives in the region had just been 'reactivated'.

The date of departure was jinxed enough to satisfy even the least superstitious. The engines of the supersonic Concorde played up and the president, accompanied by four government ministers, had to switch to a back-up aircraft. At Kourou in French Guyana, once the site of the notorious prison for transported criminals known as Devil's Island, the president watched the tenth commercial launch of an Ariane space rocket; France has a leading role in this effort, effectively runs the launching centre, and Mitterrand had only just been expressing his approval at the completion of a multi-billion dollar second launch site. It was embarrassing, therefore, when the rocket with its cargo of communications satellites began to veer out of its planned trajectory. Nine minutes into its flight the rocket was out of control and threatening to plunge back to earth. The safety officer punched the self-destruct button to activate explosive charges next to the rocket fuel and the space-flight pride of France was blown out of the sky.

The attempt to showcase French high technology had backfired ludicrously. Chatting to a bunch of reporters after his return, Mitterrand said wryly, 'If you think my bad karma stopped those engines and drove the rocket off course I think you over-estimate my powers, considerable as I would like to think they are.'

But the flag-waving could hardly have gone better. Mitterrand minced no words in re-affirming France's objectives in the South Pacific. First, France was a power in the Pacific and France alone would decide what affected her national interests. Second, France – like the other nuclear powers – would continue whatever tests were necessary for her defence needs. French language and culture in the South Pacific would be increased. 'France has no enemies in the South Pacific,' the president concluded, 'she intends only to ensure respect of her rights . . .'

The message to France and the world, especially to New Zealand, Australia and the international disarmament and environment protection movements, was blunt. France was there to stay.

The visit was denounced by Australia as provocative; Prime Minister Bob Hawke, telling France to halt nuclear testing in the Pacific, suggested Mitterrand should conduct his 'absolutely safe' tests in metropolitan France. An infuriated David Lange branded the stagey Moruroa mission 'an obscenity'. Mitterrand ignored a message from the New Zealand prime minister and announced that a planned visit to Paris by the deputy prime minister, Geoffrey Palmer, was cancelled. Mitterrand loftily instructed New Zealand to cease meddling in French affairs. When a presidential spokesman stated that opponents of France's nuclear tests would be ignored, and anyone who opposed French interests would be seen as 'adversaries', Lange launched a bitter attack. France had declared New Zealand an enemy, he claimed. And he elaborated: 'We do not declare ourselves an enemy of France. We are an enemy of the nuclear threat and we are an enemy of the testing of nuclear weapons in the South Pacific.

'New Zealand did not buy into this fight. France put spies into New Zealand. France lets off bombs in the Pacific. France sends her president to the Pacific to crow about it.

'It's not the New Zealand or the Pacific way of doing things but apparently it's the way to win a French election.'

In this last respect Lange hit the nail on the head. Mitterrand's flag-waving mission was brilliantly successful in dulling the aches of national ridicule and enhancing France's image of herself. But its benefits were short-lived. Even while Mitterrand was on the wing to the South Seas reporters in Paris, working with a photograph taken in New Zealand of a French 'tourist' by the name of Jean-Louis Dormond shooting white-water rapids, had uncovered yet another DGSE embarrassment. The tourist was shown wearing a crash helmet but intelligence sources remarked on the man's resemblance to Lt Col Dillais. The newspapers claimed the chief of the Aspretto underwater combat school had been in Auckland as controller of the DGSE operation. Tricot had made no mention of this important component.

At the same time, French intelligence sources were letting press investigators know that the order to sink *Rainbow Warrior* had not come from DGSE headquarters at all. Admiral Lacoste was quoted by *Le Canard Enchaîné* confiding to friends, 'I was asked to detach agents'. The implication is that the order to sink came from DIRCEN: its outlook was narrowed on its testing and security responsibilities in and around Moruroa, it loathed Greenpeace and its command was in a state of transition. Even if DIRCEN did go further than specifically ordered by politicians and intelligence chiefs who viewed the world from Paris, as seems likely, Hernu (apparently much more than Lacoste) shared its Pacific commanders' desire to play rough with Greenpeace. After the attack Hernu's loyalties never wavered. 'Don't expect me to break solidarity with the armed forces,' he had repeated often.

But the Tricot Report – translated into English *tricot* means 'knitting' – was now beginning to unravel and Mitterrand knew it.

While the president was still airborne on his way home from Moruroa reporters were summoned to meet him at the Elysée. First he read a brief statement on television about his trip, a tough and statesmanlike performance intended to add yet another building block to the edifice of supreme commander he was constructing to shelter his future after the March elections. Despite its disasters the long trip had reinforced his image as the man embodying France's defence and therefore her independence, a man above parties, with whom the political opposition should contemplate political co-habitation.

Then Mitterrand held an informal press conference. It was an 'impromptu' affair that was evidently carefully organised, an 'off the record' session meant to be used for publication, a florentine performance by a man of few wasted gestures. His key sentence was clearly heard by several score of the assembled reporters: 'There is a gulf between intelligence and action, a gulf that should never have been crossed.'

Listening reporters believed their ears but none dared write that the president had admitted French agents had gone beyond the limit. But forty-eight hours later somebody else would say it. Meanwhile, Mitterrand's TV performance had filled the Monday papers and on Tuesday he was off on yet another trip, this time to commemorate a dead national hero, Vercingetorix, who had united the Gauls against invading Romans. It had all happened a couple of thousand years before the *force de frappe* but it touched the same patriotic nerve. Midway through the ceremony at the remote mountain monument in Mitterrand's own consituency, the president's advisers learned *Le Monde* was poised to make sensational disclosures about the Greenpeace affair.

On Tuesday, September 17, André Fontaine, the new editor of *Le Monde*, agonised over how hard to go with a story that had hit his desk. His reporters vouched again for their sources. He decided the paper should stake its reputation against the government. The headline justified the government's worst fears. It ran nearly the full width of the front page, just short of the space *Le Monde* might allot to the outbreak of the Third World War: '*Rainbow Warrior* said sunk by third military team.'

Widely reported around the world, the story charged that a 'third team' of DGSE frogmen – unknown to Tricot, unknown to New Zealand police (though never ruled out) – had blown up the Greenpeace flagship and got clean away.

Hard on its heels came corroborating stories in other papers and news magazines. Some stories had the same sources, some had new information. They said an officer and a sergeant had actually planted the mines on the hull of *Rainbow Warrior* then escaped by plane, one to Sydney and one to Tahiti. Mafart and Prieur had played the role of lookouts. The yacht *Ouvéa* had smuggled in the munitions. Lt Col Dillais was in charge. Furthermore, *Le Monde* alleged, Charles Hernu and Admiral Lacoste had ordered the operation, or were at least aware of it, and had participated in a cover-up. France was guilty.

The government's denial was prompt – the Defence Ministry said it was unaware of any third team – and notable for its nuanced caution. The cover-up was showing cracks.

Until this point, however, the government's attempts to sustain a bold front were not an impossible dream. Defence Minister Charles Hernu, in charge of DGSE and allegedly implicated personally in the decision to sabotage *Rainbow Warrior*, was intent on protecting the military. He wanted to sit tight and stonewall all accusations. Perhaps he thought that if the government hung tough New Zealand could later be subdued, bought off or blackmailed through her important Common Market trading agreements. But any prospect of some sort of quiet deal between governments disappeared mainly because journalists obtained critical information (about the third team and the role of the DGSE) from inside sources.

Significantly, the leaks that blew the cover-up did not originate abroad but in France, perhaps within the government itself.

One source of leaks were disgruntled intelligence officers, some with a grudge against the socialists for what they had done to the secret service, others for what they might do. But the crucial leaks appear to have come from the interior ministry whose own intelligence agency, the police-oriented DST responsible for France's internal security, was historically at loggerheads with the defence ministry's DGSE. The dismissal of a strong DST chief in spring 1985 was partly blamed on the DGSE and the DST was waiting for a chance to get even. Moreover, the DST had access to information within the interior ministry because its police officers were 'co-operating' with New Zealand detectives.

Interior Minister Pierre Joxe has strenuously denied suggestions that he contributed to the public scandal and the blood-letting that followed, though interior ministry officials have been consistently cited as a source of key leaks. Joxe's aides only concede that his ministry realised earlier than the rest of the government the dangers of the situation, a realisation that might have prompted Joxe to lance the boil by leaks rather than continue stonewalling as Hernu was doing. Joxe's intention could well have been to get everything out in the open and save Mitterrand.

But ulterior motives may have been at work: Joxe, the young Turk socialist, detested Hernu politically as the man who personified the idea of 'cohabitation' with French conservatives. If the sabotage were pinned on the DGSE, Hernu would be scapegoat thus reducing the risk of political compromise. And Joxe himself might emerge as the president's confidant.

Beyond these intensive political manoeuvres a fundamental question remains. *Le Figaro*, the opposition paper, virulently denied the possibility of a third team. Did a third DGSE team in fact exist, or was it a carefully contrived smokescreen? Long after the sabotage act itself, and months after the stream of leaks suddenly dried up, few informed observers in Paris were able to make up their minds.

The theory had a lot of circumstantial support. It would certainly have been 'standard' military procedure to have at least two frogmen in the water planting the bombs. In scuba diving of any sort the 'buddy' system was fundamental to safety. Also, Auckland police did have a number of mysterious arrivals and departures of French people whose movements in New Zealand were still not fully explained. And several different journalists had learned of the third team more or less simultaneously and from different sources. This suggests that if it were a plot to lay a trail of misleading information, the orchestration of it must have involved four or five different people; in politics, four or five in one secret is a lot.

Conversely there are plenty of reasons why the third team might have been a cleverly inspired red herring.

First, a close scrutiny of the operational difficulties involved in

179

the sabotage of *Rainbow Warrior* reveals it was actually a rather simple task well within the competence of a single frogman. His job was in any case made easier by close support of the Zodiac. If the man driving the inflatable were also a trained frogman, ready and kitted up to dive at a moment's notice, the safety requirements of an 'active' military operation would have been adequately satisfied. Significantly, the men in the third team were never identified; the so-called initials that were published could mean everything or nothing.

The third team theory also happens to be convenient to the explanation of why Mitterrand's government, with nearly fatal results, was trying to persist with a cover-up. Mitterrand could claim he had been unaware of the full facts. It conveniently allowed the authorities to maintain that they had been lied to, and that as soon as the government learned of the third team it came clean. Thus the president was protected against allegations of complicity.

Above all, public knowledge of the 'third team' was necessary to help Prieur and Mafart when they appeared before the courts in Auckland. The possibility that other frogmen had set the bombs and made a clean escape reinforced the arrested agents' carefully groomed image as mere lookouts and drivers. Their defence, as it turned out, rested on the claim that they were only minor accomplices. Auckland police were not able to make stronger charges stick.

One reason the leaks dried up may well be that the agents' futures hung on this misinformation. If the third team were in fact a neat fabrication to protect the agents, the lie would surely not be betrayed while they were still in prison.

Also going on behind the scenes as the affair came to a head was in-fighting between politicians and the armed services over who should take the blame. The military top brass were determined to have nothing to do with it. A powerful national lobby, the military may have had its way in this case simply because of the political conjuncture. With elections only months off, the socialists were afraid to re-open old allegations that the left could not live with the military. The mystique of the army and the chain of nuclear command may also have asserted some sacrosanct authority.

It was proving to be a long week in French politics.

Monday (September 16), the Elysée was still trying to convince *Le Canard Enchaîné* journalists that the British had done it.

Tuesday, *Le Monde* broke its 'third team' scoop, provoking a barrage of follow-up stories.

Wednesday, the Chinese water torture of leak after leak finally penetrated Mitterrand's sphinx-like mask. During that day's weekly meeting of full cabinet he complained that he was learning more from the newspapers than from his intelligence services. He reportedly shouted: 'I want to know what happened and what's going on!' Before the assembled cabinet Mitterrand rebuked Hernu, saying he thought the defence minister was being duped by his own officers. Joxe was also tough on Hernu's handling of the affair. After the meeting Hernu remained behind with Mitterrand and left after an hour by a side door. In his first public glimmering of self-doubt Hernu told journalists waiting at his office that if anyone in his ministry had lied to him he would be punished.

Thursday, the government cracked.

Just before the evening television news a letter was made public from Mitterrand to Fabius, telling him that government ignorance had become intolerable. It ordered him to make changes in personnel and, if necessary in institutions, to clear up the situation. Clearly he had in mind Hernu and the DGSE.

Fabius had just met quickly with Hernu. What the two men discussed was never revealed. Stung by the allegations that he was not in control of his own men, Hernu called into his office a parade of top military men including Admiral Lacoste, General Saulnier and General Lacaze. He asked them to sign a statement confirming they had told everything they knew about the Greenpeace operation. Lacoste refused to sign on the grounds that he had a duty to protect subordinates. Overnight Hernu despatched a general from military intelligence to Aspretto to interview Lt Col Dillais. But no one would admit they had lied. In fact, no one would talk to him at all.

Friday morning, a haggard Hernu slipped into Matignon for a half-hour meeting with Fabius. Faced with Admiral Lacoste's refusal to sign the paper, confirming he had not been told the whole story, Charles Hernu said he would resign. His aides, he told Fabius, had 'hidden the truth' from him. Throughout the affair, Hernu persistently denied that he knew of the planned sabotage. He declared the attack to be 'scandalous, disproportionate and damnable'. And he stated: 'It would have been stupid to give the order to neutralise a ship in a foreign port.'

Early in the afternoon Fabius appeared briefly on television to read a letter he had just sent Mitterrand. It said Admiral Lacoste had been sacked and Charles Hernu had offered his resignation which Fabius recommended accepting. By the end of the day France had a new defence minister. Paul Quilès, 44, a technocrat and reserve officer, had shifted over from the transport ministry (novelist Jean Dutour commented wryly that the promotion was a natural one, for French train accidents had killed more people that summer while Quilès was transport minister than the army).

181

Staying up almost solidly for 48 hours, Quilès hunted down the facts. A prime source was apparently a report written in late July by Admiral Lacoste that detailed the affair; Hernu always denied existence of a report but the story was that Quilès had found it in Hernu's office safe when he took over. Quilès also discovered key secret service papers relating to the bombing were missing.

On Sunday evening (September 22) the government spokes-woman, fending off reporters' questions about Greenpeace, was visibly surprised to learn that Prime Minister Fabius would make a television broadcast just fifteen minutes later.

Under brilliant camera lights on the steps outside Matignon, standing alongside Quilès who looked unshaven and sleepless, Fabius announced that the truth had been discovered. 'The truth about this affair is cruel but it has been clearly and thoroughly established as I intended,' he said. 'Agents of the DGSE sank this boat. They acted on orders. This truth was hidden from state counsellor Tricot.'

Promising a new head of the DGSE whose prime task would be to reorganise the service, and saying the government favoured a parliamentary commission of inquiry, Fabius added: 'The people who merely carried out the act must, of course, be exempted from blame as it would be unacceptable to expose members of the military who only obeyed orders, and who, in the past, have sometimes carried out very dangerous missions on behalf of our country.'

The front page headlines around the world were all in much the same vein – France Confesses: 'We sank *Rainbow Warrior*.'

That day the Greenpeace yacht *Vega*, shadowed by French war-ships, took up her station hove-to in international waters just twelve miles from Moruroa Atoll.

13

CAN YOU SINK A RAINBOW?

Two days after the confession Prime Minister Fabius, interviewed deferentially on television, explicitly blamed Hernu and Lacoste for the affair without explaining exactly what had happened. He insisted nobody else in the government was implicated and the army was not to blame. It was a cold-blooded, priggish performance that shattered the young premier's image as 'fabulous' Fabius. Charles Hernu made no further statements. Two national opinion polls that day showed that most people suspected the government of knowing the whole story all along, but there was to be no 'Watergate' – two-thirds of those polled believed President Mitterrand should not resign.

The president, in a letter accepting his resignation, told Hernu: 'In the hour of travail, I am, as always, your friend.' Subsequently Mitterrand and his young prime minister appeared to drift steadily further apart.

Sound and fury erupted but no more light was shed when the new head of DGSE, General René Imbot, a former Foreign Legion officer, appeared on television. Wearing full uniform and képi, he solemnly announced that a plot within the DGSE had been discovered. 'I have chopped off the rotten branches,' he said, 'and I have battened down the hatches'.

But this extraordinary episode never had a sequel. Neither Imbot nor anyone in the government explained the crime or the punishments he had so dramatically announced. The only event that came to light was the arrest of four officers and an NCO alleged to have leaked secrets liable to damage French security. The unit set up to deal with Greenpeace, called K-cell, was disbanded. The combat-swimmer training base at Aspretto was closed as part of a general shake-up but later rehabilitated. The élite 11th *Choc* Battalion of paratroopers on which DGSE formerly relied for its muscle overseas, disbanded by De Gaulle in 1962 because it was compromised with the OAS, was re-formed.

France – or at least her leadership – had had enough. *Le Monde* did not want the Watergate it had been crusading for: in a front page editorial in the aftermath of its scoop about the third team, the paper evoked 'the limits of indignation'. French politicians stopped asking the government to disclose how the operation was funded; they no longer queried the contradiction between Hernu's denials that he had ordered the sinking and Fabius's accusations that he had.

As the president and polititicans became enveloped in this truce a holy alliance formed around France's army. Enquiries and reforms would have been inevitable in almost any other democracy but the French parliamentary enquiry into the affair never materialised. No political party (except the Communists who sought more political control of the secret services) wanted it. France was not going to blame her military for the fiasco. Hernu could be the scapegoat. 'He was so sure the military loved him that he was blind to signs that the army was distancing itself from him,' *Le Monde* commented.

The deal was simple. The politicians accepted a demand by the military that no commanders would be called to account. The DGSE, which allegedly had the missing documents that would conclusively implicate the government, agreed in return to remain silent.

With elections at hand the Socialists were haunted by the fear of allegations that the French Left could never get along with the military. Conservative politicians had no interest in arguing with the military either. So the mystique of the army – in today's terms, the nuclear deterrent – reasserted its sacrosanct position in French politics. France's military-run espionage services emerged, temporarily at least, shaken but not changed.

So there were no public sanctions or punishments in France. This angered David Lange. Calling for the prosecution of France's agents he said: 'When condemning the sinking but denying involvement in it, France pledged to bring to justice – if they were French – those responsible. What we have now is the French government saying it was responsible, that those who did it acted under orders, and therefore it will be taking no proceedings against them. This is, of course, quite absurd.'

The international press was scathing. The 'long suffering' Mr Lange had been completely vindicated in his persistent demand for a full explanation. 'He has been reviled by the French and insulted by their president,' said the *Guardian* in London, 'but his commonsense deductions after the sinking are now shown to be absolutely accurate.' *The Times* took issue with the assertion by Fabius that the actual perpetrators of the crime should be protected because they were under military orders: 'That is, to say the least, an unfashionable doctrine and has been since the time of the Nuremberg trials. A soldier, we are taught to believe nowadays, should obey only lawful commands, and it is hard to see how it could have been thought lawful to commit an act of sabotage on the territory of an ostensibly friendly country.'

In the United States President Reagan's officials sharply rejected calls to condemn the French action. Privately, for publication, they feared a knock-on effect on their own nuclear freedoms and expressed sympathy for the French. Privately, but not for publication, they were scornful of French incompetence. The European Parliament, however, did condemn the sabotage action.

France agreed to compensate New Zealand, Greenpeace and the family of Fernando Pereira for 'substantial' damages. Reparation negotiations with the New Zealand government were opened in New York. The discussions were clouded by allegations of trade-off. New Zealand had the two French agents under lock and key. France had a certain power of veto over New Zealand's key trading agreements with the Common Market. In the early stages David Lange was privately mentioning a reparation sum of NZ$20 million (about £8 million). The negotiations were continuing into 1986.

Though the French government refused to answer parliamentary questions on details of 'secret' funds, according to *Le Canard Enchaîné* sources inside DGSE put the bill for the direct costs of the Greenpeace operation at 1,600,000 French francs, plus 800,000 francs compensation for the scuttled *Ouvéa* (total cost about £200,000 or NZ$450,000). But the real cost to France was incalculable.

The government lost prestige in the eyes of France, not because it had done anything wrong but because it was caught. In short, the government had made France look ridiculous. The display of socialist incompetence sharpened the right's hope of driving Mitterrand from office. This improved the odds of a March 1986 election that left France in a state of political paralysis with a weak president pitted against a strong conservative government.

The whole episode cast France, a nuclear power professing national honour and chivalry, in the role of bully and international terrorist. It played right into the hands of Greenpeace who dressed it up as 'an act of mindless violence that reveals much about the very attitudes this organisation is trying to change.' It also spoke volumes about the importance France attaches to her *force de dissuasion* and the front she presents as a nation. Noting an almost complete absence of political criticism in the whole affair, and comparing it with the US, the *Washington Post* headlined: 'France Sinks a Peace Ship Without a Ripple.' Former right-wing President Valéry Giscard d'Estaing, explaining why he remained silent on the issue, huffed: 'Right or wrong, it's my country.' Likewise, former right-wing Prime Minister Raymond Barre sniffed, 'This is a lamentable affair on which I shall have no further comment.'

It goes to prove how highly developed in France the notion of *raison d'état* – the idea that the state has the right to resort to any

185

measures to protect its own interests – really is. Its evident strength is something peace protesters in New Zealand and the South Pacific might well contemplate, and which those striving to protect the freedoms of Western society might envy. Though it's hardly irrelevant that the last word belonged to a reader of *Le Monde* who pointed out that the quote used by Giscard to justify *raison d'état* was incomplete. The full version was in fact an argument against it: 'My country, right or wrong. If it is right, keep it right. If it is wrong, make it right.'

The 'hosepipe-to-hosepipe' confrontation on the blue Pacific waters around the atoll of the big secret took place under the eyes of the world but never amounted to much. Mitterrand reiterated his orders to the armed forces to halt – by force if necessary – unauthorised entry into air space or territorial waters around the atoll. But he was wasting his breath.

First the French Navy tried to frustrate the efforts of the new mother-ship *Greenpeace* to pick up a television film crew at the Marquesas, a remote island group in French Polynesia. Instead, the film crew flew 300 miles (480 km) to another island and dashed out in speedboats for a rendezvous in the open ocean, outside territorial waters, with Greenpeace inflatables.

Warships and aircraft shadowed the ship to Moruroa where she met up with *Vega* and the New Zealand yachts *Breeze* and *Alliance*; the fourth yacht *Varangian*, delayed by a storm near Auckland, showed up later.

The 'rainbow fleet' played stand-off war games with two frigates, three tugs, a transport vessel, two planes and five helicopters of the French Navy. The corps of reporters and film crews in both fleets waited impatiently for something to happen and fought valiantly against seasickness. A small plane chartered from Tahiti to relay live TV pictures of the confrontation, from cameras on board *Greenpeace* to a communications satellite, was refused permission to fly lower than 3,000 feet and the signal channels were jammed. But the world missed only pictures of naval ships warily circling the yachts whose crews sunbathed on deck and periodically made a Gallic fist. Official letters were delivered by small boat, warning the protest fleet to stay clear. Greenpeace sent a bottle of whisky over to the naval tug *Hippopotame* and asked to be allowed to explain why they opposed the nuclear tests but was not allowed on board.

There was a flurry of alertness when some of the nineteen crew of *Greenpeace* launched a strange vessel on the waves. But it was not an outrigger canoe bound on invasion of the reef, only a large chunk of driftwood, stabilised with empty fuel drums and rigged with a windsurfer sail.

The showdown limped to an end after only two weeks or so when the protest flotilla's mother-ship developed generator trouble and headed towards Papeete for 'urgent' repairs. French High Commissioner Bernard Gerard denied the ship permission to enter territorial waters and the Papeete harbourmaster barred the vessel 'in the interests of security, conservation and good management'.

Tahitians led by Oscar Temaru put to sea in small boats and visited the ship as she heaved-to outside the territorial limit to await engineers bringing spare parts. With the Antarctic ice season in mind, however, Greenpeace leaders called off the emergency and the ship headed for New Zealand. The brigantine *Breeze* was given dispensation to collect fresh provisions from Tahiti then sailed for Rarotonga.

On October 24 the *Vega*, remaining on station with former *Rainbow Warrior* skipper Peter Willcox and deckhand Grace O'Sullivan among her four crew, learned by radio that a nuclear device was to be detonated under the atoll. The yacht breached the prohibition zone and headed straight for Moruroa. When eight miles (12 km) off, just before dawn, the yacht was intercepted and boarded by eight marine commandos. Three hours later a five-kilotonne nuclear device was triggered. From a safe distance of 12 miles (20 km), through closed-circuit TV, it was observed by Prime Minister Fabius, Defence Minister Quilès, a bipartisan group of French members of parliament, and a party of twelve journalists. They noted that a pile of sandbags immediately above the explosion chamber was not disturbed. Pictures of a pyramid of wine glasses, which scarcely trembled during the explosion, were screened on news bulletins around the world. Two days later a 16-kilotonne device was exploded. The *Vega* crew was expelled.

As far as David Lange's government was concerned, in New Zealand the affair had brought a welcome distraction from burgeoning economic problems. Despite record interest rates, inflation exceeding 16 percent, and the farmers who were the mainstay of the economy being forced to walk off their land, the government's handling of the *Rainbow Warrior* sabotage earned it a four percent gain in public opinion polls. Boycotts of French goods, organised by peace groups, amounted to nothing. French remained the second language in schools. Restaurants with aspirations to classiness stayed with French cuisine. New Zealanders were generally in a forgiving mood. Some had found it rather exciting to be at the centre of the world stage for once. When Russell Munro moved his yacht *Django* to a new berth a few days after the sinking he heard sounds of revelry from an ocean-racing yacht nearby. Floating across the water came the strains of a new song – 'I'm a limpet mine, and I'm okay . . .'

But the attack did stiffen the government's resolve to stick to – and step up – its campaign for a nuclear-free South Pacific. The Forum of fourteen South Pacific nations meeting at Rarotonga voted overwhelmingly in favour of declaring the whole region a nuclear-free zone. The Greenpeace affair had brought nearer the day – the *inevitable* day, *Le Monde* had commented – when the nuclear test facilities on Moruroa had to be abandoned.

The attack might also be seen as something of an object-lesson to a country premising its national defence on geographic isolation. The sabotage of *Rainbow Warrior* had been the first act of foreign-inspired violence on New Zealand soil. It might not be the last. Were New Zealanders really as insulated by remoteness as they liked to think from Western society's need to maintain the vigorous and – most importantly – the *united* defence of its freedoms? Would France have been likely to commit such an act in the front yard of a stronger, more assertive country? New Zealand had made her position clear: I declare I am not a ten stone weakling but I will not help you stand up to the neighbourhood bullies. Then it was one of her *friends* who kicked sand in her face.

For the squad of Auckland detectives still investigating the case, France's confession was not much help. The prosecution could not prove anything in a criminal court unless the French officials responsible took the witness stand, and there was small chance of that. Even the admission by Prime Minister Fabius would be inadmissible as 'hearsay' in a New Zealand court. Det. Supt Galbraith had little chance of extraditing from France the *Ouvéa* crew, Cabon or Dillais. His detectives in Paris had not even been allowed to talk with any of them. Under French law it was illegal to surrender French nationals to other countries.

Galbraith's only hope now of illiciting further details was for prosecution lawyers to grill Prieur and Mafart in the witness box when they appeared in court to answer charges of murder and arson. But even this was denied him.

The preliminary hearing, set to begin on November 4, was expected to last anything up to six weeks. More than 140 reporters, photographers and film crews – including forty from France alone – were accredited. A courtroom that had been out of use for two years, in Auckland's former Supreme Court, was renovated with an overflow pressroom linked by closed-circuit television. The prosecution expected to bring more than 100 witnesses to the stand, fifteen of them from abroad, and to present no fewer than 400 exhibits.

When Dominique Prieur left Paris on the Greenpeace mission her husband Joel was out fighting a fire and they never said farewells. Now they met in her special prison in an army detention barracks. For the first time Joel Prieur learned the risks of his wife's work.

In prison Captain Dominique Prieur jogged in the exercise yard, watched television and spent a lot of time with her nose in a novel. She was haunted by the fear of being kept so long in prison that she would be too old to have children when released. Major Alain Mafart was allowed to play his guitar and piped away on the chanter of an old set of bagpipes. He played chess with other prisoners.

In France, lawyers painted a grim picture of the agents' prison conditions, claiming they were kept in small cells, were refused visitors, and that authorities were trying to break Prieur psychologically by refusing to supply beauty creams for her face. New Zealanders were both furious and amused when French radio reported that Prieur had been moved 'to an island a thousand miles from Auckland'. Listeners in France no doubt imagined conditions akin to Devil's Island. In fact Prieur had been transferred to more secure and salubrious quarters in a women's prison at Christchurch, premier city of the South Island.

French demands that New Zealand 'respect international law' in the treatment of the agents were dismissed by David Lange as 'a pompous step'. He said he was astounded that the French embassy had made no attempt to contact or visit its nationals. Tongue in cheek, Lange added that the comforts the accused couple had enjoyed when they stayed at his motel unit in Parakai, on the night before the bombing, were 'not a patch' on their current situation.

Guarded by police with pump-action shotguns, the biggest armed escort New Zealand had ever seen, the suspects were sped through Auckland in a special armoured windowless van. Access to the court building was boarded up with high fences and big gates. Journalists, lawyers and a handful of spectators were screened by metal detectors. Greenpeace members stood quietly in the drizzle with placards, balloons and banners.

But the drama was short lived.

Prieur smiled at her husband as she climbed up from the cells below and donned headphones to hear a simultaneous translation as the Crown lawyer, Paul Neazor QC, read the police summary of the facts. *Rainbow Warrior* had been disabled to ensure that her much publicised voyage to French territorial waters did not take place. To achieve the mission the two defendants were 'associated with other members of the French security forces who travelled to this country in furtherance of the action and who also played significant roles in the scuttling of the ship and the death of Mr Pereira.'

But the Crown was evidently not able to establish the role of the agents as anything more than on in 'support of those who actually placed the explosives.'

In short, the police case against the agents was not strong enough to prove murder and arson. It could not establish that the accused were personally responsible for placing the bombs. Nor did the evidence convincingly establish that the pair intended to kill anyone. The Crown had to be content with charges of manslaughter and wilful damage to which, after bargaining between lawyers, the defendants agreed to admit.

It was all over in 34 minutes. Many of the foreign journalists watching the proceedings on the TV monitors did not realise what had happened. Prieur's plea was barely audible. When Mafart said 'Guilty' in a firm voice the reporters woke up. There was astonishment in the press room. Journalists jumped to their feet. Touted in New Zealand as 'the case of the century', the *Rainbow Warrior* hearing was over in time for lunch.

Det. Supt Allan Galbraith's comment as he strode from the courtroom was a terse, 'Satisfactory.' Mr Neazor took time to explain to journalists that the admissions to the reduced charges were 'a significant acceptance' of the pair's responsibility for the sabotage and of their participation in the act. Greenpeace president David McTaggart was not a man to miss an opportunity. 'President Mitterrand promised justice at the highest level,' he said angrily. 'What we have seen this morning was justice to some extent at a very low level.'

The French press corps was furious at being deprived of a long drawn out murder trial full of juicy revelations. But the French government had every reason to be satisfied at the way its hatches had remained battened down. In an unwittingly black-humoured misprint *Le Monde* reported the charge as 'man's laughter'. Misinterpreting the seriousness of the charge, which in fact carried a maximum penalty of life imprisonment, all France was laughing. The agents, they thought, would be home for Christmas. In London *The Times*, rightly, said manslaughter was serious enough. Though David Lange at once denied allegations of a trade-off, many papers alleged a deal had been struck to exchange the agents' release for export market concessions. Trumpeted London's *Daily Express*: 'Alors, it's the great lamb-chop spy swap.'

On the morning after the sensationally abbreviated hearing the *New Zealand Herald*, Auckland's premier paper, editorialised on the subject of the beach litter problem during the holiday season. In God's Own Country, evidently, it was never too soon to return to the business of being a backwater.

Two and a half weeks later Mafart and Prieur returned to the same dock to face Sir Ronald Davison, Chief Justice of New Zealand, for sentencing. 'The courts,' Sir Ronald said, 'must make it plain that persons coming into this country cannot expect a short holiday at the expense of the government and return home as heroes.'

The 'swimming pool' warriors were sent to prison for ten years apiece. No recommendation was made for deportation.

Two days later a 50-kilotonne bomb was exploded at Moruroa. It was the 74th underground test by France, the eighth that year.

A rusting monument to French folly on a grand scale, *Rainbow Warrior* was refloated and with a patched-up hull was towed across the Waitemata Harbour to a berth at the Western Viaduct. The bombed vessel, Greenpeace said gravely, had 'become an enduring symbol for those who desire a world without the spectres of terrorism, nuclear warfare or environmental destruction.' But there was more to her than mere symbolism. Weeks after the sabotage, when I talked with those who sailed as crew on her long Pacific Peace Voyage, and others who had been aboard when the bombs exploded under their feet, I noticed that not one could speak without an awkward lump in the throat; some wept openly.

Greenpeace decided it couldn't bear the thought of its flagship being melted down to make Japanese motor cars. She was not to be treated like a whale being cut up for pet food. Instead, the old girl would be given a decent and honourable burial at sea, where she belonged. Repairs were out of the question so she would be stripped then scuttled in deep water, perhaps as an underwater monument for scuba divers to explore. Her masts were sliced off and transported by logging truck to the Northern Wairoa Museum, in Northland, where they were to be reassembled on a hilltop. Portholes were removed and one sent to every Greenpeace office around the world.

The awful irony of the sinking, Prime Minister David Lange noted, was that while the malice and venom had been directed against the ship and the life of a crew member, the cause which the *Rainbow Warrior* was pursuing was immeasurably enhanced. Many people who would not have been in Greenpeace's corner were now standing right in the ring with them.

The support and sympathy for Greenpeace in New Zealand and around the world was overwhelming. The trust funds for Fernando Pereira's family and a replacement ship swelled to NZ$180,000 in the first few weeks. Greenpeace International, meanwhile, was pursuing massive compensation claims.

In Auckland, anti-French graffiti (Frog Off La Pacifique!) flowered on every wall. But one of the most poignant of slogans popped up within hours of the sinking. Spray-painted on hoardings, stamped on lapel badges, printed on T-shirts, headlined on posters, emblazoned on collection tins, engraved on slices of copper tubing cut from the vessel's engine room and sold as NZ$10 souvenir bracelets, it was an eloquent expression of defiance, warmth and optimism – You Can't Sink A Rainbow.

Wasn't it true?